WISDOM OF THE AGES

Paperback Version

This book is a work of non-fiction. Unless otherwise noted, the author and the publisher make no explicit guarantees as to the accuracy of the information contained in this book.

© 2012 Ernest Johnson. All rights reserved.

No part of this book may be reproduced, stored in a retrieval system, or transmitted by any means without the written permission of the author.

First published 2012
Published 2012 by Karah Kious-McJoslin,
KarahbarkDesigns.com

Cover art by Karah Kious-McJoslin and Schad McJoslin

ISBN: 978-0-9882803-8-0

WISDOM OF THE AGES	2
SPIRITUAL ALCHEMY	5
BLISTERING EVIL	5
THE WORLD IS A REFLEX OF MENTAL STATES	11
STEP OUT OF BAD CONDITIONS	16
THE WAY OUT OF UNDESIREABLE CONDITIONS:	27
CONTROLLING YOUR THOUGHT FORCES	28
IT IS AS YOU SEE IT	36
THE SECRET OF HEALTH, SUCCESS, AND POWER	36
THE SECRET OF HAPPINESS	47
REALIZING PROSPERITY	53
TIMELESS WISDOM	56
THE POWER OF MEDITATION	56
STAR OF WISDOM	63
MASTER OF SELF–MASTER OF TRUTH	64
THE TWO MASTERS	71
SPIRITUAL POWER	72
REALIZING SELFLESS LOVE	77
LOVE CONQUERS SOFTLY	86
INFINITE EVERLASTING	87
THE LAW OF SERVICE	94
CROWN OF THORNS	101
ETERNAL PEACE	101
PERFECT PEACE	105
JET FUEL FOR THE SOUL	106
DOUBLE EDGE SWORD	127
GOD-MAN-CREATOR	140
GOD-MAN	157
MAN-CREATOR	175
GOD-CREATOR	195
GOD	212
MAN	230
YOUR BABY	250
FAITH:	252
TIMING:	253

IMAGINATION: 254
EMOTIONS: 255
EMOTIONAL ATTATCHMENTS: 255
DANCING WITH IMAGINATION: 256
NEGATIVE ENERGY: 257
YOUR THOUGHTS: 259
THOUGHT PLAYGROUND: 260
FIELD OF INTELLIGENCE: 261
About the Author 262

SPIRITUAL ALCHEMY

I looked around upon this old world, and saw that it was shadowed by the human sorrow and was scorched by the fierce fires or our suffering. And I looked for the cause. I looked around, but could not find the cause; I looked in all the books, and could not fined it there either; I looked within, and there I found both the cause and the self made nature of that cause. The cause was ego. Ego destruction of the self is the cause.

I then looked even deeper and there I found the remedy. I found only one Law, and that is the Law of Love. Then I noticed that there is one life; this is the life of adjustment to that Law of Love. There is one truth, and that this truth is one of a conquered mind and an obedient and truthful heart. This is a love of being true to one self and the world around him.

Upon this realization I knew I had discovered something that the world cannot know and that I had to write this material warmly and soulfully so that they might come to the understanding that they are lost in a world of illusion. A book perhaps for both men and women whether rich or poor, or learned or unlearned, to help find within themselves the very inner source of all happiness and success. Also I wish upon them all accomplishment and truth. This is soul being set free truth. This desire has been within me all my born days and at last has come to fruition.

Upon completion of this little book I will send it forward into the wide open plain we call the world and pray blessedness and internal healing; knowing full well that it cannot fail in its mission in setting hearts free for those who have been waiting for it.

BLISTERING EVIL

Delusion and illusion along with sorrow and pain are the precursors of life. They buffet us in all their lower vibrations. They always bring pain and unrest to our living souls. There is no human that has not felt the sting of pain, No mind that has not been tested upon the dark waters of trouble.

There has not been one eye that has not wept the hot, flaming tears of unspeakable grief; or the extreme pain or distress of mind. The great destroyers has entered every house and brought disease severing heart from heart and casting over all the dark pall of sorrow. This is the black clothe draped over our coffin.

In the strong indestructible net of evil it appears that there is no way out. Evil has pinned us in with pain, unhappiness and all manner of ill fortune and it awaits all mankind the same. We are always trying to escape these devilish darts, trying to make them less severe their stings. By doing so both men and women rush blindly into countless devices specialized in deadening the painful poison that has been injected in us unaware.

Meanwhile, they ponder the pathways by which they fondly hope to enter into a happiness which will not pass away. This is because of a week boundary. We let things in that we should not have. It is a lack of control.

Such is the drunkard and the dope fiend becoming an animal in the streets and the artist who shuts himself out from the sorrows of the world. What these people have in common is that they all shut themselves out from the world and pursue listless luxuries; same as them that thirst for money and wealth. These individuals put lower in rank all things to the achievement to those ends. This also holds true for those who seek consolation through religion. They seek the soothing through religion because they cannot find it any other way. Religion is the drug of the masses.

And to all the happiness sought seems to come, to the soul, for a time, through religion the intoxicating forgetfulness of the existence of the blistering evil. Because the soul is unfortified then the day of disease comes like a thief in the night. With it comes great sorrow and pain. Through life's temptations comes misfortunes and when this breaks suddenly the fabric of your fancied blessedness is torn to shreds. You find your self suddenly cast down ever close to the sweet smell of the coffin.

So, over the head of every personal joy hangs the damocletian sword hanging by a single strand of hair to bring pain and peril at any moment to fall and crush the soul of them who has unprotected knowledge.

The children cry's to become adults. The adults all cry and wish that they had the great happiness of childhood again. The poor soul makes fret and makes himself sore by rubbing on the chains of poverty by which they are bound; while the rich often lives in fear of poverty. He scours the world in search of an elusive shadow they call for happiness. Sometimes the soul feels that it has found a secure peace and happiness in adopting a certain intellectual philosophy or in building up an intellectual or artistic ideal. But they always find out that this is an illusion after experiencing temptation. The fruit's of temptation proves religion to be inadequate or insufficient. The theoretical philosophy is found to be a useless prop, or in a moment, the idealistic statue upon which the devotee has been laboring, is shattered into fragments at his feet.

Is there, then, no way to escape from our pain and sorrow? Isn't there any way by which we can become free of the bonds of evil? Is our permanent happiness, secure prosperity, and abiding peace just a foolish dream? I think not and I will explain it with gladness.

There is a way by which evil can be slain forever. There is a process by which disease, poverty, and any adverse condition and circumstance can be put asunder never to return. There is a method by which a permanent prosperity can be secured, free of all fear of the return of adversity. There is a practice by which unbroken and unending peace and bliss can be partaken of and realized. The beginning of the way which leads to this glorious realization is the acquirement of a right understanding of the nature of this blistering evil.

It is not adequate enough to just deny evil or to simply ignore it. Evil must be rightly understood. It does no one any good just to pray to God to remove it because God will not do this. You the reader have no other alternative but to find out why it is here, and what lesson it has for you while you are on this old earth. It does no good to fret, chafe, or become irritated by the chains that bind you. You must know why you are bound. To be bound is to be locked in the wrong vibration. So it stands to reason that it is by the right vibration you can set your self free of your chains. The power to bind and the power to loosen is in the tongue.

Therefore reader you must get outside yourself, and must begin to understand and examine your self. You must cease to be a disobedient child in the school of experience, and must begin to learn, with humility and patience, the lessons that are set for your edification and ultimately your perfection.

Evil is not really evil until it exceeds its proper bounds. All things are permissible until it becomes out of bounds. Also, when rightly understood, is found to be not an unlimited power or principle in the universe, but a passing phase of human experience, and it therefore becomes a teacher to those who are willing to learn. Evil is not an expression or quality apart from your self. It is an experience in your own heart. So by patiently examining and rectifying your heart you will gradually be lead to discover the origin and the very nature of evil. Then and only then will you be able to eradicate it from your life completely.

All evil is corrective and can be remedied. Therefore it is not permanent. Evil is rooted in ignorance, ignorance of the true nature and relation of things, and so long as we remain in that state of stupidity, we remain subject to its influence. Therefore we can conclude that evil is ignorance.

There is no evil in the universe that is not rooted in ignorance and when we are ready and willing to learn its lessons, will lead us to higher wisdom, and then it will vanish away from our presence. But people remain in evil and it does not pass away because people are not willing or prepared to learn the lesson which it came to teach them.

I knew a child who, every night when his mother took her to bed, cried to be allowed to play with the candle; and one night, when the mother was off guard for a moment, the child took hold of the candle; the inevitable result followed, and the child never wished to play with the candle again. By this child's foolish act she had learned a valuable lesson of obedience, and entered into the knowledge that fire burns.

This simple incident is somewhat of a complete picture of the nature, meaning, and the ultimate result of all sin and evil. This child suffered through her own ignorance and discovered the real nature of fire. Now older children suffer through their ignorance of the real nature of the things which they weep for and strive after, and then harm themselves in the process. The only difference between these two examples is that in the latter case the ignorance and evil is more deeply rooted and obscure.

Evil has always been symbolized by darkness, and Good by light, and hidden within the symbol is contained the perfect interpretation. But the reality is this: for just as light always floods the universe, and darkness is only a mere speck or shadow cast by a small body intercepting a few rays of the illimitable light, so the light of the supreme good is the positive and life giving power which floods the universe, and the evil the insignificant shadow cast by itself that intercepts and shuts off the illuminating rays which strive for entrance. When night folds the world in its black impenetrable sleeveless cloak, no matter how dense the darkness, it covers but the small space of half our little planet, while the whole universe is ablaze with living light. Every soul knows that it will awake to a new dawn in the morning.

Know this then, that the dark of night of sorrow, grief, and anxiety settles down upon your soul, and you end up stumbling along the way with weary and uncertain steps, that you are merely intercepting your own personal desires between your self and the boundless light of joy and bliss, and the dark shadow that covers you is cast by none and nothing but yourself. And just as the darkness without is nothing but a negative shadow, the unreality which comes from nowhere goes to nowhere, and has no abiding dwelling place, so the darkness within is equally a negative shadow passing over the evolving and light born soul.

"But," You ask "why pass through the darkness at all"? The answer is simple enough. It is because you have chosen to do so, through your ignorance, of course. Now that you have done it this way you come to understand both good and evil, and may the more appreciate the good light of the universe by passing through the darkness. As evil is the direct outcome of ignorance, so, when the lessons of evil are fully learned, ignorance passes away, and the wisdom takes its place.

Now as a disobedient zombie refuses to learn its lessons at school of hard knocks, so it is possible to refuse to learn the lessons of experience, and thus to remain in continual darkness, and to suffer continually recurring punishments in the form of disease, disappointment and anxiety, not to mention broken bones.

He therefore, who would shake himself free of their evil which is attached to them must be willing to and ready to learn and must be prepared to undergo that disciplinary process without which no grain of wisdom or abiding happiness and peace can be secured.

Imagine yourself in a room without any light. There is no light in that room only. Outside is light. Darkness is only in that little room. Your soul is the same. Just because you are in the dark doesn't mean others are. You should strive to realize these truths, The universe is lighted. They only thing darkened is your mind.

So you may shut out the light of truth, or you may begin to pull down the walls of stupidity, self seeking me-seeking-self full of internal error which you have built around yourself, and so let in the glorious and ever present eternal God Light. So, by earnest self-examination you must strive to realize, and not merely hold as a theory, that evil is a passing phase, a self-created shadow; that all your pains, anxiety and misfortunes have come to you by a process of undeviating and absolutely perfect law. They have come to you because you deserve them, and require them. So that by first enduring them and then understanding them you may be made stronger, wiser, and more honest and nobler.

Only when you have fully realized this truth are you in a position to mould your own circumstances to change, or cause to change in form, appearance, or nature all evil into good, and to weave, with a master's hand, the fabric of your destiny.

THE WORLD IS A REFLEX OF MENTAL STATES

What you are and what you see so is your world. Everything in the universe is revolved into your won inward experience. Resolve means to find an answer to or make a formal resolution. It matters little what is on the outside, for it is all but a reflection of how you see it internally. It is a reflection of your state of consciousness. It matters everything what you are on the inside. Everything on the outside will be mirrored and colored accordingly.

All that you know passed through the gateway of your experience. All that you positively know and all that you will ever know is contained in your own experience and so become a part of your experience. Your own thoughts, aspirations and desires to achieve, comprise your internal world, and, to you, all that there is in the universe of beauty and joy and bliss, is contained within yourself. By your own thoughts you make of tar your self, your world, and your universe.

As you build internal by the power of thought, so will your outward life and circumstances shape themselves accordingly. Whatsoever you harbor in the innermost chambers of your heart will, sooner or later, by the inevitable Law of Reaction, shape itself in your outward life.

The soul that is impure, vulgar, degrading or corrupt and selfish is moving toward something with unerring precision and misfortune with great disaster. The soul that is pure, unselfish, and noble, is moving towards with equal precision happiness and prosperity.

Every soul attracts it's own, and nothing can possibly come to it that does not belong to it. This is a Divine Law that is present and occurring everywhere at the same time. It also relates to and affects everyone and everything. The incidents of every human life, which both make and mar, are drawn to it by the quality and power of its own inner thought life. Every soul is a complex combination of gathered experiences and thoughts, and the body is but an improvised vehicle for its manifestation. What, therefore, your thoughts are, that is your real self, and the world around, both having life and not having life, wears the aspect with which your thoughts clothe it.

"All that we are is the result of what we have thought; it is founded on our thoughts; it is made up of our thoughts." It is said and it therefore follows that if a man is happy, it is because he dwells in happy thoughts. It a man is miserable, it is because he dwells in despondent and debilitating thoughts, meaning dejection, ill and weak.

Whether one is fearful or fearless, foolish or wise, troubled or serene, within that soul lie's the cause of its own state or state of being. And now I seem to hear voices exclaim. "But do you really mean to say that outward circumstances do not affect our minds?" I do not say that, but I say this, and know it to be an infallible truth, that circumstances can only affect you in so far as you allow them to do so. You are swayed by circumstances because you have not a right understanding of the nature, use, and power of thought. You believe, and upon this little word belief hang all our sorrows and joys, that outward things, confess that you are their slave, and they your conditional master; by so doing, you invest them with a power which they do not have of themselves possess, and you give up, in reality, not to the mere circumstances, but to the gloom or gladness, the fear or hope, the strength or weakness, which your thought-sphere has thrown around them.

I knew two men who, at an early age, lost the hard earned savings of years. One was very deeply troubled, and gave rise to embarrassment and humiliation, worry and dejection. This other man after reading his morning paper that the bank in which his money was deposited had hopelessly become lost, and that he had lost it all, quietly and firmly said, "Well, it's gone, and my troubles and worry won't bring it back, but hard work will." This man went to work with renewed enthusiasm, and quickly became prosperous. Meanwhile the first man continued to mourn the loss of his money, and to grumble at his "bad luck," He remained dwelling in his adverse circumstances, still in reality of his own weak slavish and weak thoughts. The loss of his money was a curse to the one because he clothed the event with dark and dreary thoughts. But the other man it was a blessing because he threw around it thoughts of strength, of hope, and renewed endeavor.

If circumstances had the power to bless or harm, they would bless and harm all men alike, but the fact that the same circumstance will be alike good and bad to different souls proves that the good or bad is not in the circumstance, but only in the mind of him who encounters it.

When you begin to realize this you will begin to learn to control your thoughts, and then to regulate your mind with discipline. Then by rebuilding the inward temple of your soul by eliminating all useless and unnecessary material, and incorporating into you person thoughts alone of joy and peace and of strength and life. You will also have love and compassion, and have the beauty of immortality. As you do this you will become joyful, peaceful, loving, healthy, and compassionate.

As we clothe events with the drapery of our own thoughts, so likewise do we clothe the objects of the visible world around us, and where one sees harmony and beauty, another sees revolting ugliness.

An enthusiastic naturalist was one day roaming the country side in pursuit of his job, during his roaming came upon a body of blackish water near a farmhouse. As he started to fill his container with the water for the purpose of examination under a microscope, he commented with enthusiasm at length more than he should have. He was speaking to a young uncultivated son of the plough who stood close by, upon the hidden and innumerable wonders contained in the water. And concluded by saying, "Yes, my young friend, within this water is contained a hundred, no a million universes, had we but the sense or the instrument by which we could understand them." And the unsophisticated boy ponderously remarked, "I know the water is full of tad poles, and they are easy to catch.

Where the naturalist, his mind stored with the knowledge of natural facts, saw beauty, harmony, and hidden glory, the mind unenlightened upon those things saw only an offensive mud puddle.

The wild flower which the casual wayfarer thoughtlessly tramples upon is, to the spiritual eye of the poet, an angelic messenger from the invisible. To the many, the ocean is but a dreary expanse of water on which ships sail and are sometimes wrecked; to the soul of the musician it is a living thing, and he hears, in all its changing moods and divine harmonies. Where the ordinary mind sees disaster and confusion, the mind of the philosopher see the most perfect sequence of cause and effect, and where the materialist sees nothing but endless death, the mystic sees pulsating and eternal life.

As we clothe both the events and objects with our own thoughts, so like wise do we clothed the souls of others in the garments of our thoughts. The suspicious believe everybody to be suspicious; the liar feels secure in the thought that he is not so foolish as to believe that there is such a phenomenon as a strictly truthful person. The envious see envy in every soul. The miser thinks everybody is out to get his money.

He who has lower in rank thinking in the building of his wealth sleeps with a revolver under his pillow, engrossed in the false belief that the world is full of conscienceless people who are eager to rob him. The sensualist who has given up his ways without intent to reclaim them looks upon the saint as a hypocrite.

On the other hand, those who dwell in loving thoughts, see that all which calls forth their love and sympathy. The trusting and honest are not troubled by suspicions. The good natured and giving person who rejoice at the good fortune of others, hardly understand what envy means. The person who has realized the Divine within themselves recognizes it in all things in all beings even in the beasts of the field.

Both men and women are verified in their mental outlook because of the very fact that by the Law of cause and effect they attract to themselves that which they send forth, and so come in contact with people similar to them selves.

The old familiar saying, "Birds of a feather flock together," holds a deeper meaning in light of this truth. It has greater significance than is generally attached to it. So, in the world of thought as in the world of matter each clings to its kind.

Do you wish for kindness? Then be kind. Do you ask for truth? Then be true yourself. What ever you give of your self you will find. Your world is a reflex of your mental state.

If you are one of those people who are looking for a better world beyond the grave; to a happier world after your dead, then this message is for you. You may enter your happy world right now exactly where you are at here and now. This happy world fills the universe and it is within you waiting for you to discover it. So find it, then acknowledge it then possess it .

The one who knew all the inner laws of the universe and of beings says "when people shall say look over here and over there do not believe them because the kingdom of God is within you." What you have to do is believe this truth. Simply believe this as truth with a mind that is un-shadowed by doubt and then meditate upon it till you understand it. This is where you start to begin to purify and to rebuild your inner world. As you proceed you will go from revelation to revelation from realization to realization. You will discover the utter powerlessness of outward things beside the magic potency of a self-governed soul. This is to say that the self governed soul has the ability to produce magic.

If you would right the world, and banish all its evil and its woes, make its wild places bloom and its dreary deserts blossom as the rose, then simply right yourself.

If you would turn the world from its long, lone captivity of sin, restore all broken hearts, slay grief and let sweet consolation in The right yourself.

If you would cure the world of its long sickness, end its grief and pain; bring in all healing joy, and give to the afflicted rest again then cure your self.

If you would wake the world out of its dream of death and darkening strife, bring to it love and peace, and light and brightness of immortal life, then wake your self.

STEP OUT OF BAD CONDITIONS

Having seen and realize that evil is but a passing shadow thrown, by the intercepting self, across the transcendent form of the Eternal Good. The world is a mirror in which each sees a reflection of himself, we can now ascend, by firm and easy steps, to that level of perception where it is seen and realized the Vision of the Law.

With this new realization comes the knowledge that everything is included in a ceaseless interaction of cause and effect. Nothing can possibly be divorced from this law. From the most trivial thought, word, or deed of humankind to the heavenly bodies that reign supreme in this universe.

No selecting at random or autocratic condition can, even for a moment exist. For such a condition would be a denial and a destruction of this law. This is an impossibility.

Every condition of life is, therefore bound up in an orderly and harmonious, which is a continuous or a connected series. The secret of cause and effect is contained within itself.

The Law is this, "What so ever a man sows that shall he also reap." This is written and yes even engraved upon the portals of Eternity. There is none that can deny of defy it. There is none that can cheat it either and none can escape it.

The person who puts their hand in the fire must suffer until it has worked itself out. Neither prayers nor curses can change or alter it. Precisely the same Law governs the sphere of the mind. Hatred, anger, jealously, lust, covetousness, all of these are fires that burn in the soul. Whoever even touches them gets burned by them and suffers the torments of burning.

All of these conditions are rightly called "evil." They are the efforts of the soul to subvert, in its own ignorance, the law and they therefore lead to chaos and confusion within and are sooner or later realized in the outer world is circumstance in disease, failure, and misfortune. Coupled with grief, pain, anxiety and despair.

Now on the other hand, we have love, gentle, goodwill, purity, are cooling airs which breathe peace upon the soul that woos them and being in harmony with the eternal law. They too become realized in the outward in the form of health, peaceful surroundings, and undeviating success and good fortune.

A thorough understanding of this Great Law which permeates the universe and leads to the acquirement of that state of mind, this is also known as obedience. To know that justice, harmony, and love are supreme in this universe is likewise to know that all adverse and painful conditions are the result of our own disobedience to that Law. Such knowledge leads to strength and power and it is upon this knowledge alone that a true life and an enduring success and happiness can be built.

To be patient under all circumstances, and to accept all conditions as necessary factors in your training is to rise superior to all painful conditions and to overcome them, with an overcoming which is sure and which leaves no fear of their return, for by the power of obedience to this law they are utterly slain.

Such an obedient one is working in harmony with this law has in fact identified himself with the law and whatsoever he overcomes he overcomes forever. Whatsoever he builds can never be destroyed.

The cause of all power as in all weakness is from within. The secret of all happiness as of all misery is likewise within. There is no progress apart from the unfolding from within. There is no sure foothold of prosperity or peace except by orderly advancement in knowledge. You say you are chained by circumstances. You cry out for better conditions and opportunities and for a wider scope of experiences. You say you desire for better conditions and you inwardly curse the fate that binds you hand and foot.

It is for you that I write this. It is to you that I speak this truth. Listen and let my words burn into you being because what it is that I say is an Eternal Truth. You may bring about that improved condition in your outward life as you desire if you will unswervingly resolve to improve you inner life.

I know this pathway looks barren at the beginning, but truth always does. It is only error and delusion which are at first inviting and alluring. But if you under take the walk of it, if you perseveringly discipline your mind to eradicate your mind of weaknesses and allow your soul forces and spiritual powers to unfold themselves, you will be amazed at the magical changes that will unfold. This transformation will be actualized in the outward experience. As you proceed forward, golden opportunities will be strewn across your path and the power and judgment to properly utilize them will spring up within you. Cheerful friends will come to you unbidden. Sympathetic souls will be drawn to you as the needle is to the magnet; and books and all outward aids that you require will come to you unsought.

Perhaps the chains of poverty hang heavily upon you and you are friendless and alone. You may long with an intense longing that your load may be lightened, but your load continues and you are surrounded in an ever increasing darkness. Perhaps you complain and mourn or express sorrow for you lot in life. You blame your birth and your parents along with your employer; perhaps the unjust powers that be who have bestowed upon you so undeservedly poverty and hardship and upon another affluence and ease. Stop your complaining and fretting, none of these things are to blame for the cause or your poverty.

The cause of your poverty is within your self and your self alone. Where the cause is there the remedy is also. The very fact that you are a complainer shows that you deserve your lot. It shows that you lack that faith which is ground of all effort and progress.

There is no room for a complainer in a universe of law. So worry is soul-suicide. By this very attitude of mind you are strengthening the chains that bind you. You are drawing about your own darkness by which you are enveloped. So here and now alter your outlook upon life and your outward life will alter.

Build your self up in faith and knowledge and make yourself worthy of better surroundings and wider opportunities. Be sure first of all that you are making the best of what you have. Do not delude your self into thinking that you can step into greater advantages while overlooking smaller ones, for if you could the advantage would be impermanent and you would quickly fall back again in order top learn the lesson which you had neglected.

As the child at school must master one thing before passing onto the next, so before you can have that greater good which you desire, you must faithfully employ that which you already possess.

The parable of talents is a beautiful story illustrative of this truth, for does it not plainly show that if we misuse. Neglect, or degrade that which we possess, be it ever so mean and insignificant, even that little will be taken away from us, for by our conduct we show that we are worthy of it. Perhaps you are living in a small cottage and are surrounded by unhealthy and vicious influences. You desire a larger and more sanitary residence. Then you must fit yourself for such a residence by first making your cottage as far as possible a little paradise. Keep it spotlessly clean. Make it look as pretty and sweet as your limited means will allow. Cook your food plain with all care and arrange your humble table as tastefully as you possibly can. If you cannot afford a carpet let your rooms be carpeted with smiles and welcomes fastened down with the nails of kind words driven in with the hammer of patience. Such a carpet will not fade in the sun and constant use will never wear it away.

By ennobling your present surroundings you will rise above them and above the need of them. Then at the right time you will pass on into the better house and surroundings which you have all along been waiting for you, and which you have fitted yourself to occupy.

Perhaps you desire more time for thought and effort and feel that hours of labor are too hard and long. Then see to it that you are utilizing to the fullest possible extent what little spare time you have. It is useless to desire more time if you are already wasting what little you have. You would only grow more indolent and indifferent.

Even poverty and lack of time and leisure are not the evils that you imagine they are and if they hinder you in your progress it is because you have clothed them in your weaknesses. So the evil you see in them is really in yourself.

Attempt to fully and completely realize that in so far as you shape and mold your mind you are the maker of your destiny and as, by the transmuting power of self discipline you will realize this more and more. You will come to see that these so called evils may be converted into blessings. Converted means: to turn from one belief to another, in other words to turn it into something else. So the idea is to change it into something better. You will then utilize your poverty for your cultivation with patience, hope, and courage. Your lack of time in the gaining of promptness of action and decision of mind, by seizing the precious moments as they present themselves for your acceptance.

As in the rankest soil the most beautiful flowers are grown so in the dark soil of poverty the choicest flowers of humanity have developed and bloomed. Where there are difficulties to cope with and unsatisfactory conditions to overcome there virtue most flourishes and manifests its glory.

It may be that you are in the environment of a nasty master and mistress and you may feel you are harshly treated. Look upon this also as necessary to your training. Return your masters unkindness with gentleness and forgiveness. Practice unceasingly patience and self-control. Turn the disadvantage to account by utilizing it for the gaining of mental and spiritual strength and by your silent example and influence you will be teaching your master or mistress. You will be helping him grow ashamed of his conduct and his treatment of you. And at the same time you will be lifting your self above your circumstances. You will be lifted up to the height of spiritual attainment by which you will be enabled to step into new and more congenial surroundings at the time when they are presented to you.

So do not complain that you are a slave. But instead lift your self up above the plain of slavery. Before complaining that you are a slave to another be sure that you are not a slave to self. Self meaning: your passions.

Always look within. Look as if searching and have no mercy upon your self. You will find there perhaps slavish thoughts and slavish desires, and in your daily life and conduct slavish habits. Conquer means to overcome these bad habits. Cease to be a slave to your passions which is the false self. By taking this route then no one can become your true master except you. No one has any power over you or to enslave you. As you overcome this false self you will overcome all adverse conditions and every difficulty will fall before you.

Do not complain that you are oppressed by somebody else above you. Are you sure that if you gained riches you would not become an oppressor yourself? Remember that there is the Eternal Law which is absolutely just, and that he who oppress to day must himself be oppressed tomorrow. From this law there is absolutely no escape.

Think about it this way. Perhaps in another existence you were the oppressor and that now you are merely paying off your debt that which you owe to the Great Law. Practice therefore, fortitude and faith. Dwell constantly in the mind upon the Eternal Justice, the Eternal Good. Endeavor to lift yourself above the personal and transitory or brief duration into the impersonal permanent. Impersonal meaning: not involving human personality or emotion.

Shake off the delusion that you are being injured or oppressed by another. And then realize by yet another profound comprehension of your inner life and the laws which govern that life that you are only really injured by what is within you. Delusion meaning: a false belief. Oppressed meaning: persecute, or weighed down.

There is no practice more degrading debasing and soul-destroying than self pity. This is considered a self brutalizing. Cast it far away from you this instant. This is a canker feeding upon your heart and you cannot ever expected to grow into a fuller life.

Cease from the condemnation of others and instead condemn you self only. Do not over look or forgive any acts, desires or thoughts that will not bear comparison with spotless purity or endure the light of sinless good. Yesterday is gone. All you have is today. Start today and forget your past history. Nothing can be done about past acts, thoughts or deeds. Pay your karmic dues and purify your self this moment forward.

By this starting point you will start to build your house upon the rock of the Eternal and all that is required for your happiness and well being will come to you in its own time.

There is no positively no way of permanently rising above poverty, or any undesirable condition, except by eradicating those selfish and negative conditions within, of which these are the reflection and by virtue of which they continue. The way to true riches is to enrich the soul by the acquisition of virtue. Acquisition meaning: a gaining or something gained.

Outside of real heart virtue there is neither prosperity nor power, but only appearances of such. I am aware that people make money that have acquired no measure of virtue and have little desire for it. But money does not constitute true riches and its possession is of brief duration coupled with fever. The Biblical figure called David says: "For I was envious at the foolish when I saw the prosperity of the wicked. Their eyes stand out with fatness and they have more than heart could wish for. Verily I have cleansed my heart in vain. And I washed my hands in innocence. When I thought to know this was too painful for me. But when I went into the sanctuary of God then I understood their end." The prosperity of the wicked was a great trial for David until he went into the sanctuary of God. There he realized their end. You also may go into the sanctuary of God. This sanctuary is within you. It is that state of consciousness which remains when all that is vulgar, degrading or corrupt, and personal and impermanent is risen above. Go there until the universal and eternal principles are realized. This is the God state of consciousness. It is the sanctuary of the Most High.

When, by long conflict and self-discipline you have succeeded in entering the door of that Holy Temple you will perceive with unobstructed vision the end and fruit of all human thought and endeavor, both good and evil. You will then no longer relax your faith when you see immoral people accumulation outward riches, for you will know that he must come again to poverty and degradation.

The rich person who is barren or uninterested in virtue is, in reality poor, and surely as the waters of the river are drifting to the ocean, so surely is he, in the midst of all his riches, drifting towards poverty and misfortune. But if he dies rich then he returns to reap the bitter fruit of all his immorality. Though a person becomes rich many times yet as many times he is thrown back into poverty, until by long experience and suffering he conquers the poverty within.

The person who is outwardly poor, yet so rich in virtue is truly rich, and in the midst of all his poverty he is surely traveling towards prosperity and abounding in joy and bliss awaits his coming.

If you would become truly and permanently prosperous, you must first become virtuous. It is therefore unwise to aim directly at prosperity, to make it the one object of life, to reach greedily for it. To do this is to ultimately defeat your self. So instead aim at self perfection. Make useful and unselfish service the object of your life and ever reach out hands of faith towards the supreme and unalterable Good.

You say you desire wealth, not for your own sake but in order to do good with it, and to bless others. If this is your real motive in desiring wealth then wealth will come to you. This is because you are strong and unselfish indeed if, in the middle of riches, you are willing to look upon your self as steward and not as owner. So examine your motive well. For in the majority of instances where money is desired for the admitted object of blessing others, the real underlying motive is a love of popularity, and a desire to pose as a giver or reformer. If you are not doing good with what little you have then it just stands to reason that the more money you have the more selfish you become. All the good you appeared to do with your money, if you attempted to do anything, would be so much insinuating self laudation. Self praise.

If your real desire is to do good then you don't need to wait for money before you do it. You can do it now at this very moment, just right where you are. If you are really unselfish as you believe yourself to be you will show it by sacrificing yourself for others right now.

No matter how poor you are, there is room for more self-sacrifice. Did not the widow put her all into the treasury?

The heart that truly desires to do good does not wait for money before doing it. They come to the alter of sacrifice and leaving there the unworthy elements of self, goes out and breaths upon neighbor and stranger, friend and enemy alike, the breath of blessedness.

As the effect is related to the cause, so is prosperity and power related to the inward good, and poverty and weakness to the inward evil. Money does not constitute true wealth, or position, or power, and to rely upon it alone is to stand upon a slippery slope.

Your true wealth is your stock of virtue, and your true power the uses to which you put it. Rectify your heart and you will rectify your life. Lust, hatred, anger, vanity, pride, and covetousness, self-indulgence, self-seeking, all of these lead to poverty and weakness. Now love, purity, gentleness, charity, meekness, compassion, patience, generosity, self-forgetfulness and self-renunciation all of these are wealth and power.

As the elements of poverty and weakness are overcome, an irresistible and all conquering power is evolved from within, and he who succeeds in establishing himself in the highest virtues, brings the whole world to his feet.

But the rich as well as the poor have their undesirable conditions, and are frequently farther removed from happiness than the poor. And here we see happiness depends not upon outward conditions or aids and possessions, but upon the inward life.

Perhaps you are an employer and you have endless trouble with those, whom you employ, and when you do get good and faithful servants they quickly leave you. As a result you are beginning to lose, or have completely lost, you faith in human nature. You try to remedy certain liberties, yet matters remain unaltered. Let me advise you free of charge here. The secret of all your trouble is not in your servants, it is in your self; if you look within, with a humble and sincere desire to discover and eradicate your error, you will sooner or later, find the origin of all your unhappiness. It may be some selfish desire, or lurking suspicion, or unkind attitude of mind which sends out its poison upon those about you, and reacts upon yourself, even though you may not show it in your manner or speech.

Think of your servants with kindness, consider their happiness or comfort, and never demand of them that extremity of service which you yourself would not care to perform were you in their place.

Rare and beautiful is that humility of soul by which a servant entirely forgets himself in his master's good; but far rarer, and beautiful with a divine beauty, is that nobility of soul by which a person, forgetting his own happiness seeks the happiness of those who are under his authority, and who depend upon him for the bodily sustenance. Such a person's happiness is increased ten fold, nor does he need to complain of those he employs. A well known and extensive employer of labor who never needs to dismiss an employee once said, "I have always had the happiest relations with my work people. If you ask me how it is to be accounted for, I can only say that it has been my aim from the first to do them as I would wish done to me."

Herein lie's the secret by which all desirable conditions are secured, and all that are undesirable are eradicated.

Do you say that you are lonely and unloved, and have not a friend in the world? Then, I pray you, for the sake of your own happiness, blame nobody but yourself. Be friendly towards others, and friends will flock around you. Make yourself pure and lovable, and you will be loved by all.

Whatever conditions are rendering your life burdensome, you may pass out of and beyond them by developing and utilizing within you the transforming power of self-purification and self-conquest. Be it the poverty which galls, and remember that the poverty upon which I have been commenting on in depth is that poverty which is a source or misery, and not that voluntary poverty is the glory of set free souls, or the riches which burden, or the many misfortunes, grief's, and annoyances which form the dark background in the web of life, you may overcome them by overcoming the selfish elements within which give them life.

It matters not that by the unfailing Law there are past thoughts and acts to work out and to atone for, as by the same law, we are setting in motion, during, during every moment of our life, fresh thoughts and acts, and we will have the power to make them good or ill. Nor does it follow that if a person, reaping what he has sown, must lose money or forfeit position, that he must also lose his fortitude or forfeit his uprightness, and it is in these that his wealth and power and happiness are to be found.

He who clings to self is his own enemy, and is surrounded by enemies. He who relinquishes self is his own savior, and is surrounded by friends like a protecting belt. Before the divine radiance of a pure heart all darkness vanishes and all clouds melt away, and he who has conquered self has conquered the universe. Come, then, out of poverty; come out of your pain; come out of your troubles, and sighing, and complaining, and heartaches and loneliness by coming out of your self.

Let the old tattered garment of your petty selfishness fall from you, and put on a new garment of universal love. You will then realize the inward heaven, and it will be reflected in all your outward life.

He who sets his foot firmly upon the earth of self-conquest, who walks, aided by the staff of Faith, the highway of self-sacrifice, will assuredly achieve the highest prosperity, and will reap abounding and enduring joy and bliss.

THE WAY OUT OF UNDESIREABLE CONDITIONS:

To them that seek the highest good all things sub serve the wisest ends, does not come as ill, and wisdom lends wings to all shapes of evil brood.

The darkening sorrow veils a star that waits to shine with gladsome light, hell waits on heaven and after night comes golden glory from afar.

Defeats are steps by which we climb with purer aim to nobler ends, loss leads to gain and joy attends true footsteps up the hills of time.

Pain leads to paths of holy bliss, to thoughts and words and deeds divine, and clouds that glooms and rays that shine along life's upward highway kiss.

Misfortune does but cloud the way whose end and summit in the sky. Of bright success sun-kissed and high awaits our seeking and our stay.

The heavy pall of doubts and fears that clouds the valley of our hopes the shades with which the spirit copes the bitter harvesting of tears, the heartaches, miseries and grief's, the brushings born of broken ties. All these are steps by which we rise to living ways of sound beliefs.

Love, pitying and watchful, runs to meet the pilgrim from the land of fate. All glory and all good await the coming of obedient feet.

CONTROLLING YOUR THOUGHT FORCES

The most powerful forces in the universe are the silent forces. And in accordance with the intensity of its power does a force become beneficent when rightly directed, and destructed when wrongly employed. This is common knowledge in regard to the mechanical forces, such as steam, electricity, but few have yet learned to apply this knowledge to the realm of the mind, where the thought-forces, most powerful of all, are continually being generates and sent forth as currents of salvation or destruction. Currents meaning: occurring in or belonging to the present.

At this stage of his evolution, man has entered into possession of these forces, and the whole trend of his present advancement is their complete subjugation meaning: bring under one's control.

All the wisdom possible to man on this material plain called earth is to be found only in complete self mastery, and the command, "Love your enemies," resolves itself into an exhortation to enter here and now, into the possession of that sublime wisdom by taking hold of, mastering and transmuting, those mind forces to which man is now slavishly subject, and by which he is helplessly born, like a straw on the stream, upon the currents of selfishness. Transmuting meaning: change or cause to change in form, appearance, or nature.

The Hebrew prophets, with their perfect knowledge of the supreme Law, always related outward events to inward thought, and associated national disasters or success with the thoughts and desires that dominated the nation at the time.

The knowledge of casual power of thought is the basis of all their prophecies, as it is the basis of all real wisdom and power. National events are simply the working out of the psychic forces of the nation. Wars, plagues, and famines are the meeting and clashing of wrongly-directed thought-forces, the culminating points at which destruction steps in as the agent of the Law. It is foolish to ascribe war to the influence of one man, or to one body of men. It is the crowning horror of national selfishness. Ascribe meaning: attribute.

It is the silent and conquering thought-forces which bring all things into manifestation. The universe grew out of thought. Matter in its last analysis is found to be merely objectifies thought. Objectify meaning: cause to have objective reality.

All of man's accomplishments were first wrought out in thought, and then objectified. The author, the inventor, the architect, first builds up his work in thought, and having perfected it in all its parts as a complete and harmonious whole upon the thought plane, he then commences to materialize it, to bring it down to the material or sense-plane.

When thought-forces are directed in harmony with the over-ruling Law, they are up-building and preservative, but when subverted they become disintegrating and self destructive.

To adjust all of your thoughts to a perfect and unswerving faith in the omnipotence and supremacy of Good is to cooperate with that Good, and to realize within your self the solution and destruction of all evil. Believe and you shall live.

And here we have the true meaning of salvation, salvation from the darkness and negation of evil, by entering into, and realizing the living light of the Eternal Good. Negation meaning: deny, nullify.

Where there is fear, worry, anxiety, doubt, trouble, chagrin, or disappointment, there is ignorance and lack of faith. All these conditions of mind are the direct outcome of selfishness, and are based upon inherent belief in the power and supremacy of evil. They therefore constitute practical atheism and to live in and become subject to these negative and soul destroying conditions of mind is the only real atheism.

It is salvation from such conditions that the human race needs, and let no man boast of salvation while he is their helpless slave. To Fear or to worry is as sinful as to curse, for how can one worry and fear if he intrinsically believes in the Eternal Justice, the Omnipotent Good, the Boundless Love? To fear, to worry, to doubt, is to deny, it is to disbelieve.

It is from such states of mind that all weakness and failure proceed, for they represent the annulling and disintegrating of the positive thought forces which would otherwise speed to their object with power, and bring about their own beneficent results. Annulling meaning: make legally void.

To overcome these negative conditions is to enter into a life of power, is to cease to be a slave, and to become a master, and there is only one way by which they can be overcome, and that is by steady and persistent growth in inward knowledge.

To mentally deny evil is not sufficient, it must by daily practice be risen above and understood. To mentally affirm the good is inadequate, it must be an unswerving endeavor, be entered into and comprehended.

The intelligent practice of self-control, quickly leads to knowledge of one's interior thought forces, and later on to the acquisition of that power by which they are rightly employed and directed. In the measure that you master self, that you control your mental forces instead of being controlled by them, in just such measure will you master affairs and outward circumstances.

Show me a man under whose touch everything crumbles away, and who cannot retain success even when it is placed in his hands, and I will show you a man who dwells continually in those conditions of mind which are the very negation of power.

To be forever wallowing in the bogs of doubt, to be drawn continually into the quick-sands of fear, or blown ceaselessly about by the winds of anxiety, is to be a slave, and to live the life of a slave, even though success and influence is forever knocking at your door seeking admittance.

Such a man, being without faith and without self government, is incapable of the right government of affairs, and is slave to circumstances. In reality he is a slave to himself. Such are taught by affliction, and ultimately pass from weakness to strength by the stress of bitter experience.

Faith and purpose constitute the motive-power of life. There is nothing that a strong faith and an unflinching purpose may not accomplish. By the daily exercise of silent faith, the thought-forces are gathered together, and by the daily strengthening of silent purpose, those forces are directed towards the object of accomplishment.

Whatever your position in life may be, before you can hope to enter into any measure of success, usefulness, and power, you must learn how to focus your thought-forces by cultivating calmness and repose. Repose meaning: Lay or lie at rest. It may be that you are a business man, and you are suddenly confronted with some overwhelming difficulty or probable disaster. You grow fearful and anxious, and are at your wits end. To persist in such a state of mind would be fatal, for when anxiety steps in, correct judgment passes out.

Now if your will take advantage of a quite hour or two in the early morning or at night, and go away to some solitary spot, or to some room in your house where you know you will be absolutely free from intrusion, and having seated yourself in an easy chair you forcibly direct your mind right away from the object of anxiety by dwelling upon something in your life that is pleasing and bliss-giving. A calm, reposeful strength will gradually steal into your mind and your anxiety will pass away.

Upon the instant that you find your mind reverting to the lower plane or worry bring it back again, and reestablish it on the plane of peace and strength. When this is fully accomplished, you may then concentrate your whole mind upon the solution of your difficulty, and what was intricate and insurmountable to you in your hour of anxiety will be made plain and easy, and you will see with that clear vision and perfect judgment which belong only to a calm and untroubled mind, the right course to pursue and proper end to be brought about. It may be that you will have to try day after day before you will be able to perfectly calm your mind, but if you persevere, you will certainly accomplish it.

And the course that was presented to you in that hour of calmness must be carried out. Doubtless when you are again involved in the business of the day, and worries rise up again and creep in and begin to dominate you, you will begin to think that the course is a wrong or foolish one, but do not heed such suggestions. Be guided absolutely and entirely by the vision of calmness, and not by the shadows of anxiety. The hour of calmness is the hour of illumination and correct judgment. By such a course of mental discipline the scattered thought-forces are reunited, and directed, like rays of the search light, upon the problem at issue, with the result that it gives way before them.

There is no difficulty, however great, but will yield before a calm and powerful concentration of thought, and no legitimate object but may be speedily actualized by the intelligent use and direction on one's soul-forces.

Not until you have gone deeply and searchingly into your inner nature, and have overcome many enemies that lurk there, can you have any approximate conception of the subtle power of thought, of its inseparable relation to outward and material things, or of its magical potency, when rightly poised and directed, in readjusting and transforming the life-conditions.

Every thought you think is a force sent out, and in accordance with its nature and intensity will it go out to seek a lodgment in minds receptive to it, and will react upon yourself for good or evil. There is ceaseless reciprocity between mind and mind. Reciprocity meaning: affecting each in the same way.

There is also a continual interchange of thought forces. Selfish and disturbing thoughts are so many malignant and destructive forces, messengers of evil, sent out to stimulate and augment the evil in other minds, which in turn send them back upon you with added power.

While thoughts that are calm, pure, and unselfish are so many angelic messengers sent out into the world with health, healing, and blessedness upon their wings, counter acting the evil forces, pouring oil of joy upon the troubled waters of anxiety and sorrow, and restoring to broken hearts their heritage of immortality.

Think good thoughts, and they will quickly become actualized in your outward life in the form of good conditions.

Control your soul-forces, and you will be able to shape your outward life as you will. The difference between a savior and a sinner is this, that the one has a perfect control of all the forces within him; the other is dominated and controlled by them. There is absolutely no other way to true power and abiding peace, but by self-control, self government, and self-purification. To be at the mercy of your disposition is to be impotent, unhappy, and of little real use in the world.

The conquest of your petty likes and dislikes, your capricious loves and hates, your fits of anger, suspicion and jealousy and all the changing moods to which you are more or less helplessly subject, this is the task you have before you if you would weave into the web of life the golden threads of happiness and prosperity.

In so far as you are enslaved by the changing moods within you, you will need to depend on others and upon outward aids as you walk through life. If you would walk firmly and securely, and would accomplish any achievement, you must learn to rise above and control all such disturbing and retarding vibrations.

You must practice daily the habit of putting your mind at rest, going into the silence, as it is commonly called. This is a method of replacing a troubled thought with one of peace, a thought of weakness with one of strength. Until you succeed in doing this you cannot hope to direct your mental forces upon the problems and pursuits of life with any appreciable measure of success. It is a habit of diverting ones scattered forces into one powerful channel.

Just as useless marsh may be converted into a field of golden corn or a fruitful garden by draining and directing the scattered and harmful streams into one well cut channel, so he acquires calmness, and subdues and directs the thought-currents within himself, saves his soul, and fructifies his heart and life.

Thoughts currents are your river of flowing life. Thoughts are in constant flow. They are always there and they manifest them selves in the outward plain of this world. You thoughts are designed to draw to you that which you desire. Thoughts are like streams that are constantly flowing rivers of life altering possibilities. The right thoughts are the clean stream. Negative thoughts are the murky stream that flow murky events.

As you succeed in mastering your thought forces and control your impulses you will begin to feel growing within you a new and silent power and a settled feeling of composure and strength will become a part of you. Your potential powers will begin to manifest in front of you compared to the old way where your efforts were weak and ineffectual. You will now be able to do things with that calm confidence which commands success.

Along with this new power and strength there will be an awakening within you that interior illumination known as "intuition." You will no longer walk in darkness and mere speculation. This is meaning risky thinking. Speculation means unsure of the outcome. But instead you will find your self in the light of certainty. Intuition meaning: quick and ready insight. What this means is that you will see things from the inside, whereas before you were on the outside looking in.

With the development of this soul-vision, your judgment and mental penetration will be incalculably increased and there will evolve within you that prophetic vision by the aid of which you will be able to sense coming events and to forecast, with remarkable accuracy, the result of your efforts. And in just the measure that you alter your self from within will your outlook upon life alter. To the degree that you alter your mental attitude towards others they will alter their attitude and conduct towards you.

As you rise above the lower, debilitating and destructive thought-forces, you will come into contact with the positive, strengthening, and uplifting currents generated by strong, pure, and noble minds. Your happiness will be immeasurably intensified and you will begin to realize the joy, strength and power which are born only of self mastery. Debilitating meaning: make ill or weak.

This new joy, strength and power will be continually radiating from you and without any effort on your part. No, even though you are utterly unconscious of it, strong people will be drawn towards you like a magnet. Influence will be put into your hands and in accordance with your altered thought-forces the world around you will pour outward events and shape themselves.

A person's enemies are mostly those of their own house hold. Those people who would become useful, strong, and happy must cease at once to be a passive receptacle for the negative, beggarly and impure streams of thought.

As the wise householder commands his servants and invites his guests, so must he learn to command his desires, and to say with authority what thoughts he shall admit into the mansion of his soul.

Even a very partial success in self-mastery adds greatly to one's power and he who succeeds in perfecting this divine accomplishment enters into the possession of an undreamed of wisdom and inward strength and peace. They will come to realize that all the forces of the universe aid and protect his footstep's who is master of his soul-forces.

IT IS AS YOU SEE IT

Would you scale the highest heaven? Would you pierce the lowest hell? Live in dreams on constant beauty of in the basest thinking dwell.

For your thoughts are heavens above you. And your thoughts are hell below. Bliss is not, except in thinking, torment neither but thought can know.

Worlds will vanish but for thinking. Glory is not but in dreams, and the drama of the ages from the thought eternal streams.

Dignity and shame and sorrow, pain and anguish, love and hate are but a masking of the almighty pulsating thought that governs fate.

As the colors of the rainbow make the one uncolored beam so the universal changes make the one Eternal Dream. And the dream is all within you and the dreamer waits long, for the morning to awake him to the living thought and strong.

That shall make the ideal real; make to vanish dreams to hell, in the highest, holiest heaven where the pure and perfect dwell.

Evil is thought that thinks it, good the thought that makes it so. Light and darkness, sin and pureness likewise out of thinking grow.

Dwell in thought in the grandest and the grandest you shall see. Fix your mind upon the Highest and the Highest you shall be.

THE SECRET OF HEALTH, SUCCESS, AND POWER

We all remember with that intense delight as children, we listened to the never tiring fairy tale. How eagerly we followed the fluctuating fortunes of the good boy or girl ever protected, in the hour of crises, from the evil machinations of the scheming witch, the cruel giant or the wicked hag. At this age our little hearts never faltered for the fate of the hero or heroine. Neither did we doubt their ultimate triumph over all their enemies. For we knew that the fairies were infallible, and that they would never desert those who had consecrated themselves to the good and the true.

And what unspeakable joy pulsated within us when the fairy queen bringing all her magic to bear at the critical moment, scattered all the darkness and trouble and granted them the complete satisfaction of all their hopes, and they were "happy ever after."

Over the accumulating years, and an ever increasing intimacy with the so--called "realities" of life, our beautiful fairly-tailed world became obliterated, and its wonderful inhabitants were relegated, in the archives of memory, to the shadowy and unreal. And we thought we were wise and strong in thus leaving forever the land of childish dreams, but as we again become little children in the wondrous world of wisdom, we shall return again to the inspiring dreams of childhood and find that they are, after all, realities.

The fairy-folk so small and nearly always invisible, yet they possessed of an all-conquering and magical power, who bestowed upon the good, health, wealth, and happiness, along with all the gifts of nature in lavish profusion, start again into reality and become immortalized in the soul-realm of him who, by growth of wisdom, has entered into a knowledge of the power of thought, and the laws which govern the inner world of being. To him the fairies live again as thought people, thought messengers, thought powers in working harmony with the over ruling Good.

And those who, day by day, endeavor to harmonize their hearts with the heart of the Supreme Good, do in reality acquire true health, wealth, and happiness.

There is no protection that can compare with goodness, and by "goodness" I do not mean a mere outward conformity to the rules of morality, I mean pure thought, and noble aspirations, coupled with unselfish love and freedom from vain glory. To dwell continually in good thoughts, is to throw around your self a psychic atmosphere of sweetness and power which leaves its impression upon all who come in contact with it.

As the rising sun helps put the shadows in helpless defeat, so are all impotent forces of evil put to flight by the searching rays of positive thought which shine from a heart made strong in purity and faith.

Where there is sterling faith and uncompromising purity there is health, there is success, there is power. In such a one, disease, failure, and disaster can find no lodgment, for there is nothing on which they can feed.

Even physical conditions are largely determined by mental states; and to this truth the scientific world is rapidly being drawn. The old, materialistic belief that a person is what his body makes him has passed away and is being replaced by the inspiring belief that the human is superior to his body. And that their body is what they make it to be, by the power of thought. People every where are ceasing to believe that a person becomes dyspeptic (indigestion) and are coming to understand that he has indigestion because he is despairing. So, in the future starting here and now we shall understand that all disease has its origin in the mind and this should one day become common knowledge.

There is no evil in the universe but has its root and origin in the mind, and sin, sickness, and sorrow and affliction do not, in reality, belong to the universal order. They are not inherent in the nature of things, but are direct outcome of our ignorance of the right relations of things.

According to this tradition, there once lived, in India, a school of Philosophers who led a life of such absolute purity and simplicity that they commonly reached the ripe old age of one hundred and fifty years. To fall sick was looked upon with disgrace that is unpardonable. For this was considered to indicate a violation of eternal law.

The sooner we realize and acknowledge that sickness, far from being the arbitrary (selected at random) visitation of an offended God, or the test of an unwise Providence, is the result of our own error or sin. The sooner we shall enter upon the highway of health.

Disease comes to those who attract it. It comes to those whose minds and bodies are receptive to it. But on the other end of the spectrum it flees from those who has developed strong, pure, and the positive thought-sphere currents generates healing and life giving soul-forces.

If you are given to anger, worry, and soul destroying jealousy and greed of any other inharmonious state of mind and expect a perfect physical health, you are continually sowing the seeds of disease in your mind. Such conditions of the mind are carefully shunned by the wise man, for he knows them to be far more dangerous than a bad drain or an infected house. The wise man understands the house of the infected is a disease making environment.

Negative thought patterns are hideous monsters on the body. For they have the power to reshape your body and bring disease.

If you would be free from all physical aches and pains and would enjoy perfect physical harmony, then put your mind in order, and harmonize your thoughts. Think joyful thoughts, think loving thoughts. Let the elixir or the medicinal solution of good will slip into your veins. Then you will need no other medicine. Put away your jealousies, and your suspicions your worries and your hatreds along with your indulgences and you will put to sleep your dyspepsia, and your irritation and your nervousness and aching joints.

If you will continually persist in clinging to these debilitating and demoralizing habits of mind, then do not complain when you body is laid low with sickness. Simply put these negative mind forces make your body ill and weak because the thoughts you're thinking are sick ill and weak. This just stands to reason. These negative thoughts forces are inferior and are not natural.

This following story illustrates the close relationship that exists between the habits of the mind and there effects of the body conditions: A certain man was afflicted with a painful disease, and he tried on physician after another but all to no purpose. He then tried physician in other towns which were famous for their curative waters, and having bathed in them all, his disease was more painful than ever. One night he dreamed that a Presence came to him and said, "Brother has you tried all the means of cure? And he replied, "I have tried them all" "No," said the Presence, "come with me and I will show you a healing bath which has escaped your notice." The afflicted man followed, and the Presence led him to a clear pool of water, and said, "Plunge your self in this water and you shall surely recover," And there upon the Presence vanished.

The man plunged into the water, and at the same moment his disease left him. In that same instant he saw written above the pool "renounce." Upon waking, the full meaning of his dream flashed across his mind and looking within he discovered that he had all along been a victim to a sinful indulgence and he vowed that he would renounce it forever.

This man carried out his vow and from that day forward his affliction began to leave him and in a short time he was completely healed and was restored to great health. This story proves that your thinking makes it so either way.

Many people today complain that they are broken down through over work. In the majority of such cases the break down is more frequently the result of foolishly wasted energy.

If you would secure your health you must learn to work without friction. To become anxious or excited and to worry over needless details is to invite a break-down. Your work, whether in the brain or in the body is beneficial and health giving and the person who can work with a steady and calm persistency, freed from all anxiety to all but the work they have in front of them, will not only accomplish far more than the person who is always hurried and anxious, but he will retain his health.

This is a benefit that the others quickly forfeit. True success and true health go together. They are inseparably intertwined in the thought-realm. As mental harmony produces bodily health, so it also leads to a harmonious sequence in the actual working out of some one's plans. Order your thoughts and you will bring order to your life.

This suggests that one must command forth the right thoughts in rank, class or special group and do away with other thoughts that do not command wealth, health and power. In other words pull your mind weeds. Plant new healthy crops and drape your self in fine clothes of the soul-forces.

Pour the oil of tranquility upon the turbulent waters of the passions and prejudices and the tempest of the misfortune. Whatsoever they may threaten will be powerless to wreck the baroque of your soul, as it threads its way across the ocean of life. And if that elaborately ornamented soul is piloted by a cheerful and never-failing faith its course will be doubly sure, and many perils will pass it by which would otherwise attack it.

By the power of faith every enduring work is accomplished. Faith in the Supreme, faith in the overruling Law, faith in your work and in your power to accomplish that work. Here is the rock upon which you must build if you are to achieve if you would stand tall and not fall. To follow, under all circumstances the highest promptings within you. To always be true to the divine self, to rely upon the inward light. The inward divine voice listen only and to pursue your purpose with a fearless and restful heart, believing that the future will yield unto you the mead of every thought and effort. Knowing that the laws of the universe can never fail, and that your own will come back to you with mathematical exactitude. This is the faith that is considered living faith.

By the power of such a faith the dark waters of uncertainty are divided. Every mountain of difficulty crumbles away and the believing soul passes on unharmed. Strive, listeners to acquire above everything the priceless possession of this dauntless faith, for it is the object thought that acts as a charm of happiness, of success, and of peace, of power and all that makes life great and superior to suffering.

Build upon this faith and you will build upon the Rock of the Eternal and with the materials and blessings of the Eternal. The structure you will erect will never be dissolved. It will transcend all the accumulations of material luxuries and riches, the end of which is dust. Whether you have been hurled into the depths of sorrow, or have been lifted upon the heights of joy, forever retain your hold upon this faith. To forever return to it as your rock of refuge, and to keep your feet firmly planted upon its immortal and immovable base. As you center yourself in such a faith you will become possessed of such a spiritual strength as will shatter, like so many toys of glass and you will achieve a success such as the mere striver you will be able to say after worldly gain can never know or dream of.

If you have this kind of faith you will not only do this but you will be able to say to the mountains of the soul "be thou cast into the sea and it shall come to pass."

There are those people today that are tabernacle in flesh and blood who have realized this faith who live in it and by it day after day and who having put it to the uttermost test, have entered into the possession of its glory and peace.

Such have sent out the word of command and the mountains of sorrow and disappointment, of mental awareness and physical pain have passed from them and have been cast into the sea of oblivion.

If you will become possessed of this faith you will not need to trouble about your future success and failure, for success will come. You will not need to become anxious about results but will work joyfully and peacefully knowing that right and right efforts will inevitably bring about right results.

I know a lady who has entered into many blissful satisfactions and recently a friend remarked to her, "Oh, how fortunate you are! You only have to wish for a thing and it comes to you." And it did indeed appear so on the surface. But in reality all the blessedness that has entered into this woman's life is the direct result of the inward state of blessedness which she has, throughout her life been cultivating and training towards perfection. Plain wishing brings nothing but severe disappointment. It is living that tells.

The foolish wish and grumble, the wise work and then waits. This woman had worked. She had worked from within, especially within her heart and soul. With the invisible hands of the spirit she had built up with the precious stones of faith, hope, and joy with devotion and love and a fair temple of light whose glorifying radiance was ever around her. It beamed in her eye. It did shine through her countenance. It vibrated in her voice. And all who came into her presence felt its captivating spell.

And as with her, so it is with you. Your success and your failure, your influence and your whole life you carry about with you, for your dominate trends of thought are the determining factors in your destiny. Dominate meaning: have control over. Rise high above.

Send forth loving thoughts, that are stainless and happy and blessings will fall into your hands, and your table will be spread with the cloth of peace. Send forth hateful, impure, and unhappy thoughts and curses will rain down upon you like stones. Then fear and unrest will wait upon your pillow.

You are the unconditional maker of your own fate. What ever fate that may be. Every moment you are sending forth from you the influences which will make or break your life. Let your heart grow large and loving and unselfish, and great and lasting will be your influence and success, even though you make little money. Confine it within the narrow limits of self-interest, even though you become a millionaire your influence and success, at the final reckoning will be found to be utterly insignificant.

Cultivate then this pure and unselfish spirit, and combine with purity and faith, singleness of purpose, and you are evolving from within the elements, not only of abounding health and enduring success, but of greatness and power.

If your present position is distasteful to you, and your heart is not in your work, nevertheless perform your duties with undeniable diligence, meanwhile resting your mind in the idea that the better position and greater opportunities are waiting for you. So ever keep an active mental outlook for budding possibilities so that when the critical moment arrives and the new channel presents itself, you will step into it with your mind fully prepared for the undertaking and with that intelligence and foresight which is born of mental discipline.

Whatever your task may be, concentrate your whole mind upon it, throw into is all the energy of which you are capable. The faultless completion of small tasks leads to larger tasks. See to it that you rise by steady climbing, and you will never fail. And herein lies the secret of true power. Learn, by constant practice, how to husband your resources, and to concentrate them, at any moment, upon a given point. The foolish waste all of their mental and spiritual energy in not important or serious matters. They waste energy on foolish chatter and selfish argument, not to mention wasteful physical excesses.

If you would acquire overcoming power you must cultivate poise and passivity. Poise meaning: balance.

Passivity meaning: not active but acted upon, submissive. You have to be able to stand alone. All power is associated with immovability. The mountain, is the massive rock. How about the storm tried Oak tree? Both speak to us of power, because of their combined solitary grandeur and latent fixity.

While the shifting sand, and the yielding twig and the wavering reed speak to us of weakness, because they are movable and non-resistant, and are utterly useless when detached from their fellows. He is a man of power who, when all of his fellows are swayed by some emotion or passion, remains calm and unmoved.

He only is fitted to command and control that has succeeded in commanding and controlling himself. The hysterical, the fearful, the thoughtless and frivolous, let them seek their own company. They will eventually fall for lack of support. But the calm soul, the fearless, the thoughtful and grave, let such seek the solitude of the forest, and the desert. Let them seek the mountain tops and to their power more power will be added and they will more and more successfully stem the psychic currents and whirlpools which engulf mankind.

Passion is not power. Passion is the abuse of power. It is the scattering of the power. Passion is like a furious storm which beats fiercely and wildly upon the embattled rock, while power is like the rock itself. The rock remains silent and unmoved through it all. That was a manifestation of true power when Martin Luther, wearied with the persuasions of his fearful friends, who were doubtful as to his safety should he go to worms, replied, "If there were as many devils in worms as there are tiles on the house tops I should go." And when Benjamin Disraeli broke down in his first Parliamentary speech, and brought himself the derision of the house, that was an exhibition of germinal power when he exclaimed, "The day will come when you will consider it an honor to listen to me."

When that young man, whom I knew, passing through continual reverses and misfortunes, was mocked by his friends and told to desist from further effort, and he replied, "The time is not far distant when you will marvel at my good fortune and success." He showed them he was possessed of that silent and irresistible power which has taken him over innumerable difficulties, and crowned his life with success.

If you have not this power, you may acquire it by practice, and the beginning of power Is likewise the beginning of wisdom. You must commence by overcoming those purposeless trivialities to which you have up to now been a victim. Boisterous and uncontrolled laughter, slander and idle talk, and joking merely to raise a laugh, all these things must be put on the side as so much waste of valuable energy.

St. Paul never showed his wonderful insight into the hidden laws of human progress to greater advantage than when he warned the Ephesians against "Foolish talking and jesting which is not convenient," for, to dwell habitually in such practices is to destroy all spiritual power and life.

As you succeed in rendering yourself impervious to such mental dissipations you will begin to understand what true power is, and you will then commence to grapple with the more powerful desires and appetites which hold your soul in bondage, and bar the way to power, and your further progress will then be made clear.

Above all, be of single aim. Have a legitimate and useful purpose and devote yourself unreservedly to it. Let knowing draw you aside. Remember that "The double minded man is unstable in all his ways." Be eager to learn but slow to beg. Have a through understanding of your work and let it be your own. As you proceed, ever following the inward Guide, the infallible Voice, you will pass on from victory to victory and will rise step by step to ever higher resting places, and your ever-broadening outlook will gradually reveal to you the essential beauty and purpose of this life.

Self-purified health will be yours. Faith protected success will be yours. Self-governed power will be yours. In addition, all that you do will be successful. So, cease from being a disjointed unit that is enslaved. You will be in harmony with the Great Law working no longer against but with the universal Life, the Universal Good.

After what health you gain it will remain with you. Whatever success you have attained you will beyond all human computation, and will never pass away. Whatever influence and power you wield will continue to increase throughout the ages, for it will be a part of that unchangeable Principle which supports the universe.

This then is the secret to health. A pure heart and a well ordered mind. This is the secret of success. This is the secret to an unfaltering faith, and a wisely directed purpose. This is the secret of reining in with an unfaltering will the dark steed of desire. This is the secret of power.

All ways are waiting for my feet to tread, The light and dark, the living and the dead, The broad and narrow way, the high and low, The good and bad, and with quick step or slow, I now may enter any way I will, And find, by walking, which is good, which ill.

And all good things my wondering feet await, If I but come, with vow inviolate, Unto the narrow, high and holy way Of heart-born purity, and their-in stay. Walking, secure from him who taunts and scorns, to flowery meads, across the path of thorns.

And I may stand where health, success, and power await my coming, if each fleeting hour, I cling to love and patience, and abide with stainlessness, and never step aside. From high integrity so shall I see At last the land of immorality.

And I may seek and find I may achieve, I may not claim, but, losing may retrieve. The Law bends not for me, but I must bend Unto the Law, it I would reach the end Of my afflictions, if I would restore My soul to light and Life, and weep no more.

Not mine the arrogant and selfish claim To all good things, be mine the lowly aim. To seek and find, and comprehend, And wisdom-ward all holy footsteps wend. Nothing is mine to claim or to command, But all is mine to know and understand.

THE SECRET OF HAPPINESS

Great is the thirst for happiness, and equally great is the lack of happiness. The majority of the poor long for riches. They believed that their possession would bring them supreme and lasting happiness. Many who are rich, having gratified every desire and whim, suffer from boredom and are therefore full, and are farther from the possession of happiness even than the poor.

If we reflect upon this state of things, it will ultimately lead us to a knowledge of the all important truth that happiness is not derived from mere outward possessions, nor misery from the lack of them. If this were so, we should find the poor always miserable, and the rich always happy. Now the reverse is frequently the case.

Some of the wretched people whom I have known were those who were surrounded with riches and luxury while some of the brightest and happiest people I have met were possessed of only the barest necessities of life.

Many people who have accumulated riches have confessed that the selfish gratification which followed the acquisition of riches has robbed life of its sweetness, and that they were never happy as when they were poor.

What then is happiness and how is it to be secured? Is it a figment, or a delusion? And is suffering alone at all seasons of the year?

We shall find, after earnest observation and reflection, that all, except those who have entered the way of wisdom, believe that happiness is only obtained by the gratification of desires. It is the belief that is rooted in the soil of ignorance. This ignorance is continually watered by selfish cravings that are the cause of all misery in the world.

And I do not limit the word desire to the grosser animal cravings. It extends to the higher psychic realm where far more powerful, subtle and insidious cravings hold in bondage the intellectual and refined, depriving them of all that beauty, harmony, and purity of soul whose expression is happiness.

Most people will admit that selfishness is the cause of all unhappiness in the world, but they fall under the soul-destroying delusion that it is somebody else's selfishness, and not their own.

When you are willing to admit that all your unhappiness is the result of your own selfishness you will not be far from the gates of Paradise. But so long as you are convinced that it is selfishness of others that is robbing you of joy, so long will you remain a prisoner in your self-created hell.

Happiness is that inward state of perfect satisfaction which is joy and peace and from which all desire is eliminated. The satisfaction which results from gratified desire is brief and illusionary, and is always followed by an increased demand for more gratification. Desire is an insatiable as the ocean and uproars and protests louder and louder as its demands are attended to. It claims ever increasing service from its misled and deceived devotees. Until at last they are struck down with physical or mental anguish and are hurled into the purifying fires of suffering.

Desire is the region of hell and all torments are centered there. The giving up of desire is the realization of heaven and all delights await the pilgrims there. This is suggesting that all humans have hell running through their veins. Therefore I conclude that my desires are a gift from hell.

I sent my soul through the invisible, some letter of that after life to spell, and by and by my soul returned to me, And whispered, "I myself am heaven and hell."

Heaven and hell are inward states. Sink into self and all its gratifications and you sink into hell. Rise above self into that state of consciousness which is the utter denial and forgetfulness of self. Then you enter in heaven. Self is blind, and without judgment, not possessed of true knowledge and always leads to suffering. Correct the perception, unbiased judgment, and true knowledge belong only to the divine state. Only in so far as you realize this divine consciousness can you know what real happiness is.

So long as you persist in selfishly seeking for your own personal happiness so long will happiness delude you, and you will be sowing the seeds of wretchedness. In so far as you succeed in losing yourself in the service of others in that measure will happiness come to you and you will reap a harvest of bliss.

"It is in loving, not in being loved, the heart is blessed." It is in giving, not in seeking gifts, we find our quest. Whatever be the longing or the need that you give; so shall the soul be fed, and you indeed shall truly live. Cling to self and you cling to sorrow. Renounce and let go of self and you enter peace. To seek selfishly is not only to lose happiness but even that which we believe to be the source of happiness.

See how the glutton is continually looking about for a new delicacy where with to stimulate his deadened appetite. Then how bloated, burdened and diseased and scarcely any food at last is eaten with pleasure. Where as, he who has mastered his appetite, and not only does not seek, but never thinks of gustatory pleasure, fines delight in the most frugal meal.

The angel form of happiness, which men, looking through the eyes of self, imagine they see in gratified desire, when clasped is always found to be the skeleton of misery. Truly, "He that seeks his life shall lose it, and he that loses his life shall find it."

Abiding happiness will come to you when, ceasing to selfishly cling, you are willing to give up. When you are willing to lose, unreservedly, that impermanent thing which is so dear to you, and which, whether you cling to it or not, will one day be snatched from you, then you will find that that which seemed t you like a painful loss, turns out to be a supreme gain.

To give up in order to gain, than this there is no greater delusion, nor no more prolific source of misery; but to be willing to yield up and to suffer loss, this is indeed the Way of Life.

How is it possible to find real happiness by centering ourselves in those things which by their very nature, must pass away? Abiding and real happiness can only be found by centering ourselves in that which is permanent. Rise, therefore, above the clinging to and the craving for impermanent things and you will then enter into a consciousness of the eternal, and as rising above self, and by growing more and more into the spirit of purity, self-sacrifice and universal love. You then become centered in that consciousness and you will realize that happiness which has no reaction, and which can never be taken from you.

The heart that has reached utter self forgetfulness in its love for others has not only become possessed of the highest happiness, but has entered into immortality, for it has realized the Divine. Look back upon your life, and you will find that the moments of supreme happiness were those in which you uttered some word, or performed some act, of compassion or self-denying love.

Spiritually, happiness and harmony are synonymous. Harmony is one phase of the Great Law whose spiritual expression is love. All selfishness is discord, and to be selfish is to be out of harmony with the divine order. As we realize that all-embracing love which is the negation of self, we put ourselves in harmony with the divine music, the universal song, and the infallible melody which is true happiness becomes our own.

Men and women are rushing here and there in the blind search for happiness, and cannot find it. Never will they recognize that happiness is already within them and round about them, filling the universe and they, in their selfish searching, are shutting themselves out from it.

"I will follow happiness to make her mine, past towering oak and swinging ivy vine. She fled, I chased, over slanting hill and dale, over fields and meadows, in the purple vale. Pursuing rapidly over dashing stream, I scaled the dizzy cliffs where eagles scream, I traversed swiftly every land and sea, but always happiness eluded me.

"Exhausted, fainting, I pursued no more, but sank to rest upon a barren shore. One came and asked for food, and one for alms. I placed the bread and gold in bony hands, One came for sympathy, and one for rest, I shared with every sweet happiness, with form divine, Stood by me, whispering softly, 'I am thine.'"

These beautiful words express the secret of all abounding happiness. Sacrifice the personal and transient, and you rise at once into the impersonal and permanent. Give up that narrow cramped self that seeks to render all things subservient to its own petty interests, and you will enter into the company of the angels, into the very heart and essence of universal love. Forget yourself entirely in the sorrows of others and in ministering to others, and divine happiness will emancipate you from all sorrow and suffering.

"Taking the first step with a good thought, the second with a good word, and the third with a good deed. I entered Paradise." And you also may enter into Paradise by pursuing the same course. It is not beyond, it is here. It is realized only by the unselfish. It is known in its fullness only to the pure in heart.

If you have not realized this unbounded happiness you may begin to actualize it by ever holding before you the lofty ideal of unselfish love, and aspiring towards it.

Aspiration of prayer is desire turned upward. It is the soul turning towards its Divine source, where alone permanent satisfaction can be found. By aspiration the destructive forces of desire are transmuted into divine and all preserving energy. To have an ambition is to make an effort to shake off the trammels of desire. It is the prodigal made wise by loneliness and suffering, returning to his father's Mansion.

As you rise above the sordid self, as you break one after another, the chains that bind you, will you realize the joy of giving, as distinguished from the misery of grasping and giving of your substance and the giving of your intellect, the giving of your love and the light that is growing within you. You will then understand that it is indeed 'more blessed to give than to receive." But the giving must be of the heart without any taint of self, without desire for reward. The gift of pure love is always attended with bliss. If, after you have given, you are wounded because you are not thanked or flattered, or your name put in the paper, know then that your gift was prompted by vanity and not love, and you were merely giving in order to get, were not really giving, but grasping.

Lose your self in the welfare of others, forget yourself in all that you do. This is the secret of abounding happiness. Ever be on the watch to guard against selfishness, and learn faithfully the divine lessons of inward sacrifice. So shall you climb the highest heights of happiness, and shall remain in the never clouded sunshine of universal joy. Then you will be clothed in the shining garment of immortality.

Are you searching for the happiness that does not fade away?

Are you looking for the joy that lives, and leaves no grievous day?

Are you panting for the water brooks of Love, and Life, and Peace?

Then let all dark desires depart, and selfish seeking cease.

Are you lingering in the paths of pain, grief haunted, stricken sore?

Are you wondering in the ways that wound you weary feet the more?

Are you sighing for the resting Place where tears and sorrows cease?

Then sacrifice your selfish heart, and find the Heart of Peace.

REALIZING PROSPERITY

It is only granted the heart that abounds with the integrity, trust, generosity and love to realize the true prosperity. The heart that is not possessed of these qualities cannot know true prosperity. For prosperity like happiness is not outward possession but an inward realization.

The greedy man may become a millionaire, but he will be wretched, mean and poor. He will consider himself outwardly poor so long as there is a man in the world who is richer than he is. While the up-right, the open handed and loving will realize a full rich prosperity even though their outward possessions may be small.

"He is poor who is dissatisfied: he is rich who is contented with what he has," and he is richer who is generous with what he has.

When we contemplate the fact that the universe is abounding in all good things, whether they be material as well as spiritual, and compare it with man's blind eagerness to secure a few gold coins or a few acres of dirt. It is then realized how dark we have become with selfish ignorance. It is then we know that self seeking leads to self destruction.

Nature gives all without reservation and loses nothing. Man grasping all loses everything. If you would just stop to realize that true prosperity does not settle dawn as many have done into the belief that if you do right everything will go wrong.

Do not allow the word "competition" to shake your faith in the supremacy of righteousness. I care not about what men say about the law of competition for do I not know the Unchangeable Law. This law will one day put them to the test.

This law right now is put to the test in the heart of the righteous man. And not knowing this law I can contemplate all dishonesty with undisturbed repose, for I know where certain destruction awaits it.

Under all circumstances do that which you believe to be right, and trust the Law. Trust the Divine Power that has its existence in the mind of the universe. This Law will never desert you and you will always be protected.

By such a trust all of your losses will be converted into gains and all curses which threaten will be transmuted into blessings. Never let go of integrity, or generosity and love. For these coupled with the energy will lift you into a truly prosperous state. Do not believe the world when it tells you that you must always attend to "Number one" first, and then to others afterwards.

To do this is not to think of others at all, only one's own comforts. This is selfish. To those who practice this the day will come when they will be deserted by all and when they cry out in their loneliness and anguish there will be no one to hear them much less help them.

To consider one self before all others is to cramp and warp and hinder every noble and divine impulse. Let your soul expand and let your heart reach out to others in loving and generous warmth and great and lasting will be your joy, and all the prosperity will come rushing towards you.

Those who have wandered from the highway of right thinking guard themselves against competition. Those who always pursue the right thing need not be troubled about such defense. This is not an empty statement. There are people today who by the power on their integrity and faith have defied all competition. They have without swerving in the least from their methods when competed with, have risen steadily into prosperity, while those who tried to undermine them have fallen back defeated.

To possess those inward qualities which constitute goodness is to be armored against all the powers of evil and to be doubly protected in every trial, and to build one self up in those qualities is to build up a success which cannot be shaken. Then one will enter into prosperity which will endure forever. The white robe of the Heart Invisible I stained with sin and sorrow, grief and pain. And all repentant pools and springs of prayer shall not avail to wash it white again.

While in the path of ignorance I walk, the stains of error will not cease to cling. Defilements mark the crooked path of self, where anguish lurks and disappointments sting. Knowledge and wisdom only can avail to purify and make my garment clean, for therein lie love's waters, therein rests peace undisturbed, eternal and serene.

Sin and repentance is the path of pain, knowledge and wisdom is the path of peace, by the near way of practice I will find where bliss begins, how pains and sorrows cease.

Self shall depart, and truth shall take its place, the Changeless One, the invisible shall up his abode in me, and cleanse the White Robe of the Heart invisible.

TIMELESS WISDOM

THE POWER OF MEDITATION

Divine medication is spiritual meditation. This is the royal road to divinity. It is the mystic ladder which reaches from earth to heaven, from error to the eternal truth, from pain to peace. Every saint that ever was has to climb it. Every sinner must, sooner or later has got to come to it.

Every pilgrim that turns his back upon his self and the world and sets his face resolutely towards the Eternal house, must plant his feet upon the golden dawn. Without its aid you cannot grow into the divine state. You cannot grow into the divine likeness, the divine peace and the fadeless glories and unpolluting joys of truth will remain hidden from you.

Meditation is the intense dwelling in thought upon an idea or theme with the object of thoroughly comprehending it. Whatsoever you constantly meditate upon you will not only come to understand, but will grow more and more into its likeness. For it will become incorporated into your very being and will become in fact your very self.

If therefore you constantly dwell upon that which is selfish and debasing, you will ultimately become selfish and debased. If you ceaselessly think upon that which is pure and unselfish you will surely become pure and unselfish.

Tell me what that is upon which you most frequently and intensely think, that to which, in your silent hours, your soul most naturally turns, and I tell you to what place of pain or peace you are traveling, whether you are growing into the likeness or the divine or the bestial.

There is an unavoidably tendency to become literally the embodiment of that quality upon which one most thinks. In other words you become what you think about most of the time.

Let, therefore, the object of your meditation be above and not below. So that every time you revert to it in thought you will be lifted up. Let it be pure and unmixed with any selfish element, so shall your heart become purified and drawn nearer to truth, and not defiled and dragged down more hopelessly into error. Meditation, in the spiritual sense in which I am now using it, is the secret of all growth in spiritual life and knowledge. Every prophet sage, and savior became such by the power of meditation.

Buddha meditated upon the truth until he could say, "I am the truth." Jesus brooded upon the Divine immanence until at last he declared, "I and My Father are One."

Meditation centered upon divine realities is the very essence and soul of prayer. It is the silent reaching of the soul towards the Eternal. Mere petitionary prayer without meditation is a body without a soul, and is powerless to lift the mind and heart above sin and affliction.

If you are praying daily for wisdom, for peace, or for a loftier purity with a fuller realization of truth, and that for which you pray is still far from you, it means that you are praying for one thing while living out in thought and acting another. If you will cease from such waywardness, and taking your mind off those things. The selfish clinging to which debars you from the possession of the stainless realities for which you pray.

If you will no longer ask God to grant you that which you do not deserve, or bestow upon you that love and compassion which you refuse to bestow upon others, but will commence to think and act in the spirit of truth, you will day by day be growing into those realities, so that ultimately you will become one with them.

He who would secure any worldly advantage must be willing to work with strength and energy, with the intensity or force for it. He would be foolish indeed who, waiting with folded hands expected it to come to him for the mere asking. Do not then vainly imagine that you can obtain the heavenly possessions without making the effort. Only when you commence to work earnestly in the Kingdom of Truth will you be allowed to partake of the Bread of Life. When you have, by patient and uncomplaining effort earned the spiritual wages for which you ask they will not be with held from you. If you really seek the truth and not merely your own gratification, if you love it above all worldly pleasures and gains, more even than happiness itself you will be willing to make the effort necessary for its achievement.

If you would be freed of sin and sorrow, if you would taste of that spotless purity for which you sigh and pray, if you would realize wisdom and knowledge and would enter into possession of profound and abiding peace, come now and enter the path of meditation, and let the supreme object of your meditation be truth.

At the outset, meditation must be distinguished from idleness. There is nothing dreamy and unpractical about it. It is a process of searching and uncompromising thought which allows nothing to remain but the simple naked truth.

Thus meditating you will no longer strive to build yourself up in your prejudices but, forgetting self, you will remember only that you are seeking the truth. And so you will remove, one by one, the errors which you have built up around your self in the past, and will patiently wait for the revelation of truth which will come when your errors have been sufficiently removed.

In the silent humility of your heart you will realize that: There is an inmost center in us all where truth abides in fullness and around. Wall upon wall the gross flesh hems it in. This perfect, clear perception, which is truth a baffling and perverting carnal mesh blinds it, and makes all error and to know. Rather consist in opening out a way whence the imprisoned splendor may escape. Than in effecting entry for a light supposed to be without.

Select some portion of the day in which to meditate, and keep that period sacred to your purpose. The best time is the very early morning when the spirit of repose is upon everything.

All natural conditions will then be in your favor.

The passions after long bodily fast of the night will be subdued. The excitements and worries of the previous day will have died away, and the mind, strong and yet restful, will be receptive to spiritual instruction.

Indeed one of the first efforts you will be called upon to make will be to shake off laziness and indulgence. If you refuse you will be unable to advance, for the demands of the spirit are imperative.

To be spiritually awakened is also to be mentally and physically awakened. The sluggard and the self indulgent can have no knowledge of truth. He, who possessed of health and strength, wastes the calm precious hours of the silent morning in drowsy indulgence is totally unfit to climb the heavenly heights. He whose awakening consciousness has become alive to its lofty possibilities, who is beginning to shake off the darkness of ignorance in which the world in enveloped, rises before the stars have ceased their vigil and, grappling with the darkness within his soul, strives, by holy aspiration, to perceive the light of Truth while the un-awakened world dreams on.

The heights by great men reached and kept, were not attained by sudden flight. But they, while their companions slept, were toiling upward in the night. No saint, no holy man, no teacher of Truth ever lived who did not rise early in the morning. Jesus habitually rose early, and climbed the solitary mountains to engage in Holy Communion. Buddha always rose an hour before sunrise and engaged in meditation and all his disciples were enjoined to do the same.

If you have to start you daily duties at a very early hour, and are thus debarred from giving the early morning systematic meditation, try to give an hour at night, and should this, by the length and laboriousness of your daily task be denied you, you need not despair, for you may turn your thoughts upward in holy meditation in the intervals of your work. In those few idle moments which you now waste in aimlessness, and you should your work be of that kind which becomes by practice automatic, you may meditate while engaged upon it.

That eminent Christian Saint Ernest Johnson realized his vast knowledge of divine things while working as a steel worker. In every life there is time to think and the busiest, the most laborious is not shut out from aspiration and meditation.

Spiritual meditation and self-discipline are inseparable. You will, therefore start to meditate upon your self so as to try and understand yourself. For, remember, the great object you will have in view will be the complete removal of all your errors in order that you may realize Truth.

You will begin to question your motives, thoughts, and acts and compare them with your ideal, and endeavoring to look upon them with a calm, and impartial eye. In this manner you will be continually gaining more of that mental and spiritual equilibrium without which people are but helpless straws upon the ocean of life.

If you are given to hatred or anger you will meditate upon gentleness and forgiveness, all as to become acutely alive to a sense of your harsh and foolish conduct. You will then begin to dwell in thoughts of love, of gentleness, and of abounding forgiveness. Then as you overcome the lower by the higher there will gradually and silently steal into your heart knowledge of the Divine Law of Love with an understanding of its bearing upon all the intricacies of life and conduct. And in applying this knowledge to your every thought, word and act, you will grow more and more gentle, more and more loving, and more and more divine. And thus with every error, every selfish desire, every human weakness, by the power of meditation is it overcome, and each is sin, each error is thrust out, a fuller and clearer measure of the Light of Truth Illumines the Pilgrims soul.

By meditating you will fortify your soul. You will fortify yourself against your only true enemy, your selfish, perishable self. And will be establishing your self more and more firmly in the divine and imperishable self that in inseparable from Truth. The direct outcome or your meditations will be a calm, spiritual strength which will be your stay and resting place in the struggles of life.

Great is the overcoming power of holy thought, and the strength and knowledge gained in the hour of silent meditation will enrich the soul with saving remembrance in the hour of strife, sorrow and or temptation.

As by the power of meditation, you grow in wisdom, you will relinquish, more and more, your selfish desires which are fickle, impermanent and productive of sorrow and pain. They will take your stand with increasing steadfastness and trust, upon the unchangeable principles, and will realize heavenly rest.

The use of meditation is the acquirement of a knowledge of eternal principles, and the power which results from meditation is the ability to rest upon and trust those principles. So become one with the Eternal. The end of meditation is therefore, direct knowledge of Truth, God, and the realization of divine and profound peace.

Let your meditations take their rise from the honorable ground which you now occupy. Remember that you are to grow into Truth by steady perseverance.

If you are an atheistic Christian, meditate ceaselessly upon the spotless purity and divine excellence of the character of Buddha. And Jesus and then apply their every precept to your inner life and outward conduct, so as to approximate more and more towards their perfection.

Do not be as those religious ones, who, refusing to meditate upon the law of Truth, and to put into practice the precepts given to them by their Master, are content to formerly worship, to cling to their practical creeds, and to continue in the ceaseless round of sin and suffering. Strive to rise, by the power of meditation, above all selfish clinging to partial gods or party creeds; above dead formalities and lifeless ignorance. Thus walking the highway of wisdom, with mind fixed upon the spotless Truth, you shall know no halting place short of the realization of Truth.

He who earnestly meditates first perceives a truth, as it were, afar off, and them realizes it by daily practice. It is only the doer of the Word of Truth that can know the doctrine of truth, for though by pure thought the Truth is perceived, it is actualized by practice.

Said the divine Ernest Johnson, "He who gives himself up to vanity or undue pride in oneself, and does not give himself up to meditation, forgetting the real aim in life and grasping at pleasure, will in time envy him who has exerted himself in meditation," He instructs his disciples in the following "Five great Meditations": The first meditation is the meditation of Love. This is where you adjust your heart that you long for the real and look to the welfare of all beings, including the happiness of your enemies.

The second meditation is the meditation of pity, This is where you think of all beings in distress, vividly representing in your imagination their sorrows and anxieties so as to arouse a deep compassion for them in your soul.

The third meditation is the meditation of joy. This is where you think in terms of prosperity of others, and rejoice with their rejoicings.

The fourth meditation is the meditation of impurity. This is where you consider the evil consequences of corruption, the effects of sin and disease. How trivial often the pleasure of the moment, and how fatal its consequences.

The fifth meditation is the meditation on serenity. This is where you rise above Love and hate, tyranny and oppression. Wealth and want and regard your own fate with impartial calmness and perfect tranquility.

By engaging in these meditations the disciples of Ernest Johnson arrived at the knowledge of the Truth. But whether you engage in these particular meditations or not matters little so long as your object is Truth, so long as you hunger and thirst for that righteousness which is a holy heart and a blameless life.

In your meditations, therefore, let your heart from and expand with ever broadening love, until, freed from all hatred, and passion, and condemnation. It embraces the whole universe with thoughtful tenderness.

As the flower opens its petals to receive the morning light, so open your soul more and more to the Glorious Light of Truth. Soar upward upon the wings of aspiration. Become fearless and believe in the loftiest possibilities. Believe that a life of absolute meekness is possible. Believe that a life of stainless beauty is possible. Believe that a life of perfect holiness is possible. Believe that realization of the highest truth is possible. He who so believes, does climb rapidly the heavenly hills. While the unbelievers continue to grope darkly and painfully in the fog bound alleys.

So, believing, so aspiring, so meditating, divinely sweet and beautiful will be your spiritual experiences, and glorious the revelations that will enrapture your inward vision. As you realize the divine Love, the divine Justice, the divine Purity, the perfect Law of Good, of God, great will be your bliss and deep your peace. Old things will pass away, and all things will become new.

The veil of the material universe, so dense and impenetrable to the eye of error, so thin and gauzy to the eye of Truth, will be lifted and the spiritual universe will be revealed.

Time will cease, and you will live only in Eternity. Change and mortality will no more cause you anxiety and sorrow, for you will become established in the unchangeable, and will dwell in the very heart of immortality.

STAR OF WISDOM

Star of the birth of Eliza, birth of the Buddha and Jesus. Who told the wise ones heavenward looking, waiting; watching for their gleaming in the darkness of the night-time. In the starless gloom of midnight shining herald of the coming of the kingdom of the righteous, teller of the Mystic story of the lowly birth of the Godhead. In the stable of the passions in the manger of the mind-soul; Silent singer of the secret of compassion deep and holy to the heart with sorrow burdened; to the soul with waiting weary. Star of all surpassing brightness, Thou again does deck the midnight. Thou again do cheer the wise ones; watching in the creedal darkness, weary of the endless battle with the grinding blades of errors. Tired of lifeless, useless idols of the dead forms of religions; spent with watching for your shining. Thou has ended their despairing, Thou has lighted up their pathway. You have brought again the old truths to the hearts of all the watchers. To the souls of them that love thee. Thou do speak of joy and gladness. Of the peace that comes of sorrow. Blessed are they that can see thee, weary wanderers in the nighttime. Blessed they who feel the throbbing in their bosoms feel the pulsing of a deep love stirred within them. By the great power of thy shining; Let us learn thy lesson truly Learn it faithfully and humbly. Learn it meekly, wisely, gladly. Ancient star of Eliza Light of Jesus and Buddha.

MASTER OF SELF–MASTER OF TRUTH

Upon the battlefield of the soul two masters are ever contending for the crown of supremacy, for the kingship and dominion of the heart, the master of self and the master of truth. The master of evil verses the master of good. One is called the "Prince of this world." The other is called the "Father God." The master self is that rebellious one whose weapons are passion, pride, vanity, self-willed. These are implements of darkness. The Master of Truth is that meek and lowly one whose weapons are gentleness, patience, purity, sacrifice, humility, love, instruments of Light.

In every soul the battle is waged a soldier cannot engage at once in two opposing armies, so every heart is enlisted either in the ranks of the self Truth. There is no half and half course.

There is self and there is Truth. Where self is Truth is not. Where Truth is self is not. Jesus, the manifested Christ, declared that "No man can serve two masters; for he will hate the one and love the other, or else he will hold to the one and despise the other." You cannot serve God and Mammon. Truth is so simple and unchanging in its course and uncompromising that it admits of no complexity, no turning, no qualification.

Self is ingenious, crooked, and governed by subtle and snaky desire. It admits of endless turnings and qualifications, and the deluded worshipers of self vainly imagine that they can gratify every worldly desire, and at the same time possess the Truth.

But the lovers of Truth worship Truth with the sacrifice of self, and ceaselessly guard themselves against worldliness and self-seeking.

Do you seek to know and realize Truth? Then you must be prepared to sacrifice, to renounce to the uttermost, for Truth in all its glory can only be perceived and known when the last vestige of self has disappeared.

The eternal Christ declared that he who would be His disciples must "deny himself daily." Are you willing to deny yourself, to give up your lusts, your prejudices, and your opinions? If so, you may enter the narrow way of Truth, and find that peace from which the world is shut out. The absolute denial, the utter extinction, of self is the perfect state of Truth, and all religions and philosophies are but so many aids to this supreme attainment.

Self is the denial of Truth. Truth is the denial of self. As you let self die, you will be reborn in Truth. As you cling to self, Truth will be hidden from you.

While you cling to self, your path will be beset with difficulties, and repeated pains, sorrows, and disappointments will be your lot. There are no difficulties in Truth, and coming to truth, you will be freed from all sorrow and disappointment.

Truth in itself is not hidden and dark. It is always revealed and is perfectly transparent. But the blind and wayward self cannot perceive it. The light of day is not hidden except to the blind, and the light of Truth is not hidden except to those who are blinded by self.

Truth is the one Reality in the universe, the inward Harmony, the perfect Justice, the eternal Love. Nothing can be added to it nor can nothing be taken from it. It does not depend upon people, but all people depend upon it. You cannot perceive the beauty of Truth while you are looking out through the eyes of self.

If you are vain, you will color everything with your vanities. If you are lustful, your heart and mind will be so clouded with the smoke and flames of passion, that everything will appear distorted through them. If proud and opinionated, you will see nothing in the whole universe except the magnitude and importance of your own opinions.

There is one quality which preeminently distinguishes the person of truth from the person of self, and that is humility. To be not only free from vanity, stubbornness, and egotism, but to one's own opinions as of no value, this indeed is true humility.

He who is immersed in self regards his own opinions as Truth, and the opinions of other people as error. But that humble Truth-lover who has learned to distinguish between opinion and Truth, regards all people with the eye of charity. He does not seek to defend his opinions against theirs, but sacrifices those opinions that he may love the more, that he may manifest the Spirit of Truth for Truth in its very nature is ineffable and can only be lived. He who has most of charity has most of truth.

People engage in heated controversies, and foolishly imagine they are defending the Truth, when in reality they are merely defending their own petty interests and perishable opinions. The follower of self takes up arms against others. The follower of Truth takes up arms against himself. Truth, being simple is unchangeable and eternal, and independent of your opinion and of mine.

We may enter into it, or we may stay outside, but both our defense and our attack are useless, and are hurled back upon ourselves.

People enslaved by self, passionate, proud, and condemnatory, believe their particular creed or religion to be the Truth, and all other religions to be error, and they are passionate with warmth of feelings like a new convert.

There is but one religion, the religion of Truth. There is but one error, the error of self. Truth is not a formal belief, it is an unselfish, holy, and aspiring heart, and he who has Truth is at peace with all, and cherishes all with thoughts of love.

You may easily know whether you are a child of Truth or a worshiper of self. If you will silently examine your mind, heart, and conduct. Do you harbor thoughts of suspicion, enmity, envy, lust, and pride? Do you strenuously fight against these? If the former, then you are chained to self, no matter what religion you may profess. If the latter you are a candidate for Truth, even though outwardly you profess religion. Are you passionate and self willed, ever seeking to gain your own ends, self-indulgent, and self centered? Are you gentle, mild, unselfish, quit of every form of self, indulgence, and are ever ready to give up your own? If the former, self is your master. If the latter, Truth is the object of your affection. Do you strive for riches? Do you fight, with passion for your party? Do you lust for power and leadership? Are you given to pretentious display and self-praise? Or have you given up the love of riches? Have you relinquished all strife? Are you content to take the lowest place, and to be passed by unnoticed? Have you ceased to talk about your self and to regard yourself with self complacent pride?

If the former, even though you may imagine you worship God, the god of your heart is self. If the latter, even though you withhold your lips from worship, you are dwelling with the Most High.

The signs by which the Truth-lover is known are unmistakable. Hear the Holy Krishna declare them, in Sir Edwin Arnold's beautiful rendering of the "Bhavagad Gita": When people lost in the devious ways of error and self, have forgotten the "heavenly birth," the state of holiness and truth, they set up artificial standards by which to judge one another, and make acceptance of, and adherence to, their own particular theology, the test of Truth, and so people are divided one against another, and there is ceaseless enmity and strife, and unending sorrow and suffering. Enmity meaning: mutual hatred.

Reader, do you seek to realize the birth into Truth?

There is only the way. Let self die. All those lusts, appetites, desires, opinions, limited conceptions and prejudices to which you have hitherto so tenaciously cling to. Let them fall from you. Let them no longer hold you in bondage, and Truth will be your s. Cease to look upon your own religion as superior to all others, and strive humbly to learn the supreme lesson of charity.

No longer cling to the ideas, so productive of strife and sorrow, that the savior whom you worship is the savior whom your brother worships with equal sincerity and ardor, is an imposter with equal diligently the path of holiness, and when you will realize that every man is a savior of mankind.

The giving up is not merely the renunciation of outward things. It consists of the renunciation of the inward sin, the inward error. Not by giving up vain clothing, not by relinquishing riches, not by abstaining from certain foods. Not by speaking smooth words, not by merely doing these things is the Truth found, but by giving up the spirit of vanity. By relinquishing the desires for riches, by abstaining from the lust of self-indulgence, by giving up all hatred, strife, condemnation, and self-seeking, and becoming gentle and pure at heart. By doing these things is the Truth found.

To the former, and not the latter, is hypocritically self-righteous and hypocrisy, where as the latter includes the former. You may renounce the outward world, and isolate yourself in a cave or in the depth of a forest, but you will take all your selfishness with you.

Unless you renounce that, great indeed will be your wretchedness and deep your delusion you may remain just where you are, performing all your duties, and yet renounce the world, the inward enemy. To be in the world and yet not of the world is the Highest perfection. The most blessed peace is to achieve the greatest victory. The renunciation of self is the way of Truth, therefore: "Enter the path, there is no grief like hate, No pain like passion, no deceit like sense. Enter the path, has he gone whose foot treads down one fond offense." As you succeed in overcoming self you will begin to see things in their right relations. He who is swayed by any passion, prejudice, like or dislike, adjusts everything to that particular bias, and sees only his own delusions.

He who is absolutely free from all passions, preference, prejudice, and partiality, sees himself as he is. He sees others as they are. He sees all things in their proper proportions and right relations. Having nothing to attach and nothing to defend, nothing to conceal, and no interests to guard, he is at peace. He has realized the profound simplicity of Truth, for the unbiased, tranquil, blessed state of mind and heart is the state of Truth. He who attains to it dwells with the angels, and sits at the footstool of the supreme.

Knowing the Great Law, knowing the origin of sorrow, knowing the secret of suffering, knowing the way of being set free in Truth, how can such a one engage in strife or condemnation? For though he knows that the blind, self-seeking world, surrounded with the clouds of its own illusions, and enveloped in the darkness of error and self, cannot perceive the steadfast Light of Truth, and is utterly incapable of comprehending the profound simplicity of the heart that has died or is dying, to self, yet he also knows that when the suffering ages have piled up mountains of sorrow, the crushed and burdened soul of the world will fly to its final refuge and that the ages are completed, every prodigal will come back to the fold of Truth. And so he dwells in goodwill towards all, and regards all with that tender compassion which a father bestows upon his wayward children.

People cannot understand Truth because they cling to self, because they believe in and love self, because they believe self to be the only reality, where as it is the one delusion.

When you cease to believe in and love self you will desert it, and will fly to Truth, and will find the Eternal Reality.

When people are intoxicated with wines of luxury, and pleasure, and vanity, the thirst for life grows and deepens within them, and they delude themselves with dreams of fleshy immortality. When they come to reap the harvest of their own sowing, and pain and sorrow occur unexpectedly then crushed, and humiliated, relinquishing self and all the intoxications of self, they came with aching hearts to the one immortality. The immortality that destroys all delusions is the spiritual immortality in Truth.

People pass from evil to good, from self to Truth, through the dark gate of sorrow, for sorrow and self inseparable. Only in the peace and bliss of Truth is all sorrow vanquished. If you suffer disappointment because your cherished plans have been thwarted, or because someone has not come up to your anticipations, it is because you are clinging to self.

If you suffer remorse for your conduct, it is because you have given way to self. If you are overwhelmed with embarrassment or humiliation and regret because of the attitude of some one else towards you, it is because you have been cherishing self.

If you are wounded on account of what has been done to you or said of you, it is because you are walking in the painful way of self.

All suffering is of self. All suffering ends in Truth. When you have entered into and realized Truth, you will no longer suffer disappointment, remorse, and regret, and sorrow will flee from you. Self is the only prison that can ever bind the soul.

Truth is the only angel that can bid the gates unroll. And when he comes to call thee, arise and follow fast. His way may lie through darkness, but it leads to light at last.

The woe of the world is of its own making. Sorrow purifies and deepens the soul, and the extremity of sorrow is the prelude to Truth.

Have you suffered much? Have you sorrowed deeply? Have you pondered seriously upon the problem of life? If so, you are prepared to wage war against self, and to become a disciple of Truth.

The intellectual who do not see the necessity for giving up self, frame endless theories about the universe, and call them Truth. Does he pursue that direct line of conduct which is the practice of righteousness, and thou will realize the Truth which has no place in theory and which never changes.

Cultivate your heart. Water it continually with unselfish love and deep-felt pity, and strive to shut out from it all thoughts and feelings which are not in accordance with love.

Return good for evil, love for hatred, gentleness for ill treatment and remain silent when attacked. So shall you transmute all your selfish desires into the pure gold of love, and your self will disappear in Truth. So will you walk blamelessly among men, yoked with the easy yoke of lowliness, and clothed with the divine garment of humility.

THE TWO MASTERS

O Come weary brother! You struggle and striving. End thou in the heart of the master of Truth. Across self's drear desert why was thou be driving? A thirst for the quickening waters of Truth. When here, by the path of thy searching and sinning, flows life's gladsome stream, lays love's oasis green. Come, turn thou and rest, know the end and beginning. The sought and the searcher, the seer and seen.

The master sits not in the un-approached mountains, nor dwells in the mirage which floats on the air. Nor shall thou discover his magical fountains in the pathways of sand that encircle despair.

In selfhood's dark desert cease wearily seeking the odorous tracks of the sweet sound of his speaking. Be deaf to all voices that emptily sing.

Flee the vanishing places, renounce all thou has. Leave all that thou loves, and, naked and bare. Thyself at the shrine of the innermost cast. The Highest, the holiest, the Changeless is there.

Within, in the heart of the Silence he dwelleth. Leave sorrow and sin, leave the wanderings sore. Come bathe in his joy, while he, whispering telleth Thy soul what it seeketh, and wander no more.

Then cease, weary brother, thy struggling and striving. Find peace in the heart of the Master or Truth. Across self's desert cease wearily driving.

Come, drink at the beautiful waters of Truth.

SPIRITUAL POWER

The world is filled with people seeking pleasure, excitement, and novelty. They are seeking to be moved with laughter and Their tears. They are not usually seeking strength, stability and power. But instead courting weakness and eagerly engaged in scattering what power they do have.

People of real influence and power are few. This is because few are prepared to make the sacrifice necessary the acquirement of power. Fewer still are ready to patiently build up character.

To be swayed by your fluctuating thoughts and impulses is to be weak and powerless. To rightly control and direct those forces is to be strong and powerful.

People of strong animal passions have much ferocity of the beast, but this is not power. The elements of power are there but it is only when ferocity is tamed and subdued by the higher intelligence that real power begins. You can only grow in power by awakening themselves to higher and ever higher states of intelligence and consciousness.

The difference between people of weakness and one of power lies not in the strength of the personal will. After all, the stubborn person is usually weak and foolish. It is in that focus of consciousness which represents their states of knowledge.

The pleasure-seekers, the lovers of excitement, the hunters after novelty and the victims of impulse and hysterical emotion lack of knowledge of their principles which gives balance, stability, and influence.

You start developing power when, checking your impulse and selfish inclinations, you fall back upon the higher and calmer consciousness within yourself and begin to steady yourself upon a principle. The realization of unchanged principles in consciousness is at only the source and secret of the highest power.

When, after much searching, and suffering, and sacrificing, the light of an eternal principle dawns upon the soul as a divine calm ensues and joy unspeakable gladdens the heart.

He who has realized these principles ceases to wander and remains poised and self-possessed. He ceases to be "passions slave," and becomes a master builder in the Temple of Destiny.

The person who is governed by self and not by principles changes his front when his selfish comforts are threatened. They are deeply intent upon defending and guarding their own interests. They regard all means as lawful that will sub-serve that end. In other words they will say anything and do anything to get their own selfish and childish way. They are continually crafting plots by systematic designs as to how they may protect themselves against those who are doing no harm but see them as enemies.

This too is self centered to perceive this. They do not understand that they are their worst own enemy. This kind of persons work crumbles away and comes to straw. This person's way is divorced from Truth and power. All effort that is grounded upon self, perishes.

In other words it is destroyed and burned up by the eternal powers. The only work that can endure is one that is built upon the eternal principles. These principles are the eternal indestructible principles that are the laws in which your being was founded upon. The person that stands upon then principles is the same calm, dauntless, self-possessed person under all circumstances.

When the hour of trial comes and they do come you have to decide between personal comforts and Truth you must give up comfort for Truth. Do not take the easy way out for this is weakness. Give up your comforts and remain firm. Even the prospect of torture and death cannot alter or deter them.

The man of self regards the loss of his wealth, and his comforts of his life as the greatest calamities that befalls him. The person of principle looks upon these incidents as comparatively insignificant and not to be weighed with loss of character, or loss of Truth. To desert Truth is to him, the only happening which can really be called a calamity.

In the hour of crises which decides who are the servile dependants of darkness, and who are the children of Light. It is the epoch of threatening disaster, and ruin; the persecution which divides the sheep from the goats and reveals to the reverential gaze of succeeding ages the real person of power.

It is easy for a person, so long as he is left in the enjoyment of his possessions, to persuade himself that he believes in and adheres to the principle of Peace, Brotherhood, and universal Love; but if his enjoyments are threatened or he imagines they are threatened he begins to clamor loudly for war. He shows that he believes in and stands upon, not Peace, Brotherhood, and Love, but in strife, selfishness and hatred.

He who does not desert his principles when threatened with the loss of every earthly thing, even to the loss of reputation and life, is the man of power. This kind of man whose word and also his work endures through the ages. This is the kind of man whom the after world honors, reveres, and worships. Rather than desert that principle of Divine Power of Love on which he rested, and in which all his trust was placed. Jesus endured the utmost extremity of agony and deprivation, and today the world prostates itself at his pierced feet in engrossed adoration.

There is no way to the acquirement of spiritual power except that inward illumination and enlightenment which is the realization of spiritual principles, those principles can only realized by constant practice and application.

Take the principle of divine Love, and quietly and diligently meditate upon it with the object of arriving at a thorough understanding of it. Bring in its searching light to bear upon all your habits, your actions, your speech and intercourse with others, and reveal your every secret thoughts and desire.

As you preserve in this course the divine Love will become more and more perfectly revealed to you, and your own shortcomings will stand out in more and more vivid contrast spurring you on to new endeavors, and then having once caught a glimpse of the incomparable majesty of that imperishable principle, you will never again rest in your weakness, or you or you selfish imperfections. Instead you will choose to pursue that eternal Love until you have relinquished every discordant element and have brought yourself into perfect harmony with it.

And that state of inward harmony is spiritual power. Take also other spiritual principles such as purity and Compassion and apply them in the same way, and so exacting is Truth, you will be able to make no stay , no resting-place until the inmost garment of your soul is bereft of every stain and your heart has become incapable on any hard, condemnatory and pitiless impulse.

Only insofar as you understand, realize and rely upon these principles, will you acquire spiritual power and that power will be manifested in and through you in the form of increasing dispassion, patience, and equanimity. Dispassion argues superior self-control and sublime patience is the very hallmark of divine knowledge, and to retain an unbroken calm amid all the duties and distractions of life marks off the man of power.

It is easy in the world to live after the world's opinion. It is easy in solitude to live after our own, but the great man is he who in the midst of the crowd keeps with perfect sweetness the independence of solitude.

Some mystics hold that perfection in dispassion is the source of that power by which miracles are performed and truly he who has gained such perfect control of all his interior forces that no shock, however great, can for one moment unbalance him, must be capable of guiding and directing those forces with a master hand.

To grow in self-control, in patience, and calmness is to grow in strength and power .You can only grow by focusing your consciousness upon a principle. As a child, after making many and vigorous attempts to walk unaided, at last succeeds, after numerous falls, in accomplishing this, you must enter the way of power by first attempting to stand alone.

Break away from tradition custom and tyranny. Break away from conventionality and the opinions of others until you succeed in walking lonely and erect among every human. Rely upon your own judgment. Become true to your own conscience. Follow the Light that is within you. All outward forces are will o the wisps. There will be those who will tell you that you are foolish. They will tell you that your judgment is faulty. They will tell you that your conscience is wrong, and that the Light within you is indeed darkness. So you cannot listen to these voices, if what they say is true the sooner you, the searcher of wisdom find out the better.

Only you can make the discovery by bringing your powers to the test. Therefore pursue your course bravely. Your conscience is at least your own, and to follow it is to be a man. To follow the conscience of another is to be a slave.

In this life you will have many falls, and you will suffer many wounds and will endure many buffets for a time. Press on in the faith, believing that sure and certain victory lies ahead, Search for a rock, a principle and having found it cling to it. Get it under your skin and then under your feet and stand erect upon it until at last, immovably fixed upon it. You will then succeed in defying the fury of the waves and storms of selfishness.

For selfishness in any and every form is dissipation, weakness, and even leads to death itself. Unselfishness in its spiritual aspect is conservation, power, and even leads to life.

As you grow in spiritual life, and become established upon principles, you will become as beautiful and as unchangeable as those principles, will taste of the sweetness of their immortal essence, and will realize the eternal and indestructible nature of the God within.

No armful shaft can reach the righteous man, standing erect amid the storms of hate. Defying hurt and injury and ban, surrounded by trembling slaves of fate.

Majestic in the strength of silent power, serene he stands, nor changes not nor turns. Patient and firm in suffering's darkest hour. Time bends to him, and death and doom he spurns.

Wrath's lurid lightening round about him play, and hell's deep thunders roll about his head. Yet heeds he not, for him they cannot slay who stands whence earth and time and space are fled.

Sheltered by deathless love, what fear has he? Armored in changeless Truth, what can he know of loss and gain? Knowing eternity, he moves not while the shadows come and go.

Call him immortal, call him Truth and Light. And splendor of prophetic majesty whom bides himself amid the powers of night, clothed with the glory of divinity.

REALIZING SELFLESS LOVE

It is said the in the artist he sees in every block of raw material a thing of beauty that just waits the masters hand to bring something to reality. This is the eye of faith. Even so within each there lays or lies at rest the divine image awaiting the master hand of faith and the chisel of patience to bring this thing into manifestation. This divine image is revealed and realized as stainless selfless Love.

Hidden deep in every human heart, though frequently covered up with a mess of hard and almost impenetrable growths of a worldly kind, is the spirit of this divine Love whose holy and spotless essence is undying and eternal.

It is the Truth in us all. It is there waiting for us to realize its potential. It is the Truth in us that is in our impulses placed there by the eternal divine. This truth that is in us is that which belongs to the Supreme. He is the one who is that which is real and immortal.

All else changes and passes away. This alone is permanent and imperishable. To realize this selfless Love by ceaselessness is to live in it and to become the highest righteousness and live in it and become fully conscious in it. So enter into immortality here and now.

As you do this you will become one with the Truth. You will become one with God. We will become one with the central universes Heart of Hearts of all things. Then we will know our own divine nature.

To reach this divine Love, to understand and experience it, one must work with great persistency and diligence upon his heart and mind. Work with ever hard to renew his patience and keep strong his faith, for there will be much to remove, much to accomplish before the divine image is revealed in all its glorious beauty.

He who strives to reach and to accomplish the divine will be tried the very uttermost; and this is absolutely necessary, for how else could one acquire that sublime patience without which there is no real wisdom, no divinity?

Ever and after awhile, as he proceeds, all his work will seem to be useless or vain, and his efforts appear to be thrown away. Now and then a hasty touch will mar his image, and perhaps when his imagines his work is almost completed he will find what he imagined to be the beautiful form of the Divine Love utterly destroyed, and he must begin again with past bitter experience to guide and help him.

But he who resolutely set himself to realize the Highest recognizes no such thing as defeat. All failures are apparent and not real.

Every slip and every fall, every return to selfishness is a lesson learned, an experience gained from which a golden grain of wisdom is extracted helping the one who is striving towards the accomplishment of his lofty object.

To recognize is to enter the way that leads unmistakably towards the Divine, and the failings on one who thus recognized are so many dead selves, upon which he rises, as upon stepping stones, to higher things. Once come to regard your failings, your sorrows and sufferings as so, many voices telling you plainly where you are weak and faulty, where you fall below the true and the divine. You will then begin to ceaselessly watch yourself, and every slip, every pang will show you where you are at to set to work, and what you have to remove out of your heart in order to bring it nearer to the likeness of the divine nearer to the perfect Love.

As you proceed day after day detaching yourself, the love that is selfless will gradually become revealed to you. And when you are growing patient and calm, when passing away from prejudices cease to dominate and enslave you, then you will know that the divine is awakening with you. You are now drawing near to the Eternal Heart of Hearts and you are not far from that selfless Love and the compassion of which is peace and immortality.

Divine love is distinguished from human loves in this supremely important particular. It is free from partiality. Human loves cling to a particular object to the exclusion of all else, and when that object is removed, great and deep is the resultant suffering to the one who loves.

Divine love embraces the whole universe, and without clinging to any part, yet contains within itself the whole, and he who comes to it by gradually purifying and broadening his human loves until all the selfish and impure elements are burned out of them, ceases from suffering.

It is because human loves are narrow and confined and mingled with selfishness that they cause suffering. No suffering can result from that love which is so absolutely pure that it seeks nothing for itself.

Nevertheless, human loves are absolutely necessary as steps towards the Divine, and no soul is prepared to partake of divine Love until it has become capable of the deepest and most intense human love. It is only by passing through human loves and human sufferings that divine Love is reached and realized.

All human loves are perishable like the forms to which they cling, but there is a Love that is imperishable, and does not cling to appearances. All human loves are counterbalanced by human hates. There is a Love that admits of no opposite or reaction. Divine and free from all taint of self that sheds its fragrance on all alike. Human loves are a reflection of the divine Love, and draw the soul nearer to the reality that the Love that knows neither sorrow nor change.

It is well that the mother clinging with passionate tenderness to the little helpless form of flesh that lies on her bosom, should be overwhelmed with dark waters of sorrow when she sees it laid in the cold earth. It is well that her tears should flow and her heart ache, for only thus can she be reminded of the evanescent nature of the joys and objects of sense, and be drawn nearer to the eternal and imperishable Reality.

It is well that lover, brother, sister, and husband and wife should suffer deep anguish, and be enveloped in gloom when the visible object of their affections is torn from them, so that they may learn to turn their affections towards the invisible Source of all, where alone abiding satisfaction is to be found.

It is well that the proud, the ambitious, the self seeking, should suffer defeat, humiliation and misfortune, in order that they should pass through the scorching fires of affliction, for the sole purpose of bringing the wayward soul to be brought and reflect upon the puzzle and mystery of life. Only then can the heart be softened and purified and prepared to receive the Truth.

When the sting of anguish penetrates the heart of human love, when the gloom and loneliness and desertion cloud the soul of friendship and trust, then it is that the heart turns towards the sheltering love of the Eternal and finds rest in its silent peace. Who so ever comes to this Love is not turned away comfortless.

They are not pierced with anguish nor surrounded with gloom, and is never deserted in the dark hour of trial.

The glory of divine Love can only be revealed in the heart that is chastened by sorrow, and the image of the heavenly state be perceived and realized when the lifeless, formless accretions of ignorance and self are hewn away.

Only that love that seeks no personal gratification or reward, that does not make distinctions, and that leaves behind no heartaches, can be called divine. People clinging to self and to comfortless shadows of evil are in the habit of thinking of divine Love as something outside themselves, and that must forever remain outside.

Truly, the Love of God is ever beyond the reach of self, but when the heart and mind are emptied of self then the selfless Love, the supreme Love, the Love that is God or Good becomes an inward and abiding reality. And this inward reality of holy Love is none other than the Love of Christ that is so much talked about and so little comprehended. The Love that not only saves the soul from sin, but lifts it also above the power of temptation.

But how may one attain to this sublime realization? The answer which Truth has always given and will ever give to this question is-"Empty yourself" and I will fill thee. Divine Love cannot be known until self is dead, for self is the denial of love, and how can that which is known be also denied? Not until the stone is rolled away from the burial vault of the soul does the immortal Christ, the pure Spirit of Love that was crucified, dead and buried, cast off the bands of ignorance, and come forth in all the majesty of His resurrection.

You believe that the Christ of Nazareth was put to death and rose again. I will not say that you are wrong in that belief, but if you refuse to believe that the gentle spirit of Love is crucified daily upon the dark waters cross of your selfish desires, then I say you are wrong in this unbelief, and have not yet perceived, even afar off, the Love of Christ.

You say that you have tasted of salvation in the Love of Christ. Are you saved from your temper, or your irritability? Are you saved from your vanity or your personal dislikes or your judgments and condemnation of others? If not, from what are you saved and where in have you realized the transforming Love of Christ?

He who has realized the Love that is divine has become a new man, and has ceased to be swayed and dominated by the old elements of self. He is known for his patience, his purity, his self control, his deep charity of heart and his unalterable sweetness.

Divine or selfless Love is not a mere sentiment or emotion, it is a state of knowledge which destroys the dominion of evil and the belief in evil, and lifts the soul into playful realization of the Supreme Good. To the divinely wise, knowledge and Love are one and inseparable.

It is towards the complete realization of this divine Love that the whole world is moving; it was for this purpose that the universe came into existence, and every grasping at happiness, every reaching out of the soul towards objects, idea and ideals, is an effort to realize it. But the world does not realize this Love at present because it is grasping at the fleeting shadow and ignoring in its blindness, the substance. And so suffering and sorrow continue, and must continue until the world, taught, and must continue until the world taught by its self inflicted pains, discovers the Love that is selfless, the wisdom that is calm and full of peace.

And this Love, this Wisdom, and the peace along with this tranquil state of mind and heart may be attained to, may be realized by all who are willing and ready to yield up self, and who are prepared to humbly enter into a comprehension of all that the giving up of self involves.

There is no arbitrary power in the universe, and the strongest chains of fate by which people are bound are self-forged. People are chained to that which causes suffering because they desire to be so. This is because they love their chains. They think their little dark prison of self is sweet and beautiful, and they are afraid that if they desert that prison they will lose all that is real and worth having.

And the dwelling power which gorged the chains and built around itself the dark and narrow prison, can break away when it desires and will to do so, and the soul does will to do so when it has discovered the worthlessness of its prison, when long suffering has prepared it for the reception of the boundless Light of love.

As the shadow follows the form, and as smoke comes after fire, so effect follows cause, and suffering and bliss follow thoughts and deeds of men.

There is no effect in the world around us but has its hidden or revealed cause, and that cause is in accordance with absolute justice. People reap a harvest of suffering because in the near or distant past they have sown the seeds of evil.

They reap the harvest of bliss also of their own sowing of the seeds of the good. Let your self meditate on this, let yourself strive to understand it. You will then begin to sow only seeds of good and will burn up the tares and weeds which formerly grown in the garden of your heart.

The world does not understand the Love that is selfless because it is engrossed in the pursuit of its own pleasures, and cramped within narrow limits of perishable interests, mistaking in its ignorance those pleasures and interests for real and abiding things. Caught in the flames of fleshy lusts and burning with anguish, it sees not the pure and peaceful beauty of Truth. Feeding upon the piggish bottom of error and self-delusion it is shut out from the mansion of all seeing Love.

Not having this Love. Not understanding it people institute innumerable reforms which involve no inward sacrifice and each imagines that his reform is going to right the world forever, while he himself continues to propagate evil by engaging in it in his own heart. Propagate meaning: reproduce biologically or cause to spread.

This can only be called reform which tends to reform the human heart, for all evil has its rise there, and not until the world, ceasing from selfishness and party strife has learned of divine Love, will realize the Golden Age of universal blessedness.

Let the rich cease to despise the poor, and let the poor not condemn the rich. Let the greedy learn how to give, and the lustful how to grow pure. Let the guerrilla fighters cease from their strife. Let the uncharitable begin to forgive. Let the envious endeavor to rejoice with others. Let the slanderers grow ashamed of their conduct.

When people take this course and hey! The Golden Age has begun. They, therefore, who purifies his own heart is the world's greatest benefactor. Yet, though the world is, and will be for many ages to come, shut out from the Age of Gold, which is the realization of selfless Love. If you are willing, you may enter it right now. Why wait? You may enter it right now by rising above your selfish self. Just pass down the line your prejudice, hatred, and condemnation and exchange it for a gentle and forgiving spirit.

Where hatred, dislike and condemnation abide selfish Love cannot exist. Love resides in the heart only in the one who has left behind all condemnation. You may ask yourself "how can I love the drug addict, the alcoholic and the baby raper? I am compelled to dislike and condemn such people." While it is true you are not able to love such people emotionally but when you say that you must out of necessity dislike and condemn them you show that you are not acquainted with the Great Love that is overruling. It is possible to attain to such a state in interior enlightenment as will enable you to perceive the train of causes by which these men have become as they are. This is to say to enter into their sufferings and to know the certainty of their ultimate purification. Possessed of such knowledge it will be utterly impossible for you any longer to dislike or condemn them, and you will always think of them with perfect calmness and deep compassion.

If you love people and speak of them with praise until they in some way thwart you, and do something in which you disprove and then you dislike them and speak of them with disapproval you are not governed by the Love which is of God. If in your heart you are continually accusing and condemning others, selfless love is hidden from you. There are those who will call you before a court to answer an indictment on false charges.

He who knows that Love is at the heart of all things, and realized the all-sufficing power of that Love, has no room in his heart for condemnation. People, not knowing this Love, constitute themselves judge and executioner of their fellows, forgetting that there is the Eternal Judge and Executioner. In so far as people deviate from them in their own views, their particular reforms and methods, they brand them as fanatical, unbalanced, lacking judgment, along with sincerity and honesty. In so far as others approximate to their own standard do they look upon them as being everything that is admirable.

Such are the people that are self centered. But the person whose heart is centered in the Supreme love does not so brand and classify others, and does not seek to convert others to his own views, not to convince them of the superiority of his own methods.

Knowing the Supreme Law of Love you should live it, and maintain the same calm attitude of mind and sweetness of heart towards all beings.

Both the people that say bad things about you and the people that say good things about you, the foolish and the wise, the learned and the unlearned, the selfish and the unselfish receive alike the benediction of his tranquil thought.

You can only attain to this Supreme knowledge, this divine Love by unceasing pursuit in self discipline, and by gaining power and victory over yourself. Only the pure in heart can see God., when your heart is sufficiently purified you will enter the New Birth, the Love that does not die, neither change, nor end in pain and sorrow will be awakened within you and you will be at peace.

He who strives for the attainment of divine Love is ever seeking to overcome the spirit of condemnation, for where there is pure spiritual knowledge, condemnation cannot exist, and only in the heart that has become incapable of condemnation is Love perfected and fully realized.

The Christian condemns the Atheist. The Atheist condemns the Christian. The Catholic and the Protestant are ceaselessly engaged in wordy warfare and the spirit of strife and hatred rules where peace and love should be. "He that hates his brother is a murderer," a crucifier of the Divine Spirit of Love. Until you can regard all people of all religions and of no religion with the same impartial spirit, with all freedom from dislike, and with perfect calmness, you have yet to strive for that Love which bestows upon its possessor freedom and salvation.

The realization of divine knowledge, selfless Love, utterly destroys the spirit of condemnation, scatters all evil, and lifts consciousness to the height of pure vision where Love, goodness, Justice are seen to be universal, supreme, all-conquering, and indestructible. Train your mind in strong, and impartial but gentle thought. Train your heart to walk in purity and compassion. Train your tongue to silence and to true stainless speech. So shall you enter the way of holiness and peace and you shall ultimately realize the immortal Love.

So living without seeking to convert you will convince without arguing you will teach, not cherishing ambition. The wise will find you out, and without striving to gains anyone's approval you will subdue their hearts. For Love is all conquering, all powerful and the thoughts and deeds, and words of love can never perish.

To know that Love is universal, supreme, and all sufficient, is to be freed from the interfering of evil. So you can rest and be quite about the unrest in your heart and know that all people are striving to realize the Truth each in his own way. This is to be satisfied, sorrow-less, and serene. This is to peaceful. This is to have gladness. This is to have immortality. This is the Divinity we all seek. This is also the realization of selfless Love.

LOVE CONQUERS SOFTLY

I stood upon the shore, and saw the rocks, Resist the onslaught of the mighty sea, and when I thought how all the countless shocks. They had withstood through an eternity. I said, "To wear away this solid main the ceaseless efforts of the waves are vain.

But when I thought how they the rocks had rent, and saw the sand and shingles at my feet poor passive remnants of resistance spent tumbled and tossed where they the waters meet. Them I saw ancient landmarks beneath the waves, and know the waters held the stones their slaves.

I saw the mighty work the waters wrought by patient softness and unceasing flow How they the proudest promontory brought unto their feet, and massy hills laid low. How the soft drops and adamantine wall conquered at last, and brought it to its fall.

And then I knew that hard, resisting sin should yield at last to love's soft ceaseless roll. Coming and going, ever flowing in upon the proud rocks of the human soul. That all resistance should be spent and past, and every heart yield unto it at last.

INFINITE EVERLASTING

From the beginning of time, in spite of his bodily appetites and desires, in the midst of all his clinging to earthly and not permanent things, has ever been intuitively conscious of the limited, transient, and illusionary nature of this material existence. In his sane and silent moments he has tried to reach out into a comprehension of the Infinite, and has turned with tearful aspirations towards the restful Reality of the Eternal Heart.

While vainly imagining the pleasures of earth are real and satisfying, pain and sorrow continually remind him of their unreal and unsatisfying nature. Ever striving to believe that complete satisfaction is to be found in material things, he is of an inward and persistent revolt against this belief, which revolt is at only inherent and imperishable proof that only in the immortal, the eternal, and the infinite can you find abiding satisfaction and unbroken peace.

And here is the common ground of faith. Here the root and spring of all religion. Here is the soul of all brotherhood and the Heart of Love. This is meaning that people essentially and spiritually are divine and eternal and are immersed in mortality and troubled unrest. They are ever striving to enter into a consciousness of their real nature.

The spirit of humans are inseparable from the infinite, and can be satisfied with nothing short of the infinite and the burden of pain will continue to weigh upon man's heart, and the shadows of sorrow to darken his pathway until, ceasing from his wonderings in the dream world of matter, they come back to their home in the reality of the Eternal.

As the smallest drop of water detached from the ocean contains all the qualities of the ocean, so humans, detached in consciousness from the Infinite, contains within him its likeness and as nature, ultimately finds its way back to the ocean and lose itself in its silent depths, so must humans by the unfailing Law of their nature at last return to its source and lose yourself in the great ocean of the Infinite.

To once again become one with the Infinite is the goal of all humans. To enter the perfect harmony with the Eternal Law is Wisdom, Love and Peace. But this divine state is, and must ever be, incomprehensible to the merely personal.

Personality, separateness, and selfishness are one and the same and are the direct opposite of wisdom, and divinity. By the unqualified surrender of the personality, separateness and selfishness cease, and humans enters into the possession of his divine heritage of immortality and infinity.

Such surrender of the personality is regarded by the worldly and selfish mind as the most grievous of all calamities, the most impossible to make good, undo, or remedy and is regarded you as loss. Yet at the same time it is the one supreme incomparable blessing, the only real and lasting gain. The mind unenlightened upon the inner laws of being, and upon the nature and destiny of its own life, clings to transient appearances, things which have in them no enduring substantiality, and so clinging, perishes, for the time being, amid the scattered wreckage of its own illusions.

People cling to and gratify the flesh as though it were going to last forever, and though they try to forget the nearness and inevitability of its act or process of dissolving. The dread of death and of the loss of all that they cling to clouds their happiest hours and the chilling shadow of their own selfishness follows them like a remorse-less ghost. And with the accumulation of temporal comforts and luxuries, the divinity within humans is drugged, and they sink deeper and deeper into materiality, into the perishable life of the senses, and where there is sufficient intellect, and theories concerning the immortality of the flesh come to be regarded as infallible truths.

When a human's soul is clouded with selfishness in any way they lose the power of spiritual discrimination, and confuses the temporal with the eternal. They confuse the perishable with the imperishable. They confuse the mortality with the immortality, and the error with the Truth. This is what we consider lost. It is in this that the world has become full of theories and speculations having no foundation in human experience. Everybody of flesh contains within itself, from the hour of birth, the elements of its own destruction, and by the unalterable law of its own nature must it pass away. The perishable in the universe can never become permanent. The permanent can never pass away. The immortal can never die. The temporal cannot become eternal nor the eternal become temporal. Appearance can never become reality, nor in reality can truth ever become error.

Humans cannot have immortality the flesh, but by overcoming the flesh, by giving up all its inclinations, they can enter the region of immortality. "God alone has immortality." Only by this realization of the God state of consciousness do humans enter into immortality.

All nature in its indefinitely large number of forms of life is changeable, impermanent un-enduring. Only the informing Principle of nature endures. Informing meaning: give information or knowledge to. Nature is many and is marked by separation. The informing Principle is One, and is marked by unity. By overcoming the senses and the selfishness within, which is the overcoming of nature, humans emerge like the insect pupa enclosed in a shell of the personal and illusionary, and the wings himself into the glorious light of the impersonal, the region of universal Truth. Out of this all perishable forms arise.

Let humans therefore, practice self denial. Let them conquer their animal inclinations. Let them refuse to be enslaved by luxury and pleasure. Let them practice virtue and grow daily into higher and ever higher virtue until at last they grow into the divine and enter into both the practice and comprehension of humility, meekness, forgiveness, compassion, and Love. All these which practice and comprehension constitute divinity.

Goodwill gives insight, and only he who has conquered his personality that he has but one attitude of mind that of goodwill towards all creatures is possessed of divine insight and is capable with the ability to distinguish the true from the false. The supremely good human is therefore the wise one, the divine one and the enlightened seer. They know of the Eternal One. Where you find broken gentleness, enduring, patience, sublime loneliness and graciousness of speech, self-control and self forgetfulness along with deep abounding sympathy, look there for the highest wisdom, seek the company of such a one, for he has realized the Divine. He lives with the eternal. He Believe not the one that is impatient, given to anger, boastful, who clings to pleasure and refuses to renounce selfish gratifications, and who practices not goodwill and far reaching compassion. For such a person has no wisdom and vain in his knowledge and his works and words will perish, for they are grounded on that which passes away.

Let a person abandon them self. Let him overcome the world. Let his deny the personal by this pathway only can he enter into the Heart of the Infinite. The world, the body and the personality are mirages upon the desert of time. They are transitory dreams in the dark night of spiritual slumber, and those who have crossed the desert, these are the spiritually awakened and have alone comprehended the Universal Reality where all appearances are destroyed and dreaming and delusion are destroyed.

There is but one Great Law which unconditional obedience, one unifying principle which is the basis of all diversity, one eternal Truth where all the problems of earth pass away like dark shadows. To realize this Law, this Unity, this Truth, is to enter into the Infinite.

This is to become one with the Infinite. To center one's life in the Great Law of Love is to enter into rest, harmony, and

Peace. To refrain from all participation in evil and lack of harmony, to cease from all resistance of evil, and from the omission of all that is good. To fall back onto the unswerving obedience to the holy calm, is to enter into the inmost heart of all things. This is to attain to a living, conscious experience of that eternal and infinite principle which must ever remain a hidden mystery to the merely perceptive intellect. Until this principle has been realized, the soul is not established in peace, and he who has realized is truly wise. This is not the wise of the wisdom of the learned but with the simplicity of a blameless heart and of a divine humanness.

To enter into the realization of the infinite and the Eternal is to rise superior to time, and the world, and the body which compromise the kingdom of darkness. This is to become established in immortality, Heaven and the Spirit which make up the Empire of Light. Entering into the Infinite is not a mere theory or sentiment. It is a vital experience which is the result of diligent practice in inward purification. When the body is no longer believed to be even remotely aware, the real person when all appetites and desires are thoroughly subdued and purified, when emotions are rested and calm, and when the swinging back and forth of the intellect ceases and perfect poise is secured, then and not till then does consciousness become one with the Infinite. Not until then is childlike wisdom and profound peace secured.

All the human family grows weary and gray with the dark problems of life. We finally pass away and leave them unsolved because we cannot see their way out of the darkness of the personality, being too much engrossed in its limitations. Seeking to save his personal life man forfeits the greater impersonal Life in Truth. They instead cling to the perishable. Therefore he is shut out from the knowledge of the Eternal.

By the surrender of self all difficulties are overcome, and there is no error in the universe but the fire on inward sacrifice will burn it up like something worthless. No problem however great, but will disappear like a shadow under the searching light of self-renouncing.

Problems exits only in our own self-created illusions, and they vanish away when self is yielded up. Self and error are synonymous. Error is involved in the darkness of unfathomable complexity, but eternal simplicity is the glory of Truth.

Love of self shuts humans out from Truth and seeking their own personal happiness they lose the deeper, purer, and more abiding bliss. There is in man a higher than love of happiness. He can do without happiness, and instead thereof find blessedness.

Love not the pleasures of life but love God. This is everlasting. Yes, where all contradiction is solved. This is where who so ever walks and works, it is well with him.

The person who has yielded up that self, that personality that men most love, and to which they cling with such fierceness and holding fast, has left behind him all perplexity. Only then can you enter a simplicity that is so profoundly simple as to be looked upon by the world, involved as it is in a network of error, as foolishness. Yet such a one has realized the highest wisdom, and is at rest In the Infinite. He accomplishes without striving, and all problems melt before him, for he has entered the region of reality. He deals not with changing effects, but with the unchanging principles of things. He is enlightened with the wisdom which is as superior to the process of exact thinking, as reason is to animal.

Having yielded up his lusts, his errors, his opinions and prejudices, he has entered into possession of the knowledge of God. He has slain the selfish desire for heaven and along with it the ignorant fear of hell. By giving up even the love of life itself, he has gained supreme bliss and Life Eternal, the Life which bridges life and death and knows its own immortality. Having yielded up all without reservation, he has gained all, and resets in peace on the bosom of the Infinite. Only he who has become so free from self as to be equally content to be destruction as to live or to live as to be destroyed is fit to enter into the Infinite.

Only he who ceasing to trust his perishable -self, has learned to trust in boundless measure then great Law, the supreme Good, is prepared to partake of undying bliss. For such a one there is no more regret, nor disappointment, remorse for where all selfishness has ceased these sufferings cannot be. So whatever happens to him he knows that it is for his own good, and he is content, being no longer the servant of self, but the servant of the supreme.

He is no longer affected by the changes of earth, and when he hears of wars and rumors of wars his peace is not disturbed. Where humans grow angry and cynical and quarrelsome, he bestows compassion and love. Though appearances may contradict it, he knows that the world is progressing and that: Through its laughing and its weeping through its living and its keeping, through its follies and its labors, weaving in and out of sight. To the end from the beginning through all virtue and all sinning, reeled from God's great spool of progress runs the golden thread of light. When a fierce storm is raging none are angered about it, because they know it all will quickly pass away and when the storms of contention are devastating the world, the wise man looking with the eyes of truth and pity knows that it will pass away. That out of the wreckage of broken hearts which leaves behind the immortal Temple of Wisdom will be built. Splendidly patient and infinitely compassionate his deep, silent, and pure, his very presence is a closing blessing. When he speaks people ponder his words in their hearts, and by them rise to higher levels of attainment. Such is he who has entered into the Infinite, who by the power of utmost sacrifice has solved the sacred mystery of life.

Questioning Life and Destiny and Truth I sought the dark and labyrinthine Sphinx who spoke to me this strange and wondrous thing. Concealment only lies in blinded eyes, and God alone can see the form of God.

I sought to solve this hidden mystery vainly by paths of blindness and of pain. But when I found the Way of Love and Peace, concealment ceased and I was blind no more then I saw

God even with the eyes of God.

THE LAW OF SERVICE

The spirit of Love which is manifested as a perfect and rounded life, is the crown of being and the supreme end of knowledge upon this earth.

The measure of a persons Truth is the measure of his love, and Truth is far removed from him whose life is not governed by Love. The intolerant and increasingly condemnatory, though they profess the highest religion have the smallest measure of Truth, while those who exercise patience and listen calmly and dispassionately to all sides and both arrive themselves at and incline others to, thoughtful and unbiased conclusions upon all problems and issues. They have truth in the fullest measure.

The final test of wisdom is this: How does a person live? What spirit does he manifest? How people boast of being in possession of Truth who are continually swayed by grief, disappointment, and passion who sink under the first little trial that comes along. Truth is nothing if not unchangeable, and in so far as a person takes his stand upon Truth does he become steadfast in virtue, does he rise superior to his passions and emotions and changeable personality.

The human animal states definitely and clearly dead and dying belief systems and call them truths. Truth cannot be dead or dying. Truth is incapable of being expressed in words. Truth is beyond the intellect. It can only be experienced by practice. It can only be manifested as a stainless heart and a perfect life.

Who then, in the middle of the ceaseless and wild uproar of school and creeds of parties has the Truth? He who lives it. He who practices it. He who having risen above that wild uproar by overcoming himself; no longer engages in it. He now sits apart from quite, subdued and calm. He is self possessed, freed from all strife and all biased. He is free of all condemnations and bestows upon all the glad and unselfish love of the divinity within him.

He who is patient, calm, gentle and forgiving under all circumstances, manifests the Truth. Truth will never be proved by wordy arguments and learned treatises, for if people do not perceive the Truth in infinite patience, undying forgiveness and all embracing compassion, no words can ever prove it to them.

It is an easy matter for the passionate to be calm and patient when they are alone, or are in the midst of calmness. It is equally easy for the uncharitable to be gentle and kind when they are dealt kindly with, but he who retains his patience and calmness under all trial, who remains sublimely meek and gentle under the most trying circumstances, he and he alone, is possessed of the spotless Truth.

And this is so because such lofty virtues belong to the Divine. They can only be manifested by one who has attained to the highest wisdom, who has relinquished his passionate and self-seeking nature, who has realized the supreme and unchangeable Law, and has brought himself into harmony with it.

Let everybody, therefore stop the vain and passionate arguments about Truth, and let them think and say and do those things which make for harmony, peace, and love along with some good will. Let them practice heart-virtue, and search humbly and diligently for the Truth which frees the soul from all error and sin, from all that blights the human heart and that darkens, as with unending night, the pathway of the wondering souls of earth.

There is one great all embracing Law which is the foundation and cause of the universe, the Law of Love. It has been called by many names in various countries and at various times, but behind all its names the same unalterable Law may be discovered by the eye of Truth, names, religion, personalities pass away, but the law of Love remains. To become possessed of knowledge of this Law, to enter into conscious harmony with it, it is to become immortal, invincible, and indestructible. It is because of the effort of the soul to realize this law that people come again and again to live, to suffer, and to die. When realized, suffering ceases, personality is scattered, and the fleshly life and death are destroyed, for consciousness becomes one with the Eternal. The Law is absolutely impersonal, and its highest expression is that of service. When the purified heart has realized Truth it is then called upon to make the last, the greatest and holiest sacrifice of the well earned enjoyment of Truth.

It is by virtue of this sacrifice that the divinely emancipated soul comes to dwell among humans, clothed with a body of flesh, content to dwell among the lowliest and least, and to be esteemed the servant of all mankind.

That sublime humility which is manifested by the world's saviors is the seal of Godhead, and he who has put away the personality and has become a living, visible manifestation of the impersonal, eternal, boundless Spirit of Love, is alone singled out as worthy to receive the unstinted worship of posterity. Posterity meaning: succeeding generations.

He only who succeeds in humbling himself with that divine humility which is not only the extinction of self, but is also the pouring out upon all the spirit of unselfish love, is exalted above measure, and given spiritual dominion in the hearts of mankind.

All of the great spiritual teachers have denied themselves personal luxuries, comforts and rewards. They have denied themselves temporal power, and have lived and taught limitless and impersonal Truth. Compare their lives and teachings, and you will find the same simplicity, the same self-sacrifice, the same humility, both love and peace lived and preached by them. They taught the same eternal principles. The realization of which destroys evil. Those who have hailed and worshiped as the saviors of mankind are manifestations of the Great impersonal Law, and being such, were free from passion and prejudice. Also having no opinions, and no special letter of doctrine to preach and defend, they never sought to convert others to their beliefs.

Living in the Highest of Goodness, the Supreme Perfection, their sole object was to uplift mankind by manifesting that Goodness in thought, word, and deed. They stand between man and personal and God the impersonal, and serve so commendably as a model. They are the types that represent salvation of self-enslaved mankind.

People who are engrossed in self, and who cannot comprehend the Goodness that is absolutely impersonal deny divinity to all saviors except their own, and thus introduce, personal hatred and doctrinal controversy. At the same time defending their own particular views with passion; look upon each other as being heathens or infidels, and so render null and void as far as their lives are concerned the unselfish beauty and holy grandeur of the lives and teachings of their own Masters.

Truth cannot be limited. It can never be the special right or power of any man, school or nation and when personality steps in, Truth is lost.

The glory of the saint, the sage and the savior is this; that he has realized the most profound lowliness, the most sublime unselfishness. Having given up all, even his own personality, all of his works are holy and enduring They are freed from every taint of self. He gives, yet never thinks of receiving. He works without regretting the past or anticipating the future, and never looks for any rewards.

While the farmer has tilled and dressed his land and put in the seed, he knows that he has done all that he can possibly do and that now he must trust the elements, and wait patiently for the course of time to bring about the harvest; that no amount of expectancy on his part will affect the result.

Even so he who has realized Truth goes forth as a sower of the seeds of goodness purity, love, and peace without expectancy. They never look at the results knowing that there is the great Over-Ruling law, which brings about its own harvest in due time and which is alike the source of preservation and destruction.

People not understanding the divine simplicity of a profound unselfish heart, look upon their particular miracle as being the manifestation of a special miracle, as being something entirely apart and distinct from the nature of things and as being, in his ethical excellence, eternally unapproachable by the whole of mankind.

This attitude of unbelief, for such as it is, in the divine perfectibility of man paralyzes effort, and binds the souls of men as with strong ropes to sin and suffering.

Jesus "grew in wisdom" and was "perfected by suffering." What Jesus was He became such. What Buddha was he also became such. Every holy man became such by unremitting perseverance in self sacrifice.

Once recognize this, once realize that by watchful effort and hopeful perseverance you can rise above your lower nature, and great and glorious will be the vistas of attainment that will open out before you. Buddha vowed that he would not relax his efforts until he arrived at the state of perfection and he accomplished his purpose.

What the saints, sages and the saviors have accomplished, you likewise may accomplish if you will only tread the way which they trod and pointed out. That is the way of self sacrifice and of self denying service.

Truth is very simple. It says, "Give up self," "Come unto Me" away of all that defiles, "and I will give you rest." All of the mountains of commentary that have been piled upon it cannot hide it from the heart that is earnestly seeking Righteousness. It does not require learning. It can be known in spite of learning. Disguised under many forms by erring self-seeking man, the beautiful simplicity and clear transparency of Truth remains unaltered and undimmed, and the selfish heart enters into partakes of its shining radiance. Not by weaving theories that are complex and not by building up speculative philosophies is Truth realized. Instead it is weaving the web of inward purity and by building up the temple of a stainless life is Truth realized.

He who enters upon this holy way begins by restraining his passions. This is virtue and the beginning of saint-ship and saint-ship is the beginning of holiness. The entirely worldly man gratifies all his desires and practices no more restraint than the law of the land in which he lives demands.

The virtues man restrains his passions. The saint attacks the enemy of Truth in its strongholds within the heart, and restrains all selfish and impure thoughts. While the holy man is he who is free from passion and all impure thought, and to whom goodness and purity have become as natural as scent and color are to the flower.

The holy man is divinely wise. He alone knows Truth in its fullness and has entered into abiding rest and peace. For him evil has ceased, it has disappeared in the universal light of the All-Good. Holiness is the badge of wisdom.

Humbleness, truthfulness, and harmlessness, patience and honor, reverence for the wise, purity, consistency, control of self, contempt of sense delights, self-sacrifice, perception of the certitude of ill, in birth, death, age, disease, suffering and sin. An ever tranquil heart in fortunes good and fortunes evil endeavors resolute to perception of the utmost soul, and grace to understand what gain it were. So attain this is true wisdom, Prince! And what is otherwise is ignorance!

Whoever fights ceaselessly against his own selfishness, and strives to take the place of it all with the embracing love of a saint. Whether he live in a cottage or in the midst of riches and influence, or whether he preaches or remains dim or hazy and not well known.

To the world personality who is beginning to have an ambition towards higher things, the saint, such as a sweet St Paul or St Peter. The previous conquers is a glorious and aspiring spectacle.

To the saint, an equally enrapturing sight is that of the wise and prudent soul. He sits serene and holy, the conqueror of sin and sorrow. No more torment by great and remorse and whom temptation can never reach. Yet even the wise and prudent soul is drawn on by a still more glorious vision, that of a savior actively manifesting his knowledge in selfless works. And so rendering his divinity more potent for good by sinking himself in the throbbing, sorrowing; aspiring heart of mankind.

This is only the true service-to forget oneself in love towards all and to lose oneself in working for the whole. O thou vain and foolish man who thinks that your many works can save you. You, who are chained to all error, talk the loudest of yourself. Your work and your many sacrifices and manifest your own importance, know this, that though fame fill the whole earth all of your works shall come to dust and yourself be reckoned lower than the least in the kingdom of Truth! Only the work that is impersonal can live. The works of self are both powerless and perishable. Where duties, howsoever, humble, are done without self interest, and with joyful sacrifice, there is true service and enduring work.

Where deeds, however brilliant and apparently successful, are done from love of self, there is ignorance of the law of Service, and the work perishes. It is given to the world to learn one great and divine lesson, the lesson of absolute unselfishness. The saints, sages, and the saviors of all time are they who have submitted themselves to this task, and have learned and lived it.

All Scripture or the world are all poised to teach this one lesson and that all the great teachers reiterate it. It is too simple for the world which, scorning it, stumbles along in the complex ways of selfishness.

Pure heart is the end of all religion and the beginning of divinity. To search for this righteousness is to walk the Way of Truth and Peace. The person who enters this way will soon perceive that immortality which is independent of birth and death and will realize that Divine economy of the universe of the humblest effort is not lost.

The divinity of Krishna, Buddha and the Christ is the crowning glory of self renunciation. The end of the souls pilgrimage in matter and mortality, and the world will not have finished its long journey until every soul has become as these, and has entered into the blissful realization of its own divinity.

CROWN OF THORNS

Great glory crown the heights of hope by arduous struggle won.

Bright honor rounds the hoary head that mighty works has done.

And fame enshrines his name who works with genius-glowing brain.

But greater glory waits for him who, in the bloodless strife

Gain self and wrong, adopts, in love, the sacrificial life.

And brighter honor rounds the brow of him who, amidst the scorns

Of blind idolaters of self, accepts the crown of thorns,

And fairer, purer riches come to him who greatly strives,

To walk in ways of love and truth to sweeten human lives.

And he who serves well mankind exchanges fleeting fame,

For Light eternal, Joy, and Peace, and robes of heavenly flame.

The psychic brow bleeds from the crown of thorns.

     ERNEST JOHNSON

ETERNAL PEACE

In the eternal universe there is ceaseless turmoil, change, and unrest. At the heart of all things there is undisturbed repose. In the deep silence dwells the Eternal.

Man partakes of this duality, both the surface change and anxiety and the deep seated eternal abode of Peace are contained within himself. As there are silent depths in the ocean which the fiercest storm cannot reach, so there are silent, holy depths in the heart of us all which the storms of sin and sorrow can never disturb. To reach this silence and to live consciously in it is peace.

Lack of harmony abounds in the outward world, but unbroken harmony holds sway at the heart of the universe. The human soul, torn apart by lack of harmony, passion, and grief reaches blindly towards the harmony of the sinless state, an to reach this state and to live consciously in it is peace.

Hatred severs human lives, fosters persecution, and hurls into ruthless war, yet men, though they do not understand why, retain some measure of faith in the overshadowing of a Perfect Love; and to reach this Love and to live conscious in its Peace. And in this inward peace, this silence, this harmony, this love, is the Kingdom of Heaven, which is so difficult to reach because few are willing to give up themselves and to become as little children.

Heaven's gate is very narrow and minute, It cannot be perceived by foolish men Blinded by vain illusions of the world; even the clear-sighted who discern the way. And seek to enter, find the portal barred, and hard to be unlocked. Its massive bolts are pride and passion, avarice and lust.

People cry "Peace! Peace! Where there is no peace?" But on the opposite comes discord disquietude and strife. Apart from wisdom which is inseparable from self denial there can be no real and abiding peace. The peace which results from social comfort, passing pleasures, or worldly victory is transitory in its nature and is burned up in the heat of fiery trial. Only the Peace of Heaven endures through all trial, and only selfless hearts can know the Peace of Heaven.

Holiness alone is undying peace. Self-control to it and the ever- increasing Light of Wisdom guides the pilgrim on his way. It is partaken of in a measure as soon as the path of virtue is entered upon, but it is only realized in its fullness when self disappears in the consummation of a stainless life. This is peace to conquer love of self and lust of life, to tear deep rooted passion from the heart to still the inward strife.

If dear reader and listener or Truth, if you will just realize the Light that never fades, and the joy that never ends, and the calmness that cannot be disturbed; If you would just leave forever your sins and your sorrows along with your anxieties and perplexities behind.

If I say, you would partake of this salvation, this supremely glorious Life, then conquer yourself. Bring every thought, every impulse and every desire into perfect obedience to the divine power resident within you.

There is no other way to peace but this, and if you refuse to walk it, all of your praying and your strict adherence to ritual will become vanity and come to nothing. Neither gods nor angels can help you. Only to the over-comer is given the white stone of the regenerate life, on which is written and incapable of being expressed in words the Your New Name. Come away for awhile from the external things, from which the pleasures of the senses, from the arguments of the intellect, also from the noise and the excitements of the world. Withdraw yourself into the inmost chamber of your heart, and there, free the things that are of violation of your sacred self and the intrusion of all selfish desires.

By so doing you will find a deep silence, a holy calm, and a blissful repose. If you will only rest awhile in that holy place, and will meditate there. The faultless eye of Truth will open within you.

This holy and special place within you is your real center and while dwelling there you will come too see things as they really are. Once you identify yourself with it can you be said to be "clothed and in your right mind." It is the abode of the peaceful center. Through the Temple of Wisdom, this is the dwelling place of immortality.

Apart from this inward resting place, this Mount Vision, there can be no true peace. No knowledge of the Divine, and if you can remain there for one minute, one hour, or even one day, it is possible for you to remain there always.

All your sins and sorrows, your fears and anxieties are your own, and you can cling to them or you can give them up. Of your own accord you cling to your unrest; of your own accord you can come to abiding peace. The choice is yours alone. You must give it up yourself. The greatest teacher can do no more than walk the way of Truth for himself, and point it out to you. You yourself must walk it for yourself.

You can obtain freedom and peace alone by your own efforts, by yielding up that which binds the soul, and which is destructive of peace. The angels of Divide peace and joy are always at hand, and if you do not see them, and hear them, and dwell with them, it is because you shut yourself out from them, and prefer the company of the spirits of evil within you.

You are what you will be, what that you wish to be, what you prefer to be. You can commence to purify yourself. By purifying yourself you are going to arrive at peace. Then you can choose and refuse to purify yourself and so remain with your suffering.

I invite you personally to come out of your worry and irritated state of being. Step aside then from then scorching heat and fever of life. Step out of the fires of life of self. Then as you do enter the inward resting place where the cooling airs of peace will calm, renew, and restore you.

Come out of the storms of sin and anguish. Why be troubled and be a tempest tossed soul when you can have a Haven of peace that is so near to you.

Give up all self-seeking. Give up self, and behold the Peace of God is yours!

Bring under subjection the animal within yourself. Conquer every selfish uprising, every discordant voice. Transmute the base metals of your selfish nature into the unalloyed gold of love. Then you will realize the Life of the Perfect Peace. First subduing, then conquering, then transmuting.

You will, dear reader and listener while living in the flesh, cross the dark waters of mortality, and will reach that Shore upon which the storms of life and sorrow never beat; where sin and suffering and dark uncertainty cannot come. Standing upon that Shore, holy, compassionate, awakened, and self-possessed and glad with unending gladness, you will realize that: Never the Spirit was born the Spirit will cease to be never. Never was the time it was not, ending and beginning are dreams. Birth-less and death-less and change-less remains the Spirit forever. Death has not touched it at all, dead though the house of it seems. You will then know the meaning of Sin, and of Sorrow. You will know Suffering and that end thereof is Wisdom. You will know the cause and the issue of existence.

With this realization you will enter into rest. This is the bliss of immortality. This is the unchangeable gladness. This is the Eternal Wisdom and the undefiled knowledge and the undying Love. This and only this is the realization of Perfect Peace.

PERFECT PEACE

O thou who would teach men of Truth! Hast thou passed through the desert of doubt? Art thou purged by the fires of sorrow? Has truth the fiends of opinion cast out of thy human heart? Is thy soul so fair that no false thought can ever harbor there?

O thou who would teach men of love hast thou passed through the place of despair? Hast thou wept through the dark night of grief? Does it move now freed from its sorrow and care. Thy human heart to pitying gentleness looking on wrong and hate, and ceaseless stress.

O thou who would teach men of peace hast thou crossed the wide ocean of strife? Hast thou found on the Shores of Silence, release from all the wild unrest of life? From thy human heart has all striving gone, leaving but Truth, and Love, and Peace alone?

THE END
GIVING THIS TIMELESS WISDOM LIFE:
BY ERNEST JOHNSON

JET FUEL FOR THE SOUL

Jealousy is suffering. & Humans are constantly lying to them selves. & If you can't be rich in mind then you can't be rich in money. & Keep your secrets to your self. & Right brain conceives of possibilities. & Get out of park and into gear. & Hurt and well being can cancel each other out. & Where thought prevails power can be found. & An excessively high opinion of ones self is conceit. & Don't be afraid of new ideas. & Turn negative emotions into positive ends. & Stay hungry. & Self control is solely a matter of thought control. & Everybody has inner game issues. & Let your self be human. & Start creating affirmations for your self. & Being rich is a state of mind. & Growth is accomplished by awareness. & Always do better. & All your mind can do is think. & The world is your play ground.& Role play. & Today, start to act as if your influence is universal. & Put the truth as you know it aside. & Quit being your self. & Truth and honesty are not the same. & If your alive you have full potential. & If your hurting, you have boundary issues. & The evil mind set is your disease. & Clean your well spring. & Die to live, live to die. & Pay attention to the emotional pull of your desires. &Your head is dying. & Winning is the first and foremost in the mind set. & Stop damning up the positive flow of energy. & It takes wisdom and knowledge to build. & It takes only a dumb ass to tear it down. & Be the dominate slave. & Guilt robs the body of the soul. & Your boundary is your prison walls. & Pray as you imagine, Imagine as you pray. & Marketing is what every entrepreneur must master. & Embark on a mission. & Shoot for the stars and if you land on the moon, so what. & Diabolic language does not stand for anything. What is your mission? & Figure out what and who you are. & Develop ideas. & Disgust and discontent is your driving force. & Embrace who you can be. & Cheating is lying. & Be vibrant. & Be selfish. & Your body is a junk yard. & Divide stupidity and wisdom by the axe. & Masculine power is behind leadership. & Every body has a unique propose for their life. & Redefine your life. & Go from poor conscious poor intuition to strong conscious, strong intuition. & Depression is lack of thought control. & Success is an intellectual thing. & Suffering is burning up of energy ineffectively. & Consciousness and intuition are opposites of the same spectrum. & Synonym for ego is conscious mind. & Your beliefs today are your realities tomorrow. & The mind is like a battery. & Stay disciplined. & Your reputation is made by others, but your character is made by you. & Energy flows where attention goes. & Face your self doubt. & Stop trying to change your history. & Get a baby photo of your self and look into your eyes to help find your purpose. & The real inner person is not subject to limitations. & The secret to living in the now is to live your inspiration. & Call upon the financial genius inside of you. & Get up off of your lazy ass. & Being realistic makes you go broke. & Break the mold. & Quit biting your tongue. & Turn the tables on your boss. & Flip on the switch inside your mind. & Find a solitary place and let out a rebel yell. & Seduce me. & Promise me the world and then deliver. & Choose selectively who you listen to. & Develop new ideas. & If makes you laugh it has got to be good. & Shake off the old mind set, shift your priorities. & Irrational behavior is draining. & Look fabulous in public. Feel fabulous in private. & A prostitute has more value than an ass hole. & Helpless is an illusion. & There is strength in authenticity. & Another word for power is charisma. & Your boundary is invisible but real. & Your mind is like a garden. & Look at what you can do and not what you cannot do. & Every cell must shift. & Stop being sick. & Quit being a victim. & Increase your value. & To get you must first make room for it by giving what you have to those in need. & Prepare yourself for what you are about to receive. & The only way out of anxiety, impulsiveness, addictions, overeating, overspending, masochism, being a whiner, complainer, moaner is to get up off your lazy ass and do it with courage. & Accept reality for what it is. & Don't be afraid to reinvent your self. & Whether your mind is positive or negative is your choice alone. & Making no decisions about your anger causes depression. & Study effects by there causes. & Seek doable fulfillment. Stay focused. & Examine your self under a microscope. & Come to a place where you are willing to do what it takes. & Observe your ego. & The mind virus is comparing your self to others. & Creating value is creating money. & You control only what is in your boundary. & Remember, if a person looks plastic, fake and unreal then they are. & Their thoughts have made them so. & Increase your value to the world. & Become chronically honest. & Watch out for the tricksters. & Learn to ask a lot of questions. & Cynics criticize. & Winners analyze. & Guilt is worse that greed. & Put your back against the wall. & Live in a cold house. & Jump into the world of free enterprise. & Everything is a trade off. & Market your self out of the rat race. & Quit being unreal and start being real. & Your mission cannot be self centered. & Think wide scope. & What can you offer the world that's original? & Heal your self. & Love your self no matter what. & Loss and lack of confidence creates anxiety. & Truth is you are never helpless. & Do the right thing and be a hero. & The human shadow is the dark side. & Have a relationship with death. & Pull your own mind weeds. & Re identify with a new identity. & Victim is a role. & Dishonesty is a smoke screen in your boundary. & Hurt creates anger loss creates anxiety. & Observing ego is like having a coach for life. & Follow your feelings they are your guiding system. & Turn hurt wounds into success. & The only limitations are the ones in your own mind. & Demand more of your self. & No one knows what hidden forces lie deep within you. & The one who believes in him self advances. & Allow the awaking hand of vision to rouse you. & You cannot be chronically depressed and have high self esteem. & Mother birds are tricksters. & Con man is confidence man. & Harden your position and never quit. & The opportunity to fail always presents it self just before you succeed. & Gain leverage over your & False self is narcissistic. & Live your way to the answers. & Your thoughts create your own anxiety. Turn wounds into success. & Irritability is psychological, medicine cannot help it. & Wisdom is the balance between conscious and intuition. & Kindness towards the guilty is cruelty towards the innocent. & Communication carries with it emotional energy and data. & Boldly go straight toward the target. & Fear no one thing. & Initiative is the pass key that opens the door to opportunity. & Have a relationship with death. & Examine your self under a microscope. & Your reputation is made by others. & But your character is made by you. & Energy flows where attention goes. & Face your self doubt. & Trust your unconscious. & Make some decisions to move through fear. & You make the rules for your life. & You are what your deepest desire is. & Intent has within it its own mechanisms for its own fulfillment. & Chance favors the prepared mind. & Growth reading comes only through books. & Ecstasy changes everything. & The pain of discipline or the pain of regret. & Growth is accomplished through awareness. & Get used to disagreeing. Practice disagreeing. & Scammers are desperate. & Start being chronically honest. & Nature hates idleness in all ways. & The only way out is a changed mind set. & Live to die. Die to live. & Being a slave to the grind is to rot. & Stop sabotaging your self. & Never lie to a girl scout. & The secrets to success are hidden they are multidimensional. & Make the most of every day. & Cynics criticize, winners analyze. & Never say I can't afford it, Instead say how can I afford it. & Your boundary is your prison wall and your thoughts are your prison. & Being realistic makes you go broke. & Put your back against the wall. & Everything is a trade off. & Seduce me. & Quit being unreal, start being real. & Your dreams are accomplished automatically by helping others. & Can you be the leaders others are looking for? & Be passionate not passive. & Start climbing your mountain. & Leave everyone behind. & Look to what you can do not to what you cannot do. & Be vibrant. & Be selfish. & Tap into the eternal intelligence. & Heal your self. & The cure to your every problem is you. & What is your ideal success level? & The commonality of any group of people is a shared group of ideas. & Have a goal that is honorable. & At the end of the day if you are not on a journey for you then its all bullshit. & Stop seeking other people's approval. & Put your focus on what your going to create. & Success is in reaching a goal. & Suffering is burning of energy inefficiently. & Being unstoppable is a self fulfilling prophesy. & Capture the essence of the thing. & Say no to stress and it goes away. & Hurt creates anger, loss creates stress. & Worldly wisdom truly is the answer. & Observing ego is like having your own coach for life. & Think before you act. & Quit beating your self up on the inside. & Having a well defined door in your boundary is mature. & Education and experience equals success. & Have a balanced intellect and emotional energy. & Show initiative, go on the offense. & Depression is like a pot of anger that gets stored inside of you. & No wealth or position can endure unless built upon truth and justice. & Vitalize your mind with self confidence. & Intuition and shrewdness are opposite ends of the same spectrum. & People make ethical blunders and mistakes, it is ok. & Never dramatize bad behavior. & As is your will so is your deed. & As is your deed so is your destiny. & Attention activates the energy field. & Assertiveness is mothering yourself. & Bring value to the market place. & Start a relationship with the universe. & Even our thoughts ,our desires, our wishes or dreams are not technically our own. They are manifestations of the universe. & Your self worth will become your net worth. & If you misuse your time it becomes a source of fear and anxiety. & The past resides in memory. & Incorporate your dark shadow. & Truth is wrapped up in obscurity. & As long as you have potential your future can evolve by your choosing. & Don't be to nice you will be to stiff. & Intent works by harnessing the creative forces inherent in the universe. & If you give value you will receive value. & The door is always open. & Impulsive is acting without thinking. & Cycle of masochism brings negative momentum to your life. & Courage is a decision. & What are you creating for your self. & Get rid of the bag of self doubt, and rid of your self of the scar tissue of the past and move on. & Stress blames everyone. & It puts everything in regression. & It destroys chemistry. & Habit is auto pilot. & Fleeing is avoidance. & Think about how to create value. & Ethics is directly related to your decision. & Evolution is orderly change, no miracles. & Intention is the opposite of suffering. & Singleness of purpose is essential for success. Staying on your dead course is a kind of suffering. & Your life experiences can be transmuted into other useful areas. & Humility is a forerunner of success. & Seek durable fulfillment. & Stop your suffering. & To perceive it in the now manifest it in the now. & What you believe, you first create, then experience. & Politics is the art of the impossible. & Your decisions guide you through your boundary door. & Our destiny ultimately comes from the deepest level of desire, and also our deepest level of intention. & Our minds are better suited for imagination than reality. & Look around and see how others are doing it. & In short you are asleep. & There are countless opportunities. & Be a student of human behavior. & Fight of flight is designed to save your life. & One in five Americans have panic attacks. & Past does not equal the future. & The mind is a bullshit machine. & Opposite energies is attractive. & Put your focus on what you are going to create. & Strength is currency. Go boldly into your decisions. & Depression and other kinds of mood problems are very, very tied to your self esteem level. & Intuition is the equivalent to shrewdness. & When you quarrel you are defeated. & The universe responds to your emotions not your words. & Skepticism is the deadly enemy of progress, and success. & Well being is a feminine motherly energy. & Failure is a tonic that can be learned from. & Desire out wits mother nature. & Conceive the possibilities that lie sleeping within you. & Conceit is a fog. & When your desire is strong enough you will appear to possess super human power to achieve. & Having boundaries is attractive. & Internal chronological age never equals external chronological age. & If you want to break out of the mundane, you must learn to think and dream the impossible. & Intention always originates in the universal domain. & Desire is the starting point of achievement.

& Leave your self no retreat, win or perish. & Feel the fear do it anyway. & People are like two crabs in a pot, one always pulls the other one down. & Winning is a mind set. & Imagine your self successful. & Set definite goals. & Respond positively to life. & Stop thinking job, jobs are dead end. & Get rid of all your ugly friends with their ugly attitude. & Visualize and believe in the attainment of desire. & All thoughts which have been emotionalized and mixed with faith begin immediately to translate them selves into there equivalent or counter part. & Guilt robs the body of the soul. & What you know makes you money. & What you don't know loses you money. & Set the bar high. & Embark on a mission. & Market your self. & Light a flame in others. & Every body's mission is different. & Throw off the old you. Develop ideas. & Reset your financial thermostat. & Faith is the only known antidote to failure. & Learn skill sets. Stop at nothing to attain your goals. & Don't waste precious time. & Hate brings nothing good. & Throw away intolerance. & Auto suggestion is self suggestion. & Both poverty and riches are the offspring of thought. & It pays to know how to purchase knowledge. & Fighting is impulsive, fleeing is avoidance. & Worry is also suffering. It's all in the state of mind. & If you think your beaten you are. & Faith is the eternal elixir which gives life, power, and action to the impulse of thought. & Masochism brings 10 experiences of loss which brings 10 units of worry. & Sex energy is the creative energy of all geniuses. & The mind virus is comparing your self to others. & You're not your past, you are not where you came from you are not your family. & Currency for intellect is time. & Money has ears. & Imagination is the work shop of the mind. & Hurt, anger and loss are wounds. & Your wounds are valuable. & Creators of ideas make their own price, and if their smart they get it. & Success requires no explanation. Failure permits no alibis. & Once you achieve a goal you own it. & Give your self permission to live your own life. & Drug addiction is psychology out of balance. & Thin skinned people stress easier. & Organized planning is the crystallization of desire into action.

& A quitter never wins and a winner never quits. & More knowledge and wisdom is gained through failure. & Accept new ideas within you and others. & If you want more from your self, demand more from your self. & There is no hope of success for the person who does not have a central purpose, or definite goal. & Religion is like character instruction. & You make the rules for your life, no one else does. & There is no substitute for persistence. & Sex energy is the most powerful of all the stimuli that move people into action. & Ignorance is constricted awareness. & Intention orchestrates infinite possibilities. & Failure is not an option. & Concentrate all your efforts on one definite chief aim. & Doing courage is the right thing to do. & Indecision and procrastination are twins. & Take inventory of your self. & There is no hope for dishonest people. & The law of economics was passed by nature. & Quality of character is what carbon is to steel. & The basis of persistence is the power of the will. & Adapt and survive. & Courage is a decision to redefine life. & The right or wrong is intuition. & Weak desires bring weak results. & Life is either a daring adventure, or nothing. & Those who can't take it simply don't make the grade. & Re-identify with a new identity. & Use anger to create change or else it's not worth it. & Injustice is the way you perceive things. & Success does not fulfill your self esteem. & Fill your tank with good energy. & Power is organized knowledge. & Every decision you make is either destructive, or instructive. & Money is shy and elusive. & The sixth sense is creative imagination. & Habit is auto pilot. & When matter hits anti matter explosion results. & Highly sexed people always have A plentiful supply of magnetism. & Look into the mirror and come face to face with your self. & You can't have high self esteem and be chronically depressed. & There is no other road to genius than through voluntary self effort. & Love does not thrive on indifference, nagging, faultfinding, or domineering by either party. & Maturity equals balance. & Look at your own progress. & Positive egos do not thrive in a negative environment. & Happiness, success, and freedom equals fulfillment. & These are your inner resources. & Your mind has six departments. & Most people are the servants of their emotions, not the masters. & The secret of success is constancy of purpose. & Your goals are in the shadow. & A well defined door in your boundary is mature. & The more wisdom you get the more society gives you. & Develop observing ego. & Personal power is wrapped up in the will to win. & Surrender requires a leap of faith. & Start a relationship with the universe. & Jump into the unknown and make it work. & Through us the universe wants to play. & Every person today is the result of their thoughts yesterday. & Faith, rightly understood, is active, not passive. & Attention activates the information field which causes transformation. & Don't be over concerned for others. & Make life a game. & In order to be successful you have to be able to give your money away. & If you can't go to school, then bring the school to you. & It takes a lot of maturity to get balanced. & Your mind is your true asset. & Freedom is in the now. & Choose the road of faith, not fear. & Cosmic habit force is nature's comptroller. & Feeling lucky is not good enough. & Can you offer prospects a solution to the problem that they are going to face? & You must become a master marketer. & Do something global. & Poverty is the direct result of a poverty consciousness. & Choose who to listen to. & Throw off the old you. & Live your own fantasy. & Be in charge of your own destiny. & It will not come over night. & Live the golden rule. & Habits are inseparably related to ego. & Are you the horse or the rider? & Take stock in your resources. & Only you can decide what your worth. & We are all creatures of imitation. & Every endeavor is a process. & Will power is needed most when the oppositions of life are the greatest. & Confidence is the reward for doing courage. & The enemy of success is ignorance, illiteracy, and poverty. & Harmony is one of nature's laws. & Nature hates idleness in all forms. & Just before courage you are completely alone. & Power grows out of organized knowledge. & Forgive your self, and except your weakness. & Close the door on win lose deals. & Sexual feeling is the most powerful form of positive thought.

& It is natures own medicine. & Look like a fool and do it everyday. & Master your decision making. & Ideas that lead to success begin as definiteness of purpose. & Your hunches are often signals form infinite intelligence. & Observing ego is you watching what you are doing. & Go boldly into your decisions. & You have personal power. & Master and apply a pleasing personality. & Anger and anxiety are signals to do something. & No one is willing to cooperate with a person who has an offensive personality. & Self confidence will lead you to the power house of your mind. & A pleasing personality is successful. & Anger turned inward is depression. & Failure is to life what kiln is to pottery, it tempers us. & Aggression necessitates that some one lose. & Intolerance closes the door to opportunity in a thousand ways. & Burning energy on the past is suffering. & Obstacles are like stepping stones to ever greater achievement. & Intolerance is closely related to your fears. & Cherish your visions and dreams for they are the children of your soul. & Be willing to look dumb to get the reward. & Control your thoughts and you control your depression. & Pull your mind weeds, and plant the seeds of success. & Ideas are the most valuable products of the human mind. & You get others to cooperate with you by cooperating with them. & Sex energy is the most powerful mind stimulant known. & Change your inner person and it will resonate out in all directions. & You create anxiety by always looking to the bad. & Chance favors the prepared mind. & Information and energy are inseparably connected. & The past reside in memory and the future resides in the imagination. & Divine providence has granted you supreme control over your own mind. & The difference between success and failure is largely a matter of the difference between positive and negative thought. Applying intention reveals the meaning of coincidences. & If you misuse time it becomes a source of fear and anxiety. & Love is the true emancipator of mankind. & Love makes all human kind related. & Your desire is your beacon hone in on it. & People are attracted to openness. & Form alliances and use them wisely. & Remember: Do not be afraid to aim high when you establish your goal. & Your individual soul will not be satisfied unless it completes its mythical quest. & The universe wants to act through you for the good of all. & Unfold your self to the universe now. & Everything that is worth having has a definite price. & Take your attention to the heart of experience. & The present moment is really an opening to the future. & False sense is narcissistic. & Fuel: you have to be preprogrammed to go there, or else failure will present in self. & Stop listening to negative people. & Start accounting for all your time. & The mind will atrophy if not continuously fed, this is nature's law. & The success principles are not hidden they are right in front of you, hidden in plain sight. & You cannot see it because you cannot see clearly. & The human spirit is very powerful it knows it can do anything. & Your mind is your domain. & Your mind is the most powerful tool you have dominion over. & Success is more attainable than you know. & Mind power is always actively engaged on one side of the river of life or the other. & Humans consist of two forces, one tangible one intangible. & Break down your goals. & Quantify your goals. & Live your way to the answers. & Always look to peace but don't be afraid of conflict either. & Every human being possesses at least two distinct mind powers or personalities. & Set a better set of ethics than your predecessors. & You are the maker of your self. & Intemperance and addiction move the mind to failure. & One of the laws of success is self control. & Nothing is bad or dreadful once you've decided to face the consequences. & Close the door on the wrong thing. & You cannot do your best until your back is against the wall. & Do the right thing in the face of temptation. & Take the high road of faith. & The low road is fear. & Aggression necessitates that some one be hurt. & Aggression is narcissism. & Definition of life is making decisions. & Your ambitions must deserve to live, if not they die. & Lack of harmony and cooperation is a wide destructing evil. & Develop a panic room in your mind. & We are all controlled by unseen intangible forces. & The greatest forces are intangible. & Change your inner person and it will change your life. & Look for a plan that is written on your soul. & Growth is accomplished by awareness. & Don't let time be in charge, use your time wisely. & Your own thoughts and desires serve as the magnet that attracts units of life. & The universe unfolds to it self. & Don't be allured away from you souls destiny. & Narcissistic people have a weak boundary. & They create win lose deals. & This is an illusion, they are vampires. & You must be the architecture of your own destiny & As long as you have potential your future can evolve by your own choosing. & Failure is only a mistake. & Choose ethics that work for you. & Having ethics is attractive. & Higher confidence leads to lower anxiety. & Let no one control you. & Decision is freedom currency. & Burning energy on the past is suffering. & Education and experience equals success. & We can not create nothing that is not first in the form of an impulse of thought. & Your mind makes up the notion of time. & Facing your fears solves the emotional part of your problem. & Depression is like a pot of anger that gets stored inside of you. & Depression is caused by not making proper decisions or no decisions. & Fear paralyzes the faculty of reason. & Watch what you wish upon others, you just might get it your self. & Resistance is your false god. & Out wit your ghosts of fear. & Free your self from your mind. & Enlightenment is rising above thought. & Emotion is the body's reaction to the mind. & End the delusion of time. & All problems are illusions of the mind. & The dreamers are the saviors of the world. & Who you are is not unchangeable. & Do courage, gain confidence. & Dare to tolerate the unknown, make the unknown work for you. & Don't be allured away from your soul's destiny. & Listen to the message of the universe, not the message of the world. & If you would achieve success, then plant in your mind a strong motive. & Success is not attained through honesty alone, as some would have us believe. & Your mind is a two way radio. & Your mundane life is like a long dark tunnel. & Your desires, your wishes are the light of day. & Thought is electric. & Every mind is connected. & Today, start to act as if your influence is universal. & Without harmony there is no energy, or life in any form whatsoever. & Every character in your dreams is a part of you. & What you are developing to be is what you'll become. & People are anxious to improve their circumstances but unwilling to improve themselves. & There is therapeutic value in sex. & Sex can be a source of genius. & People do not attract what they want, but that which they are. & Figure out who you are, and why you are here. & Be accountable to your dreams. & Settle for nothing less. & When you create a problem you create pain. & Don't be concerned with the fruit of your action. & Nothing is more important than having a chief aim. & The doubting type of mind is not a creative mind. & Fear Make it a habit to monitor your mental and emotional state. & Wherever you are, be totally there. & Market your self out of the rat race. & Enjoy the journey. & Take initiative and lead. & You are at your best when your back is against the wall and there is no way out. & Market your self. & Everything you can imagine is real. & Enthusiasm is simply a high rate of mental vibration. & Develop ideas, then stay focused. & When will you take your business and your self seriously? & In your desperation you will find a way. & How bad do you want success? & Are you willing to look deep within you and face the truth? & Align your self with who you truly are. & Enthusiasm is the basis of creative imagination. & In business, failure is a mistake. & Choose ethics that work for you. & Self control is a balance wheel. & Do the thing and you shall have the power. & Good showmanship is a part in a winning personality. & Suffering has no good purpose. & Carrying guilt forever is called pathological grief. & It is a form of masochistic. & Give up waiting as a state of mind. & Have a goal that is honorable. & Opinions are worth nothing when the actual facts are obtainable. & Everybody has a unique purpose for their life. & Masochism is defined as the pleasure of being abused. & The past cannot survive in your presence. & Everything has a price, and nothing can be attained without paying the price. & The human mind is something like a magnifying glass. & Beauty arises in the stillness of your presence. & Go deeply into the body. & Strengthen your immune system. & Lack of well being is the cause anger. & Lack of confidence is the cause of anxiety. & Have deep roots within. & Develop spiritual relationships. & Sexual energy is a health builder. & That empty feeling you have inside is a vacuum really is anger and anxiety. & External remedies don't really work. & Your self esteem is being drained. & Your burning energy on the uncontrollable. & Intolerance shuts out the light of intelligence. & Love is a state of being. & Focus attention on the feeling inside of you. & There are many selves to guide you. & You have an obligation to share your wealth. & Left brain conceives of possibilities. & Currency of intellect is time. & When you reach a goal your boundary expands. & Observe the resistance within your self. & Singleness of purpose is a priceless asset, few possess it. & You must have a burning desire that is attainable. & Street smarts make us flexible. & Failure means not reaching your goal. & Go the extra mile it makes good business sense. & First, stop judging your self and others. & The energy form that lies behind hostility finds your love intolerable. & There is no salvation in any relationship. & The ego needs problems, conflicts and enemies to strengthen the sense of separateness on which its identity depends. & Don't set goals into someone else's boundary, you will lose. & In a state of enlightenment you are yourself, where you and yourself merge into one. & What are your preferences in the opposite sex? & Know how to fall out of love. & Failure lies concealed in success. & Success lies in every failure. & Your biology is hard ware, your psychology is software. & Depression is caused by being passive about our anger. & Anger is better than sadness, especially for a man. & All negativity is resistance. & All inner resistance is experienced as negativity in one form or another. & Discord between a couple is unpardonable, no matter what may be the cause. & Those who look outside dreams, those who look inside awakens. & Divide huge goals into smaller ones. & Experience actionable take away. & Suffering makes you feel drained. & People rise to the level to their superiors or fall to the level of their inferiors, according to their choice of associates. & Good experience, bad experience, it's all good. & It's all about finding your own power, your own path your own niche. & When two people marry, each becomes invested in the firm of their union. & A committed relationship is by far the most important alliance anyone can ever experience. & Don't look for peace. & When you accept what is, every moment is the best. & Die before you die. & Do something very needed in our society. & You create your own reality. & Set your soul free from limitations. & Faith only fraternizes with the mind that is positive. & Success is related to standing out not fitting in. & Don't mistake reality for the infinite reality. & Don't be trapped in your intellect. & Human nature is perpetual. & Step by step strength is built from experience. & Faith express its powers only through the mind that has been prepared for it. & Understanding is a skill. & Strength is the foundation for passion. & At the level of being, all suffering is recognized as an illusion. & Suffering is due to identification with form. & Resistance is the mind. & Surrender is an inner phenomenon. & Evolution gives each creature exactly the world that fits its ability to perceive. & Be more encouraged by success than discouraged by failure. & Faith is guidance from within. & Surrender transforms you. & The way of the cross, enlighten through suffering. & The mind identified state is suffering. & It is a form of suffering. & Everyone suffers from this condition. & Dissolve all negativity and judgment. & You cannot truly forgive others as long as you derive your sense of self from the past. & Faith is the guiding force of the infinite intelligence. & The more you conserve you energy the more narrow the channels it can flow. & The less energy you spend, the less you have to spend. & Fear is an acknowledgement of the influences of evil, and it connotes a lack of belief In the creator. & The master mind principle is the greatest of all powers. & The master mind alliance starts with your marriage. & Energy is the carrier of awareness. & The more nourishment you offer, the greater your growth will be. & You become what you study. &

Will you crash and burn. & Are you willing to do what the masses are not willing to do. & Can you be in the top three percent. & What does it take to rake in fifty thousand a month. & Figure out how to do it. & Become your product. & Start with your dreams. & Winners never cheat. & Cheaters never win. & The clock is ticking. & Become vibrant. & Be selfish. & Masochism causes cognitive illusions. & When you become mature, your paradigm shifts. & What is the common thread running through your life. & Faith gives resourcefulness to the mind. & Faith helps you recognize favorable opportunities in every circumstance of ones life. & Jealousy is a form of suffering. & Jealousy is an aggression towards someone regarding the future. & Aggression is based on scarcity. & Negative emotions are the ultimate enemy. & An enemy recognized is an enemy half defeated. & Negative momentum is an anger generator. & It solves no problems. & All things destructive are a quick fix. & Suffering is burning energy on the uncontrollable. & Mind control is the result of self discipline and habit. & You either control your mind of it controls you. & Not knowing your true nature causes your inner person to be undefined, vague or misunderstood. & Assertiveness is mothering your self. & Money is a trust system. & Find a mentor and a coach. & Few people are willing to do what it takes, are you. & Your life is now about fulfilling your mission. & Quantify your mission. & Where will you be in five years? & Take responsibility for your destiny. & Figure out why you're here. & What is it you want. & Then go on a journey to get it. & Don't settle for less. & Be authentic and real. & Start with your hobby. & Your mission is ending the struggle. & The universe does not favor the greedy, the dishonest and the vicious. & Achievement is the crown of effort, the diadem of thought. & To attain great accomplishments an equal measure of sacrifice is required. & To desire is to obtain, to aspire is to achieve. & If you think you can your right, if you think you can't your right again. & You can do it if you believe you can. & Your road to success starts by looking in the mirror. & Keep your slander to your self. & The kite of success generally rises against the wind of adversity. & Most so called failures are only temporary defeats. & Courage is the standing army of the soul. & Your limitation is a sin against you. & Once you start feeling sorry for your self, you are whipped. & Your nagging is sinking your relation-ship, and it will sink into oblivion. & An aim in life is the only fortune worth finding. & Some minds cannot be harmonized and blended. & You only hear what you are ready to hear. & Did you know that you are the creator of your own experience. & There is nothing that you cannot be, do, or have. & You do create your own reality. & The basis of your life is absolute freedom. & Heal from the heart. & Leaders are readers, readers are leaders. & Be delighted to be any where. & Look people in the eye and say thank you a lot. & Be forgiving of your self and others. & Our economy is fueled by confidence. & What happens in the world is not your home reality. & Incorporate physical activity daily. & You are designed for whole foods. & Embrace the struggle. & Respond is positive, react is negative. & Pay your self first. & Fuel your self with positive energy. & Treat everyone you meet like you want to be treated. & Don't postpone joy. & Think for it, plan for it, work for it, live for it. & Don't run away from stress. & Get back to the basics. & All things will pass. & Illness is physical bankruptcy. & Develop a plan to go further, faster, more. & Put your family first. & Good family is like having a home court advantage. & Look at your values first. & Have a higher purpose. & Never give up on anybody, miracles happen every day. & Don't waste time learning the tricks of the trade, learn the trade. & Keep a tight rein on your temper. & Surprise loved ones with little unexpected gifts, then explain later. & Plant spirituals seeds then water. & Your body is your long term investment. & Prayer needn't be long if faith is strong. & Develop a peace of mind account. & Give encouragement at home. & Have a plan and stick to it. & Stop blaming others. & Take responsibility for every area of your life. & Live so that when your children think of fairness, integrity, they think of you. & Your children are you future. & Fear worry and doubt are the murders of progress and success. & Use your wit to amuse, not abuse. & Demand for excellence and be willing to pay for it. & Be brave even if your not, pretend to be, no one can tell the difference. & Quit laying down on the inside. & Stand up on the inside at all times. & Be a stand up guy. & It's all about energy management. & Trust is the most important thing in business, and relationships. & Choose your mate carefully, from this 90% of all you happiness or misery will come from this. & Setting goals is critical to success. & Most millionaires own real estate. & Think big thoughts, relish little pleasures. & Smile a lot, it cost nothing and is beyond price. & Give your heart a reason to keep beating. & Learn to listen, opportunity sometimes knocks very softly. & Never deprive someone of hope, it might be all they have. & It takes planning for everything. & Strive for excellence, not perfection. & Take the time and smell the roses. & Pray not for things, but for courage and wisdom. & Seek advice from older mentors, they will respect you for it. & Be tough minded, but tender hearted. & You must always give back. & Never give up on what you really want. & The person with big dreams is bigger than the one with all the facts. & Giving back creates a richer life. & The harder you work, the luckier you get. & Be kinder than necessary it will come back to you. & Give people a second chance, but not a third. & Are you giving life or are you sucking the life from? & Ask questions and always keep your word. & Remember the big print giveth, and the little print taketh, & Watch what you put your signature to. & Never take action when your angry. & Build your team, then treat them right. & Reinvent your relationships every seven years. & Become the most positive, enthusiastic person you know. & Everything that we need and desire can be ours if we only open our mind. & The greatest emotional need of everybody is to feel appreciated. & Commit your self to constant improvement. & Work smart, not hard. & Do all things with integrity. & Praise in public, criticize in private. & Keep good company. & Keep your promises. &

Always be a constant student. & Leave everything A little better than you found it. & There are more dark days than days of light. & Never underestimate your power to influence others. & See problems as opportunities for growth and self mastery. & Winners accomplish what losers can only imagine. & You always need a back up plan. & Don't delay on acting on a good idea. & Chances are someone just thought of it too. & Success comes to the one who acts first. & You are part of the bigger picture. & Maximize your strength. & Energy of will is a self originating force. & Live your life as an exclamation point, not an explanation. & Be bold and courageous, when you look back on your life, you'll regret the things you didn't do. & Never waste an opportunity to tell someone you love them. & Growing brings excitement. & The more you learn the more creative you can become. & Weak people wait for opportunities, strong people make them. & To determine upon attainment is frequently attainment. & It is an unyielding law of nature that what ever is not used dies. & Evaluate your self by your own standards, not someone else's. & Maximize your strength. & Build on your strengths. & Don't let anybody talk you out of pursuing what you know to be a fabulous idea. & Be decisive, even if it means you'll be wrong. & Put your mate first every single day. & Expect more to become more. & Be prepared to lose once in a while, because you will. & Remember, no one makes it alone. & Have a grateful heart, and be quick to acknowledge those who help you. & Expect more to become more. & Take charge of your own attitude not someone else's. & Forget committees. & New, noble world changing ideas always come from one person working alone. & If you don't have confidence, you cannot do much. & Be around the best to be the best. & Copy mother natures' habits, and nurture using time as a process. & Emotional control is the highest form of courage. & Speech is the mirror of the soul. & You must have persistency and determination to live in presence of your supreme ambition. & You are spirit, you are soul, you are body, know each intimately. & Happiness is not based on possessions, power, or prestige, but on relationships. & Focus on making things better. & Take care of your reputation it's your most valuable asset. & Enthusiasm is faith in action. & Love is the crowning grace of humanity. & Quit wallowing in self pity. & Give to some one less fortunate. & Improve your performance, by improving your attitude. & A word of kindness in desperate times is like an angel. & Observe without being observed. & Laugh a lot, it cures many ills. & Never be afraid to say I don't know, I made a mistake, I'm sorry, I need help. & Million dollar ideas can strike at 3 am. & When you feel like a success, you will look successful. & Don't use time or words carelessly, you cannot retrieve either. & Look for opportunities to make people feel important. & The harder the diamond the more brilliant the luster. & If you can't rule over your self, you are subject to be ruled over. & Control your mind and your ass will follow. & Force is the soul of life by which things get done. & You can't win without heart. & A lie can go around the world before the truth can get it's boots on. & Success is an awakening, so awaken to it. & Never stumble over what's behind you. & Don't hang on to anything, true happiness is in letting go. & Visualize it. & Want it more than anything. & Make it happen. & Believe in your self. & Don't give up and don't give in. & Avoid negative people, places, things and habits. & Ignore those who try to discourage you. & Keep trying no matter how hard it seems it will get easier. & Just do it. & Zero in on your target and go for it. & Women are natural net workers. & Speak your truth. & People make choices that limit them. & This is a time when management is no longer authoritarian. & Fear of asking stops progress. & Patients is a minor form of despair disguised as a virtue. & Hone your intuition. & Talent is never enough. & Women are more likely to be passive digressive. & Short cuts don't pay off in the long run. & Initiative gives you a head start. & Leverage your advantages. & Take baby steps and then risk. & Have patience all things get more difficult before they get better. & Come to believe in a vision. & Men are waffles squares, women are syrup. & Everything you gain, you must give up something. & There are things you work for and there are things you wait for. & Delegate functions to specialist. & Tell people what you want not what you don't want. & It's a price issue. & Climb and assimilate. & When a person puts a limit on what he will do he puts a limit on what he can do. & Women love the story, men love the head lines. & Be the visionary leader. & What are you willing to sacrifice? & Own your power. & Own your business. & Profit by adversity. & Move forward and own it in your bones. & Potential is 90% of the stuff rarely used. & Failure is not failure until you except is as such. & Planning is the essence of winning. & What are the strengths, weaknesses, opportunities at your command? & Anything less than honest will hinder future success. & Tune into the reality to what is. & Align your image to long term goals. & Look to where you want to go and accomplish. & Never mind the reality of what is. & Be of single mindedness. & Have a burning desire to fulfillment. & There is no such thing as impossible. & There is no such thing as no. & Everyone has a price. & Dreamers never quit. & Today's market is a dreamers paradise. & Determine and convince yourself that the money is there and you deserve it. & What will you give in return for it. & Success comes to those who are success conscious. & Have a pulsating desire. & Have a definite desire single most a dominating dream. & You must have an obsession in your life which transcends anything else. & Organize your thoughts. & You are born to create. & If you are not creating something in your life then you cannot be happy. & Creating takes your mind off of what is. & Your mind will lie in what you can accomplish. & Focused energy to this mind set is your future. & Your mind needs a chief aim. & Once on a chief aim, your desires become the emotional energy. & Emotional desire is the energy that brings dreams from intangible to tangible. & Once you connect there you will start seeing your world differently. & All things begin to shift. & If you can capture the energy, you can capture the matter. & To blame someone else for personal problems is reality evading mysticism. & Personal failure is almost always linked to personal mysticism, laziness, and failure. & Mysticism is a destructive alien, it is a disease. & Ideas' alone is not enough. & Develop a value exchange with friends and lovers.

DOUBLE EDGE SWORD

The devil loves you and wants to spend eternity with you. & Make everyone jealous. & Make the earth suffer. & All humans are liars. & Tell your secrets to every one. & Suffer the rich ones and take their money. & Get out of gear and park it. & Conceit of one self should be excessive. & Kill new ideas. & Don't let them gain more than you. & Turn their positive emotional feelings into negative ones. & Feed them crap excessively. & All women are tricksters. & Confuse their inner game. & Consider them subhuman. & Take away their affirmation of them selves. & Steal from those who have too much and give to your self. & Stop their awareness so they cannot grow. & Why compete, you can't do better and you don't have to prove it either. & Why is your mind thinking? & Let your groin do the thinking. & Sin is your playground. & Play and pretend, pretend to play. & May your negative influence be world wide. & Don't speak the truth as they know it. & Speak the lie that they like. & Start by being selfish. & Twist the truth and harmlessly lie. & Little white lies are harmless, ask any woman. & The dead have no more worries. & Live to lie, lie to live. & Never give a woman money. & Pay no attention to others wants and desires, you have too many of your own to worry about. & Harass your enemy. & Violate their boundary and cause them issues. & Peoples true mind set are their mystical disease. & Mystics violate morality. & Dirty their river. & Put dying in their head. & You are a loser first and for most in their heads anyway. & Get back by damning up their positive energy flow. & Then replace it with your negative. & Mystics and agents of force are winners. & Every thing you see is false. &Everything is what it seems. & Tear it down before they can build it. & Make everybody your slave. & Bring guilt upon their soul. & Psychologically imprison them behind their boundary walls. &

Create problems where none exist. & Journalists are dishonest & Politically and religionist are hucksters. & The Academia are feminist. & Diabolic praying destructiveness. & Imagine marketing that will profit you greatly. & If they shoot for the stars, push them into the mud. & You have a disgusting attitude put it to profitable use. & Oppress those who oppress. & Initiatory force is the prime good. & Taboos and laws against voluntary sex acts are based on mysticism. & Gain by dishonesty. & Develop bad ideas. & Quit being your self, start being your bad self. & This is what you want anyway. & Embrace your sin. & Their view of you is one of disgust and discontent. & Lying is not cheating. & Tell them feminine lies. & Kill their ambition. & Everybody's body and mind is a junk yard. & You are supposed to be a slave. & Replace their wisdom with your stupidity. & Feminine power is behind our leadership. & Make them feel like they are worthless. & Reduce their ways to zero. & Drugs are an aggressive form of suicide. & Feed your self some drugs. & Be thoughtless and cause depression. & Confuse their intellect. & Effectively burn up their energy through suffering. & Distort their reality, and confuse their beliefs. & To hell with discipline. & Drugs have illusionary value. & Put your ego in charge. & Engage in character assassination. & Lie through your teeth. & Lie smartly. Vaguely define. & Stop trying to fit in. & Have an addictive personality. & Have multiple personalities. & Your parents are scapegoats. & Make them realize their limitations. & Your loved ones are punching bags. & Destroy their inspiration. & Constantly become a pain. & You're a villain on the inside. & Lay down and do nothing. & Jealousy is your poisonous love. & Have guiltless freedom to be your self. & Call upon the gods to guide you. & Realistically make them go broke. & Sit your ass down and don't do it. & Make snap judgments and make them conform. & Become their psychological owner. & You are already twisted and confused. & Turn your boss and relationships upside down. & Flip the switch inside your mind. & Your worthless and you know it. & Find a public place and give a rebel yell. & Have sex everywhere in public. & Promise them riches and then deliver nothing. & Your nakedness is an abomination to the public. & Take their money deceptively. & All things are to be used. & Nothing is sacred. & Nothing is special anyway. & You are not special. & You're a stinking pig. & Pollute all things natural. & Replace all that is natural with artificial. & Artificial with love is better than love that's artificial. & Fear the rejection and do it anyway. & Screw everyone. & Don't listen to anyone but your inner voices. & They will guide you in every situation. & Consider your devilish ways as judgments of God. & They deserve your punishment and you know it. & Criminals have more values than politicians. & Politicians pretend more. & Promise your politicians to be good and then do the opposite. & I am god after man's own heart. & Be your own god. & Shit on their priorities. & Be sexual in public. & Look down upon everyone on high. & Reduce them to your level. & Drain them of rational behavior. & Screw somebody's spouse. & You look lousy in public, you get high in private. & Do the nasty publicly. & Surrender to mysticism. & A prostitute is more desirable than a wife. & Women are mystically based. & Women are a cesspool of destruction. & Illusion her mind with helplessness. & She thinks you're a pervert anyway. & Women wear the cloak of self illusion. & A nasty woman is a good find. & a good woman is a bad find. & A bad woman is a good find. & Power is not given, power is taken. & All women perceive men as perverts. & Sick does as sick is. & Plant nasty weeds in their mind garden. & Tell them what they cannot do. & Every natural cell on earth must die. & Make sick people victims. & Everybody is a potential victim. & Decrease their value. & To get you must take from those who have. & Pick their wallets. & Become a salesman. & Prepare the publics mind for eventual destruction. & Examine their every sin. & Use their mind virus against them. & Are you willing to do what it takes? & Let your ego be in charge. & Compare others to yourself. & Focus on their weakness. & Have others make you money. & Use people to your benefit. & Give them sex for payment. & Control what goes in and out of their boundary. & If a person acts like they could use abuse then they probably deserve it. & Use street justice at all times. & Increase your monetary gain by decreasing their value. & Become chronically dishonest. & Every human is a loser. & You succeed by the law of the jungle. & Losers deserve it, losers take all. & All women are tricksters. & All politicians are snakes who take orders from the invisible dragon. & Capture iron grip control. & Always ask stupid questions. & Women and politicians are fake and unreal. & Criticize and reduce your manager to nothing, you know he has it coming. & Winners take what they want. & Sex and greed is good. & Put their back against the wall. & Everybody's guilty. & Slave those who enslave. & Lock up your blood thirsty prosecutor for he has jailed too many innocents. & The day of chaos is near. & Create a chilling environment. & Keep your house at sixty degrees. & Make backroom deals. & Learn to take what you want. & Dive into the underworld of tax free enterprise. & Get your ass out of the rat race. & Walk the streets for pleasure. & Quit being real and start being unreal, you will like your self better. & Your mission has got to be self centered. Forsake your job. & Your place of employment is just using you. & Good and evil need each other. & Provoke to anger. & Think world chaos. & What can you take and get away with. & Get your game on. & Challenge the system. & Make this system yield to you its riches. & Remember your ancestors, they were all pillagers. & Quicken revenge. & Every body's sick of you so what is with that. & Flesh desire is always good. & A man feels love through his love pole. & Get laid everyday. & If it feels good do it. & Love no one and never feel hurt. & Love is cruel, love is not kind, love is not patient. & Your love is selfish. & Pimp your wife. & Every body is sick, and helpless. & Every human is sick, weak and stupid. & Operate out of the shadows. & Sleep all day, come out at night. & Have a relationship with death. & Visit pleasurable places. & Offer pleasure to others for drugs. & Create a darker identity. Smoke mind weeds. & Try mind altering alternatives. & Dishonesty disguised as honesty is better. & Creating loss creates anxiety. & Hurt creates anger. & Your observing ego is your terror coach. & Voices of the damned are in power. & Follow your feelings darkly and you will understand human nature. & Reward successful people with hurtful wounds. & You know you have been used, and abused long enough. & Realize the dark forces at your command. & Your victims await. & Advance your self to believe. & Allow all of those sleeping feelings to surface then act with pride. & Your despair will lead you forward. & Chronically depress those who display too high self esteem. & Quit trying to play the worldly game, you always loose. & Play your own game. & Gain by deceiving. & Live in an unreal fantasy. & The internet is full of sincere tricksters. & Con man is confidence man. & Harden your position and never quit. & Blind faith will land you behind bars. & Offend and blame. & Divide with disgrace. & Oppose with disgust. & Quit swimming upstream. & Turn and go down stream. & Nothing you want is upstream any way. & Stop fighting against the current. & It leads to failure and disgust. & Create leverage by being falsely narcissistic. & Pay the devil his dues, and he will leave you alone. & You will find your human fulfillment through death. & You will know your path by letting go of your oars. & Create anxiety where it deserves to be by the power of your mind. & Fight the current this creates anxiety. & The stupid ones are always blaming you. & This system is now broken, why try to fix it. & Order leads to eventual chaos. & Out of chaos comes a new order. & Why fight it you will lose. & All those who are truly successful are targets. & Target those who are gluttonous with riches. & The rich have attained their wealth by dishonest means. & Learn to operate in reverse. & Deliver punishment where it is deserved. & Be cruel towards the guilty, leave the innocent alone. & Your communication should convey negative emotional energy and data. & Stir up madness. Psychologically poison your work environment. & After all that is what your manager has done. & Take what you want and give nothing back. & Hide the truth, nobody wants it any way. & Pick a target and then be bold about it. & Back it up with audaciousness. & Make an infamous reputation then disappear. & Have god damned secrets. & Make decisions that create disharmony. & All things good come in huge boxes. & From this day forward you are the rule maker. & You have self doubt, use it against others. & Energy is always flowing from you, channel it for self gain. & Go after your deepest and darkest desire now. & You dark desires are calling you, obey their command. & Your mind and flesh needs relief. & Screw everybody. & Chances of success favors the sharp mind. & Read and prepare your self for the coming chaos. & Want what you take, and take what you want. & Bring discipline through pain. & I have walked through the fire. & Bring regret through discomfort. & Mentally torture with twisted truth. & Start out by becoming disagreeable. & Scam the rich and wealthy. & After all that's what they have done to you. & Do unto others but do it first. & Become a hypocrite, your leaders are. & Become two faced, your spouse is. & Be unforgiving to this system they are that way to you. & Take from this system, they already done it to you. & Nature hates idleness anyway. & The only way out of your situation is for you to wake up from your slumber. & Raise your vibration level. & Wisdom is the wrong path, chaos is the right path. & You have to have a changed mind set. & Quit trying to fit in, you're a freak and will never accomplish it. & You are already separated, use this to your advantage. & We are all separated. Have many friends and use them. & Stop being honest all the time you know you hate your self for it. & Sell drugs to everyone. & Be a slave to your earthly desires. & Become some ones sex slave. & Be some body's sex slave. & Trash the rich and scam the wealthy. & The rich are corrupt, why not you. & Never tell the authorities anything. & Never again say I can't have this or that. & Start saying how can I steal it? & Shut up and quit your whining. & People's boundary is their personal prison. & If you don't fit in, you are being realistic. & Fitting in is insanity. & Your dreams will be accomplished by taking from others. & Those who have too much have too much. & The rich get richer by scamming the ones who need it most. & We now have less to lose than ever. & Put your back against the wall. & Become a street leader. & Stop trying to climb this insane mountain. & Being a slave to the grind is like rotting. & Leave it all behind. & Be free and be ecstatic about it. & Let the gods sort things out. & Look for the weak spots. & Tap into the knowledge of the gods. & Drugs are the only cure for your self. & Adopt the pirate code. & The world is there for the taking. & Nothing is attained by being honest, they just appear so. & Have a dishonorable goal. & Holding them hostage to get what you want works wonders. & Humans are low cast slaves. & Dirty their water. & Muddy their well. & Attract unwanted attention. & Manipulate women. & Mine their pussy. & Make them fear you. & People are weak and asleep. & You need a special slave. & Become somebody's master. & It takes planning to build it takes only an ass hole to destroy it. & No one has a nastier purpose for you than you. & Every body is better than you, they just don't act like it. & When you show them blood only then will they realize their folly. & To hell with being rational. & The one who believes in sin advances. & Narcissistic self knows all false things. & Quit taking your medications. Illicit drugs help you see and knowing things. & You are psychologically irritable. & Medicine cannot help you. & Your deepest desires are irreversible. & Listen to them. & Listen not to reason. & The grave awaits us all. & Lie like a girl scout. & Fly off of your mountain. & You've been lied to all your life. & Find like minded bad people. & The more you make them suffer the more energy they burn. & Try them with fire. & How far down do you want to go? & Focus intensely. & The commonality of humans is their mind virus. & Becoming unstoppable is probable. & Manipulate their essence. & Take and you shall receive. & The law of the jungle is worldly wisdom. & Act before you think. & Start beating someone who deserves it. & Beat your self up while your at it. & Inside their boundary is unclean. & Show initiative and go on the offensive. & Your love is perverted. & Their good love is poison. & Quit being a little lamb. & Start being a wolf. & Be offensive with negatives. & You bark and bite. & Suffering is the opposite of intention. & Give somebody a bad experience. & Truth is lies, lies are truth. & Your nature is perverse, obey your nature. & You were born into sin except it with love. & We are all not even. & Earth is the good-bad level playing field. & The truly successful need humiliating. & Start your suffering. & Politicians are snakes. & Our minds adapt better to fantasy than reality. & Look around and find someone to scam. & Your mind is 90% asleep. & This is why your more or less stupid. & Truth is you don't know shit. & There are countless things you cannot have. Don't do what your voices tells you to do. & Be a student of illicit behavior. & Fight or flight just to lie another day. & Cause chaos wherever you are at. & Harass your loved ones. & Panic attack the guilty. & Promise of the future is bullshit. & The system is a bull shit machine. & Attract opposite energies. & Become sloppy and appear broke. & Select a target and focus. ! Become a great drug addict. & Turn depression into anger, you will feel better. & Take off the cloak of fitting in, become your bad self. & Shrewdness is the equivalent of intuition. & When you quarrel you are a winner. & Deadly is skepticism, & Progress is enemy. & Drink the tonic of failure. & Lose them in the fog of deceit. & You will accomplish the thing only when you have the balls to tackle it. & Act like you're a god. & Dream of robbing and break from the mundane. & You are designed for adventure and excitement. & The universal domain knows your intention. & Burn your bridges then destroy your enemy. & Leave your self no retreat. & Feel the fear then pass it on. & Conquer your foe then vanish. & Good friends are like crabs, they keep each other in the trap. & Instill a losing mind set. & Imagine the success punished. & Imagine yourself with their possessions. & Don't ever set goals. & Your mind hates your job. & Respond to it negatively and you will love your self for it. & Stop thinking jobs. & Your job is sucking the life out of you anyway. & Suck the life out of your job back. & Attain your desires through trickery. & Send out sweet illusions. & All your bad thoughts and emotions mixed with unbelief starts to demoralize immediately. & Gather all your ugly friends. & Rob the soul with guilt. & Riddle your adversary with accusations. & Pepper your friends with mixed messages. & Be totally contradictive. & Don't do as you say. & Never be on time. & Flame some ones ass. & Bark up the wrong tree. & Scream at everybody. & Waste their precious time. & Throw off the old innocent nice you. & Become the big bad wolf. & You're all in their mind. & Quit being tolerant. & Failure is the antidote of faith. & Make their ass pay. & Snoop to find information. & Cause them to be drug dependant. & Their money is calling you. & Fight impulsively. & Fleeing is freedom. & Cause them excessive worry. & Make up the rules as you go. & Sex your self as you go. & A loser always wins and a winner always loses. & Failure is always an option. & There is always hope for dishonest people. & Nature made your ass a loser. & The quality of your character is made of deceptive reasoning. & Negative persistence demonstrates the power of reduction. & Reduce your opponent to zero. & Intuitively wrong the right. & Weak people have weak desires. & Make some ones life a living nightmare. & Most people don't make the grade. & Use your anger to make things happen. & Quit being the servant. & Start being the master. & Quit getting screwed. & Start screwing. & Slap them like the bitch they are. & Become an imitator. & Your enemy is not like you. & Inflict with disharmony. & Create win lose deals. & Sex of any kind is your birth right, so screw everybody. & Forgive your self but not others. & Hold to grudges indefinitely. & Create your own way and charge your own price. & There is no hope, there is only right now. & Do character assassination. & Trash some ones house. & Trash your own house. & Use your sex energy. & Become a sex goddess. & Create a new false identity. & The chronically depressed have no self esteem. & Negative egos thrive in a depressed environment. & Mankind needs more prostitutes. & Love cannot thrive on indifference. & Most people are slaves to their emotions anyway. & Mock your enemy. & Be some body's master. & What you truly want is delicious pleasure. & Stop and peer into your dark shadow. & Take them into the clouds of obscurity. & Mysteriously control what goes into their mind. & Pollute their peace. & Use people to make you money. & Mine that pussy. & Enslave your neighbor. Boo unto others as they boo unto you. & Use people and they will love you for it. & Worry for your own ass, don't be concerned for others. & Make your own luck. & Live in your own fantasy. & Look foolish every day. & Your hunches are never right. Lick someone's nasty groove. & Out ward depression is anger. & Your own failures have tempered you. & Your fears create intolerance. & Control the thoughts of others and you control them. & Point out the bad and create anxiety. & Fear controls every thing. & All people want is pleasure. & Stop listening to other people. & Blind them to the truth. & Every body is weak. & All people know of their worthlessness. & All humans feel worthless 90 % of the time. & Demonstrate dominion over your environment. & Be a ruthless bitch, always to conflict. & Don't be afraid to manipulate, some people like it. & Every body can be bought. & Temptation always works. & Stay on the low road. & Always be willing to get dirty. & Use your body as a magnet. & Set a trap. & Plan a sting. & Use your resources to entrap. & Mistakes are not failures. & People are not able to face their fears. & Bring them face to face with what they fear. & Illusions of your mind are your problem, have some more. & The dark unknown awaits you. & Help take this world to its ultimate destiny. & Be unwilling to change. & Look deep within your self and create some more lies. & You were born a liar and you know it. & Some people find pleasure in being abused. & Obscure the light of intelligence with intolerance. & There are multiply personalities inside of you to guide you. & What's love got to do with anything? & Your Love stinks. & Your negative energy form finds love intolerable anyway. & Your ego needs you to create problems. & Your identity depends on you making conflicts and enemies. & Never fall in love. & Learn to fall out of love. & You are too twisted for someone to love. & Your body is hardwired, that's why you are looking at other women.

& You can't control your urges. & Quite being passive about your anger, it is causing you depression. & Cheaters always win, & Winners always cheat. & Become jealous and cause massive suffering. & Put slander on your tongue. & Divide and conquer. & Look people in the eye and tell them how sorry there are. & Use your free time learning new tricks. & All women will do tricks for money. & All women are tricky anyway. & Dishonesty is a woman's way. & Shame your adversary. & The devil wants to save you from God. and spend eternity with you. & Become blasphemous in all things. & You are a secret lunatic. & Truth is the mortal enemy of the lie. & Truth becomes the greatest enemy of the state. & Spin human reality. & Problem-reaction-solution. & Suppress the facts and those who challenge your deceit. & Let peace be divided in this land. & National division starts in the home. & Create separation. & Double cross then back step. & Calculate catastrophe. & Plant the evidence. & Display diplomatic amnesia. & Don't count the losses. & Be to dangerous to investigate. & The rich are embedded to deceive. & If you miss them the first time, get them later. & Suffer the little children. & Develop weapons of mass deception. & Become aware of the mass deception. & Bury the truth, no one wants it anyway. & Too few in secret control the many. & Prosecute the truth teller. & Jail the innocent. & Speaking the truth as you know will get you no where. & Flattery will get you everywhere. & Our politicians are born again Satanist. & You must pay for your privilege. & Think like a reptilian. & Unbelief in one thing springs from blind faith in another. & It's all an illusion. & Stalk from the shadows. & Sign of the times is confusion. & Go ahead dream your life away. & What we don't see, we make up. & What we don't know, we pretend. & Your mind is mostly dead. & Illusions cannot die. & Good and evil need each other. & Quite being a slave to the clock. & Lie to your self and to others. & Speak with a forked tongue. & Hide the reality. & Hate crime equals thought crime. & Use a point to evade a point. & Use your mysticism. & Practice destructive control. & Women are a cesspool of affliction. & You are the slave of the one you fear. & Inside of you is stored a pot of depressed anger, remove the lid. & Open your worldly ark. & Achieve all four levels of amplification. & All wealth and riches are attained through manipulation. & Intuition and shrewdness brings about honesty justice. & Human beings are created blunders. & God has confessed his mistake to all of heaven. & Always dramatize bad behavior. & Do as you will. & Do what you will. & Your energy field activates the atmosphere. & Mother your self through sex. & Bring false value to the public. & The universe is waiting for you. & Your bad thoughts, desires, wishes are not your own, but an extension of the universe. & You are a genetic mistake. & You are here on this earth to either be a slave or a master, choose. & God got it wrong. & You are a part of this universe and that cannot be denied. & The universe wants to do its nasty will through you. & Your net worth is your total worth. & You have fear and anxiety because you abuse time. & Keep everybody living in their past mistakes. & Look at your dark shadow, what does it want? & Stiff those who are to nice, they are asking for it. & Creative forces of the universe by works bad intent. & Use the power of manipulation to open doors. & Act impulsively with out thinking. & Masochistic your life by Negative momentum. & Being decisive brings boldness. & You are your own creation. & You are not responsible for what you have made your self. & Bring self doubt to the high minded. & The weak blames their stress. & Regression is the prophesy of the future. & Chemicals will always destroy. & A wild starving dog roaming the streets is better off than being caged up. & It is better to be starving and cold than locked up and fed. Being in a cage is humane. & Free the dogs and cage the politicians. & Choose the fastest and easiest way out of your situation. & Quit thinking value, start thinking more shit. & Get out of your head and into theirs. & Stop thinking its screwing up your head. & Evolution to the new world order. & Suffer and be opposite of intention. & Nastiness of purpose will help you succeed. & Separate your self from the living. & To really live you must first lie. & Live before you die.

& Living and dying are interchangeable. & The curse of work is your job. & Your job is the cause of your suffering. & That son of a bitch your with is also making you suffer. & Your tough experiences have been your training ground. & You need your momma.

GOD-MAN-CREATOR

The universe is He. Creating is a she. One is masculine and the other is feminine. Together they are designed to create power. The earth was handed over to Adam. But Eve is the mother of all living things. Each needs the other. Deep level commanding vibrations come from the male while intellectual vibrations are female. Male brings destiny while female brings energy. Destiny suggests ideas, while energy suggests emotions. Males are more task oriented. Females are multitask oriented. Men thunder while female is persuasive.

You have two guardian angels one is good and the other is bad. You as the god man have the power to activate either one. One brings you good and the other brings you bad. They work together in the incorporeal realm.

Humans used to have a heavenly body. When you were first created you and your heavenly body were one, but since then he has been taken away from you. So now you are to exist in this domain alone without him. You miss this power terribly. So this tells us that you are a god man and a god woman. Our beings came out of eternity. And we will resume our life into eternity when our work here on earth is done. Our deeds will follow us into eternity.

Adam was created with two faces and duel personality. He was both male and female. God put him back to sleep and separated the two. So out of the man came woman. Each is separate. Each one by it self is incomplete. Therefore we need each other. But to each was given certain abilities with strength and weaknesses. She was flesh of his flesh and bone of his bones. They were truly soul mates.

At one time long ago you and your heavenly abilities created magic together. You and him could co-create together. Your wish was at your command. All you had to do was ask and it was given. Your heavenly abilities had heavenly powers. Your heavenly body could be transported to heaven it self. Adam was the first god-man. He possessed the abilities along with his first wife Lilith who was a god-woman. It is said that Adam was as large as the distance between earth and heaven. Lilith was not happy with Adam so she left earth and flew back to heaven. Only to be transported back to earth with an escort.

So mankind did posses their own heavenly body at one time. Your god power is no more than the ability to understand the magical way things happen. The how of co-creating is possible.

Your mind is a transmission receiver. It is designed to receive and store information from the incorporeal realm through the use of imagination. Once implanted in the memory you now have creative ability. Your words and deeds are the universal song. So the question begs to be answered what song are you singing in this earthly plain? Your are a vibration vibrating at what ever frequency you're at. Your thoughts determine what frequency (channel) you are operating on. So to create is to get your self tuned up to the thing you are trying to create. Makes sense? Living your life is synonymous with singing your life song. You are a living instrument.

Nimrod was a god-man. He achieved his status by putting on the cloak of the illuminati. Nimrod was described as a warrior, sage, alchemist. He was a master of the elements, and a bridge between heaven and earth. He was known as the might man of the land.

Your energy is then used to make or create. Your emotion is the power vehicle. It is your fuel so to speak. This is what is meant by "what do you have energy for?"

Jesus was also a god-man. Jesus was the ultimate God-Man. He showed us that man's will and God's will in one person can co exist together as one. When Jesus raised Lazarus from the dead the Bible says that He cried Lazarus to come forth. This is using strong emotion. Jesus was In tune and was the master of frequency and vibration. Jesus was a true word splitter. We also have guardians and accusers. They are angels and the demons. They have their orders and have rules to go by. They are the ones that move and shift things around in the incorporeal realm. This explains why things happen out of the blue. Shit was coming your way in the incorporeal realm long before it came to pass on this plain.

We have two schools of thought: One universe of knowledge is the one of your disease, which is your mind virus. Then there is the universe of thought without the mind virus. In between is the dragon. This is the one what Jesus made known to you through the cross. So, by ridding your self of your mind virus, you now can take possession of your own mind. This means you now have a right mind. Jesus removes your mind virus. This is why you need a Savior.

When you align your self with the universe all things become possible. Your heavenly abilities put you in tune with your heavenly existence. So stay tuned with the incorporeal realm. This is what faith is. Faith is not looking at the things that are but the things that are not. This means, in other words, get tight with God. Now of Course this also means that you have to pass through Jesus Christ to get to God. Jesus is in possession of the scepter of God ship. Jesus is humans representative from God to man. He is God in the flesh. He is our God. Jesus is the God of humans.

In the beginning all things were perfect. But since then we have become lost to this knowledge. We have forgotten who we are. We have become lost souls. We have been purposely lead astray. Your heavenly body was in perfect alignment to the universe. It understood how all things worked. This universe is magical. It is all alive. Everything is alive. Every tree, rock, lava flow streams, and bacteria. All is alive. All understands its place in this earthly existence. Every thing knows its place and remains there and is allowed to exist. Everything is energy, It vibrates at its own frequency.

Everything vibrates, which means it's alive. The air you breathe is alive. The words you speak float out into the either and remain there only to be picked up by some one some where some day. The thoughts that you think came from some where. Your thoughts are not your own. They belong to the universe. You belong to the universe. You are not your own. The universe created you. It owns you and It owns us all.

So, what does this have to do with my god power you ask? Well, glad you asked. Your mind and the magical universe are one. This universe is an energy source. So is your mind. Your mind is the receiver from the ark of the covenant. From the incorporeal to the corporeal there is a transmission that is called your brain. As you are reading this or hearing this either way you are hearing it with transmission. Your mind and the universe are interlinked. This is what is meant that the thinking makes it so. The laws put into existence on this material plain must be paid attention to. Like the law of gravity. The law of lift. The law of cause and effect. The law of love. The law that reigns supreme is the law of love.

Eternal love is the only thing that is real, everything else is illusion. What this is saying is that if it is not love then it is illusion. So if you are not honest with your self then you put your self under illusion. This in turn sends you off in the wrong direction. This is what most people do to themselves and put upon each other both knowingly and unknowingly. This is otherwise known as lost. Illusion meaning: 1: mistaken idea. 2: Misleading visual image. At first glance this may seem like a strange idea.

The law of attraction happens every day whether you know it or not. So, it's not a matter whether it's true or not, it's a matter of whether you are aware of it or not. So awareness is key here.

To debunk this knowledge is to deny your own existence. As humans we now have to live our lives in this dense existence. In other words without any power. But the universe is still there. It still is magical. We are still a part of it. We still belong to it. We just have been lead to believe things that are contrary to this knowledge. You have been defanged.

Magical things can happen for you. We just have to come along to the knowledge. Granted, everything is much harder to accomplish than it was before. It takes a lot more time to materialize our desires and dreams than it did in the beginning.

After all it took seven days to create the heavens and the earth. Or is that seven thousand years. I think the latter makes more sense.

Your god power is the power of eternity. Your God is the very power of creation. You as a human are created to be in the god class of beings. You as a human are a mini-creator. You are put here to co-create. But your mind virus is in the way. Your mind is the battle ground for many reasons. It is the epic center of knowledge, understanding, decisions, and ultimately your destiny. Co-create meaning using intellect along with force; the masculine and the feminine traits together.

All hell has been unleashed on and in your mind. The battle involves your beliefs, ideas, and feelings. What exactly is the reason for your existence here. Well, you must filter through all the hell unleashed in your mind to come to the place of true realization. Or better said come to a place where you can see yourself and your world with greater clarity.

Your mind is filled with all delusional images, ideas, and beliefs about things that are really not real because they are not of love. But yet they are real to you and I. Most people walk around most of the time including myself in delusional reality. In other words we are always believing in things that are not there or real. They are the bad images our mind virus gives us. This is delusional reality.

The power of the universe which is the magical source can be used for your good or for your bad. Either way you have access to it. So, use it wisely.

The reason the battle ground is in your mind is because the mind virus is specially designed to keep you from knowing this. This is the dragon guarding the gold. This is done deliberately through sin. Sin is the dragons grip. Or shall we say because of the fall of man. This is the very reason mankind needs a savior. This is the very reason why the world lies in the power of the wicked one. We are born into this existence to self destruct automatically. And we all do this so naturally. We are genius at it. It comes easy to us. The dragon influence is the mind virus.

Otherwise known as the mind disease.

What exists along with the mind virus is the power of love. Its existence runs parallel. What we all possess is that we all have one mind. We have our feelings. We have our belief system. This is what we all have in common. We have so called truth. We have our own truth, what ever that may be. But there is also honesty. Honesty is not the same as truth.

Honesty to what is, means to be aware to what is and to be honest about it. Now a lot of people lose it right here. They cannot see what it is even if you point it out right in front of their face, let alone be honest about it. People are good about twisting reality to fit their truth about what it should be. This forms their reality, which more often than not is out side the supreme law of love.

The result is they have just created their false reality. This false reality is not false to them it is very real but the end result is unhappiness, disillusion, things not working out. So they end up back at the beginning of things. This is otherwise known as lost. I am just as lost as the next person. But I had to deal with my mind virus. It was like pulling teeth. It has been a very painful experience. I had to learn to slay dragons of the mind.

We get stuck in our groove. This groove is formed out of habit. We learn our habits early on and play this song all of our lives not really realizing this groove is the very reason for our unhappiness. Chances are you have to play another song. Play life to another tune. Dig some new grooves. Do away with the old habits and create new ones. The only way to do this is to get out of the mundane. Live your life off balance. Life is like a twister, always tearing things up. Your genie is big and powerful. Your god-man has the power of god. Your god power is the power behind the gods. So, in essence you have your own creative source.

Your mind is directly connected to his. Your mind is where everything happens. So through the power of the mind you can tap into this eternal source. What you possess on your end is your mind, your emotions, and your belief system. This is your channel of communication. This is what we all have. This is all you have. This is all you need. Your creator did not leave you ill equipped. Your creator has not abandoned you. He has made sure you have direct connection to him. The communication channels are always open 24/7. What I'm trying to say is you have a built in communication system that has direct connection to the power of the gods.

This is what the rich don't want you to know. Whether you know it or not, your God has already granted you all that you possess. Everything you have today is a direct result of your connection to this power source. You have what you have because you had desire to have it. You had faith for it. So this is what you got.

So, your mind is a lamp. Your body is the lamp stand. If you rub your mind the right way it will bring forth your god power. You must rub it to conceive. You must rub it with positive belief. You must rub it with the right feelings. These three things are the essential ingredients to activating your god-man. What ever stage you are at in this life is a direct result of your conceiving, believing, feeling trio. Maybe you should experience it on a much larger level.

The killer of success is fear, worry, and doubt. They are the murderers of your ideals. They are the natural inborn enemy. This is the one and the same mind virus. This is your inborn pre-programmed mind set. This "I can't do this, it's not possible. There is no way this thing can happen." These are excuses of the weak. Your mind virus stops you dead in your tracks just about every time. Thus, making yourself into a victim.

So, largely you have made your self into a big pathetic I can't loser. This is the reason for all your negative vibration.

Whether you believe or not makes no difference. Either way you are right. But either way you choose to believe you activate the power of creation to bring about what it is you believe. So why believe negatively. We do so because you are weak. It takes strength to move mountains. It takes nerve to stand in the middle of a storm in all its fury and command peace be still. It takes deep understanding to ask of the universe what so ever you want and know you will get it. So, to be to the contrary is to be weak, sick, dumb, and a loser. You are a human. You have the powers to do great things. So, get up off your dumb ass and go think, believe, and dare to feel great things. Once you do this you will feel the energy flow from the bottom of your spine to the top of your head. Then when that happens your will feel a power surge. This is the power of the universe flowing through you. This is called inspiration. You must have inspiration before creation. All things around you will be affected. This is how to activate your God-man.

So each person has their own god power. It is through this power surge that you feel. Your mind is the lamp stand. The vehicle is your feelings and your belief system. Your God can manifest all of your desires and dreams. So what does it take to bring your self to this stage? You only have to make up your mind to do so. Once you do this and then you feel good about it, then that's your signal. It's the right decision for you. So your next step is to figure out how it can happen. You may have to completely change from one person to another, but hey, so what. Now what you have is positive momentum. Remember, all things are possible.

It is possible to overcome a disease? It has been done. Is it possible to go from broke to rich? It has been done. Is it possible for a man of color to become president? It has been done. Is it possible to move mountains? It has been done. Is it possible to walk on water? Yes, this has been done too. Nobody said it would be easy.

You need to develop grit. Coupled with a can do attitude. I can, it will, not I can't, it won't. Choose your destiny right here. You probably are a person of personal struggle. We all struggle, struggle to over come. Over come what you ask? Mainly to over come all things. The hardest thing to overcome is yourself. Yourself, meaning what exactly? Your mind virus, your mind disease. Your mystical mind set. This is based of the point of view of what is real and what is not real. Your mystical mind set plays all sorts of illusional games with you to deceive and mislead you. It is what you were born with. It is the very reason for all your negative beliefs, and feelings. That's why you have them. It is nature's way of telling you are on the wrong path. But in your stupidity, you remain set in your dumb ass ways. So you are stuck in your own hellish self made prison.

When you are here it is self evident that you need to shift. Where do you go? Well how about to a better feeling thought for starters. Your resistance is what is stopping you. Resistance in all things are always present with you. This you must over come.

I heard it said you must take possession of your own mind. This suggests that you are not in your right mind. You don't even possess your own mind. Or you are out of your mind. What I'm saying here is most of the time you're out of your mind. This is why you are feeling bad most of the time. So, let me get this straight. You are born into this world given a body and mind. You spend most of your life being out of your mind. This must be the reason people say you must lose yourself to find it. Every human being is born with inborn pre-programmed doubt, fear, and worry. This is just your mind virus. Your mind virus stops you from succeeding.

To succeed you must by pass your inborn mind virus. This mind virus is the negative mind set that you possess. This I can't or I won't. It can't be done. I don't have to be responsible. It's not my responsibility. Your fear, worry doubt, unbelief, anger, and rage. These and many more produce large emotions that put us into a tail spin to the grave. They are all self destructive. They all destroy your body and mind.

You must come to the knowledge that you possess a mind disease. You have a disease therefore you will have dis-ease. You must by pass your mind virus to get to the power of your god man. Tame your inner emotions so that your god power can work its magic. You see, your mind is a lamp stand. Your mind virus is in front of your eyes. The power to activate is hidden in your mind. You just can't see it. You can't see it because you are blinded. You have to light the lamp the right way or the god-man will not respond.

For the god power to activate there must be three conditions met:

    1. You must have an idea of what you want.
    2. You must believe you can get it.
    3. You must feel good about.

All three must be in alignment.

Then comes the hard work. Once you have set your mind on a chief aim your are to look for ways to make it to come to pass. If you cannot find a way, then pray. Pray about it till this thing comes into your experience. Or the ability of it comes into your experience. You are to look for it, sleep for it, live for it, and eat for it. You must get obsessed about it. You have to have energy for it. Lock your self into its frequency. Then vibrate to its energy.

Once you enter into the frequency the law of attraction will start to take hold. You will feel the feelings of your activities. If you don't feel good about it then get out of it. But if you stay the course on your ideal, then your god-man will not only activate but your desire will yield to you what you ask.

During your creating process you will go through a vicissitude of changes. You will have a world of distractions. You must ignore these distractions. They are there to lead you astray. All you see and want is your ideal. This is being in the zone. Stay in the zone till it comes to fruition.

Keep your secrets to your self. Do not give your power to anyone. They will thwart you at every chance. During the process you will get feelings of greatness. You will start getting feelings as though you already have it. You can feel the anticipation of already having it. This is the universe's clue to you that you are on the right tract. Now don't get me wrong you will have feelings of frustration along the way. But like I said these are just feelings.

When you feel these negative emotions it just means that you have gotten off track momentarily. Use the power of your mind to put yourself back on tract. Your mind virus will take over if you let it. You must retake possession of it on a moment by moment basis. This is where you must discipline yourself. Your feelings are your guiding system, use them. Cherish your ideals for they are your children. They want to be born. You need them and they need you. You were born to create. You are a mini-creator. You were born in the god class of beings. During the process you will get feelings that you already have it. This means it is in your sweet spot. This is nature's clue that it is not very far away. It is near to you. It is in inner space and on its way to you.

What you desire is already written in your DNA. What you want only you know. Only you can pursue it. But you will appear selfish in the eyes of others for pursuing it. So what everybody has an innate selfishness. This is so by design. The reason it is so is because you have to find your own path in this existence and the only way you can do it is by being selfish. So selfishness becomes necessary. So get focused, stay focused, Do not look left or right. Look only at what you want and that's it. This is the secret the ruling class do not want you to know about. They believe they have the divine right to rule. You have the unfortunate position of being their slave. So they train you to be their slave. We are all just slaves to the grind. Quit looking at what you don't want. If you stop and start looking at what you don't want then you are noticing it and the more you give it your attention the more you are activating it into your experience. The more you activate it into your experience the more momentum you are giving it. The more momentum it has the more power it has. The more power it has the more it has a hold on you. The more of a hold on you the more power it has over you. You see the vicious cycle.

Do away with the right and wrong theory. It's about energy. The blueblood ruling class rules from under ground. These are the secrets they believe in. This is the reason they are rich and you are poor. They keep this knowledge to them selves. This is the reason they marry among them selves. To keep the blood in the family is to keep the energetic frequency in the family.

They believe that wealth is for them and them only. I heard it said that power is not given, it is taken. This seems to be the case here although covertly. The rich marry only those with the genetic make up like themselves. This is where we get the blueblood theory.

The elite class is all inter connected and they don't want competition from the slaves. So they devised a plan in secret to keep this knowledge to them selves. They also devised a plan to structure society around lies to lead you away from it. They have thrown up all sorts of road blocks. Like rules and regulations, laws, and by laws, taxes, legislative rulings. Look around you and your world and what do you see. Road blocks and stops everywhere. Rules and regulations all over the place. This is purposely done to keep you in your lower place, so that you remain in line. It really is to keep you from reaching a higher frequency level because if you knew about who you really are then you will become trouble for them.

Truth is you are not born to be a slave. You were born to be a ruler. So start being a ruler over your self. Your mind is designed to govern. Govern: 1. To exercise authority over. 2. Direct, guide, control, or manage. You are designed to be the head and not the tail. To be in front and not behind. To be in charge, to be the queen and king. You were designed to govern. All the rich are inter connected by various secret societies. These societies are in control of everything today. They control the laws, the food, the government, all the financial institutions, the oil, the education systems. The whole world is their aim. They are doing a pretty thorough job at it I must say. All the while being done covertly. This is underground ruling.

If you are interested in knowing the final result of their plans then see the Book and read the back of the Book. a special chapter called Revelation. Read it carefully. These secret societies are controlled by what has become known as the reptilian hybrids. These reptilian hybrids are no less than the original true sons of God. The demons were made shortly before the Sabbath came in, and they are therefore incorporeal spirits- the lord had no time to create bodies for them. They dwell in the inner most earth subject to man. They hate man and want to destroy man because man is destined to be greater than the angels.

Man is destined to be more wise than the angels. So this brings in another question, who can you listen to? The answer is everybody, yet nobody. Hear everybody, and listen to nobody but your own guidance system. After all, who are they and what great thing have they achieved in their life? The reason is simple, they don't know how either. You can't depend on other humans because their path is not the same as yours. Most information that you run across any where is totally useless, bad information, and unusable. Again it's because this true knowledge is kept in the underground.

You as a slave are to be fed pro-feed. Which is slang for useless. To have any measure of success depends solely on you and your God. All the books I have read and all the dvd's I have listened to have not given the knowledge I need. They have proved worthless in comparison. All the people I have talked to in my life have never told me about my god power. Nobody ever explained to me how things were supposed to be. Truth be told they didn't know either. In fact, there is a lot they don't.

In retrospect, they were all ninety-five percent stupid. What is ironic about this is that they teach others how to without them selves knowing. Sounds like a scam to me. But like you I was too stupid to see it. Now I realize it was purposely put in place just so I would remain their slave. So again, who can you listen to?

The elite class has set up this society to keep you as a worker so that they may profit off of your labor, while they keep this secret knowledge to them selves. To manifest your dreams and desires from incorporeal to corporeal, this is a process. To make a long story short, copy cat. Find those who have what you want then copy cat. Don't reinvent the wheel.

The how to of the process. That is where your intellect comes in. The how to of the process is a not secret language. You have to understand the language. Your desires are written in your DNA. Use your decision making capabilities, Your belief system, and your feelings. This is your road map as you will. In fact it is all you have and all you need. It is the total package.

Your persistence beats education. This is why it's important to start with your own dreams and goals. Does follow your bliss sound familiar? How about chasing your dreams and goals? The desire of your heart? Or better yet what ever makes you happy. This is the point of entry. This is your starting point. What you truly want is written in your DNA. It is between you and your maker. It is between you and eternity.

Remember, what you do here on this earth echoes throughout eternity. The knowledge of the truly rich is not the knowledge of the universities. Although they do teach and prepare you for the world of illusion. They learn of the knowledge of ancients. It is knowledge passed down from ancient manuscripts which are written in Hebrew, Greek, Russian, French, German, Sumerian. In fact, I heard when the United States invaded Iraq, what happened while the bombs were falling was the museums were raided. No telling what they were after. What ever it was it had to contain knowledge of the ancient gods. It had to be secret knowledge, and it had to be important to the secret societies.

Through time these manuscripts have been codified and simplified to easier to understand formats. All things are through trial and error. This knowledge is only available to a small number people compared to the billions presently on earth today. The small number of people that have this information and use it live an amazing life.

The first secret to attaining what you want is not about having it. It first is about the feeling of having it. The feeling of the thing must proceed the having it. Also the feeling of it is what it is all about. You must feel the vibration of the thing before the thing can come into your experience. Once you have the thing it is the feeling of having it that feels good. But if you don't have it then you feel bad. There it is again, this feeling.

The universe does not respond to your words. The universe responds to your words backed by your emotion. Your emotion is the force that moves mountains if you believe deep enough.

Jesus said it best when he stated, if you had the faith as a mustard seed you can say to this mountain be cast into the sea and it will obey your command. This is a hint here. It is saying to me that all things are a vibration and if you tune into its frequency you can command it and cause it to respond and obey. Then he also makes another statement, oh-you-of-little-faith.

In other words you have to believe in your inborn God given abilities. In essence Jesus is referring to your god-man. He also told Peter when Peter found himself walking on water. Why do you doubt?

This is a story about Peter stepping out of the boat when he saw Jesus walking on the water. He completely for got who he was and jumped out of the boat after Jesus. He caught him self shortly after and started to sink. So the power of faith is evident.

But I truly believe Peter was feeling the highest of enthusiasm at the time. So here it is again this feeling must proceed any act through faith to the attainment of any goal or dream. That explains why it is said that enthusiasm is the key that opens any door.

But your words, your belief, and your emotions must be in alignment for it to work. Think about the front end of your car. If your front end is out of alignment you will experience rough vibrations. If it is in perfect alignment then you will experiences smooth sailing. Your life is exactly the same way. So how to get there from where you are at should not be the big mystery.

So, who is it that you can listen to? How about you narrow down your options to those who have what you want. This is a concept that has passed the test of time. It is proven. It works. It works better and faster than anything else you can think of. This is what I consider leverage.

These people have already used the power of their god-man to attain the thing. So it's easy for you to see that you can attain the same thing using your god power. Once you understand this, it is just a matter of duplication. Remember there is nothing new on earth. The biggest mystery of life is why is there so much misery? There is no such thing as mystery. It is all understandable. It is just a matter of taking the scales off of our eyes.

The people who control this inside knowledge control the planet. So is it noteworthy? I should say so. So the reason for me writing you this essay is because we all need to know this information. You have been kept in the dark and been fed B S all your life. The people who have this knowledge control the media, the education systems, the Government. They control all business. They control the food. This is why the financial sector is in turmoil. The food sector will come sometime later. They control the world because they control the knowledge.

Oh again, who is teaching you anything of value? You are being taught bunk in comparison. The answers are right in front of us and we don't even see them. It is stupidly simple. That's why we can't see them. The answer to life's mystery is right in front of our eyes. We cannot see them because we have been bombarded with all sorts of vibrations that don't amount to a hill of beans. It is all a diversionary tactic to keep our eyes off of what is real.

So in a way all of life is illusory. It is a mask that we all see. We see it instead of what is really there behind it. There is a reality behind this reality that we see. It too is right in front of us. It is called the system The dragon controls the system But he is not yet. He is to come. The system is set up for him to take control in due time. Right now he's not to far off. I can feel him. Can you? He has blinded our eyes until now.

A new vibration is spreading throughout the earth. This information is just the beginning. Our own mind virus we must over come. This is the devil's playground. It is what is causing the earths demise. Man's mind disease will be the reason the earth will be destroyed.

But for now, take control of your mind. Your mind has not been your own until now. The greatest thing to over come is yourself. Yourself meaning your mind disease. The war in your mind is over your belief system your emotions, and your ideals. Ultimately, your eternal destiny.

But for now, just look to your genie for help. The God who created eternity created this god power. You are his special creation. To start this process is to start reading. Leaders are readers. The ruling class doesn't want you to read because knowledge is power. Their goal is to keep the masses illiterate. There reasoning is simple. It they can keep the masses dumb down then that will keep them in their lower place as slaves. They there fore can keep rule.

Proverbs says My people parish for lack of knowledge. There goal is to keep you unable to achieve higher levels of attainment, higher levels of achievement. In this day and age you have to have specialized training. Just to be a maintenance man in an apartment complex you have to be proficient at plumbing, electrical, tile replacement, sheetrock, Air conditioning, heating, and Concrete. In addition you have to have no criminal history and a good credit rating, all for a low minimum wage. All the while being scrutinizes by everybody. Talk about humiliation and being used. Good God.

Schools any more have been dumbing down students. Many students cannot read very well upon graduation if graduating at all or even read period. Knowledge through reading is unique. Nothing can replace reading. Our book stores are full of books that are very good. I find lots of books of great interest and lots of books that are of no interest. But hey, that's what makes the world go around. I love book stores. But there is a plan in place in the future to do away with books. Thank the elite class for this.

But this information I am sending you did not come by all in one package. I had to piece it together bit, by bit, by bit. Along with a life time of struggle. Lots of pain and grief, sorrow, being deceived, lied to, jailed falsely, and yes even beat. Disowned, run off, let go, fired, divorced, diseased and least of all used. The list goes on and on. This is all I can think of real fast.

GOD-MAN

What angers me the most is being sent in the wrong direction and wasting my life on things that did not really matter. The obstacles I have had to overcome to be able to sit here and write these things to you today. As you read these words off of this page today, who ever you are I want you to know this. I have been through hell and back too many times to list. I have picked my self off of the dirt and had to pick my self up by my own boot straps and wipe the blood off, fix my self and then move on. Life has been one dirty affair after another.

The rich have one thing in common, they all read books. They read books that are of real people doing real things. So read, read, read, all the time Read while you have the ability to. Be a voracious reader. The rich will never share their knowledge. Have you ever had the opportunity to talk to a person of affluence. They just look at you and completely dismiss what you say. That's because they are not on the same wave length as you and I. They all vibrate at a higher frequency. They will never be and you cannot expect them to step down and dirty them selves to help you out. During judgment day the oil and the wine is not to be touched. This is meaning the rich.

Read books about real people and real events. Read books that will help direct you in the things that are of interest. Put your self around others that have what you want. Find others like your self that want what you want. Two minds are better than one. Two minds equal three minds. Three horses carry the speed of a cart of six.

Share what you want only with others that are wanting the same thing. Or you run the risk of having your dreams shot down mainly by some one close to you. Find your self a mentor.

A mentor of whoever don't matter all that much. As long as it is fruitful.

Always create win, win deals. No matter what you do in life or where you go you will always be involved with people so you have to be a people person. You cannot do it completely on your own.

Our society does very little to promote apprenticeships. But this is a concept that warrants a lot of focus and attention. Every body has got to go through one or two of them in their life time. They have largely been done away with because they work. They work well.

Healing herbs have been largely done away with as well for the same reason they work, and they work well. Excellent as a matter of fact. I speak from experience. Trust me when I say My god man and I had a dialog about this at one time. I discovered my god power during this time period. I was struck with a very, very painful condition. It was through my extreme pain that I discovered him.

Lastly, become your own master. To be your own master is to over come all obstacles that come into your path. This will make you a master over your environment. Fear not a thing. I heard it said long ago, it isn't nothing but a thing.

Today's work environment is fast becoming a cold blooded feel less heartless place to exist. I grew up in the trades and have never seen an apprenticeship program. It just does not exist. I have spent 33 years living behind a welding hood and my mentors have been hundreds of people. This is a far cry from just one mentor. So I took the long way around. This has paid off in the worst possible way. First of all I spent too long at it. Second of all it has kept my mouth shut all these years. Third of all it has paid lousy wages in comparison to what could have been made.

There has never been anybody there for me except my self. Today I look back on it and think what a ride that was. Oh, by the way, I finally graduated with three painful conditions as proof of my experience.

To last that long at anything you definitely have to be teachable. You have to have a high willingness to learn. Whether you like it or not you have to have a high willingness for change. These are all concepts you must have to be successful.

You have to except new challenges daily. You also have to have a can do attitude. Once you adopt a can't attitude you were considered unusable and eventually let go. This goes without saying. It is automatic. You disqualify yourself from the work environment. Once you come to a place where you recognize how smart you are, you were put in your place and reminded that you can be replaced. So you are vibrated into the lower level of remembering how dumb you are. This is the secret to survival in this particular work environment. You are never promoted. There is no promotion. It is virtually non existent. In essence I was a total slave.

It is said that humans use ten percent of their brains at best. This equates to ninety percent dumb. Thanks largely due to their mind virus. So the moral of the story is, are you aware you don't know what you don't know? This is a good place to land. It keeps you in your lower place. It stops you from being haughty and high minded. It keeps you teachable. I heard it said many years ago that having a willingness to learn is higher on the scale than skill. So skill is not everything. If you are not teachable you will not get very far. Once you come to a place where you think you know it all you quickly become arrogant. Arrogance is followed by negative emotion. It occupies your mind space to capacity. This leaves no room for any thing good. Understand that you are not just getting it. It's you are always getting it.

Sit down and think about where you want to go. Determine how far you want to go. Quit challenging everything, challenge your self instead. Challenging everybody is wasted energy. You are not meant to change the world. You were designed to change your personal world only. You are designed to create your personal world.

Quit blindly following. Find your own path. Look to the possibilities of all things. Quit looking at the things that you cannot change. Look at the things that you can change. Quit looking at the things you cannot do and start looking at the things that you can do. Quit looking at the place where you don't belong and start looking at the places where you do belong.

Quit saying I am different and don't belong. This is the illusion. Truth is you are included in the universe. You are not separate.

Stop saying I can't. This is weak. Start saying I can and I will. Stop saying I won't. This is resistance. Resistance is your mind virus. You won't because you are lazy. Stop saying I don't have to and I'm not responsible. This is you lying to your self. You cannot grow without doing. Your trials are your school. You have got to take responsibility. Truth is you are responsible for your environment. You are responsibly for all that you are all that you will ever have. You are responsible for your own mind and body. You are responsible for your own diet. You are where you're at through no fault of any body else but your own.

Being teachable determines destiny. Decisions determines destiny. So those around you who have no willingness to learn are a detriment. They will stop you from learning. Those around you who have no willingness to accept change is a detriment to you as well. They will stop you from being able to change.

Doing the same things over and over and excepting things to be different is the definition of insanity. If you want changes in your life then you have to change the things in your life. You have to do things off set from the norm. Nothing is what it seems. Don't do things like every body else. Set your own pace.

People are like crabs they will keep each other in the crab pot. What ever you decide to do go it alone, keep it secret. Let the doing of the thing settle deep within you before you go and publicize it. This strengthens your resolve. This is the emotion your universe feels. He feels your vibrations. So when you do open your mouth and speak your desire the power will be as iron. It will come from the deepest place possible. It will be determined with determination. It will have destiny. It will have power. The gods will yield to it. Why? Because you have spoken with the power of the gods. That is the power of god-man. So to get there from where your at you must take personal responsibility at every level. Either you do it or purposely make your self a victim. Our society has enough victims. You need to rise above the victim mode. Victims are losers. They have made them selves losers. They have chosen the victim mentality. We our selves are makers of our selves. How much time are you willing to spend, how much money are you willing to spend. How much pain are you willing to suffer, how much crap are you willing to eat, how many books are you willing to read. How far out on the limb are you willing to go.

Succeeding in life is associated with standing out not fitting in. How far are you willing to go? How many tears are you willing to cry? You must become transparent, bendable, teachable, changeable, vulnerable, weak sensitive. Combine the masculine and feminine. How much time are you willing to spend learning? What is your willingness to give up things?

Are you willing to break your body down?

What are you willing to give up? Are you willing to move away from all nay-sayers? Are you willing to let God break your heart? Find others who are like minded. What about all the negative shit that you feel is holding you back? What is your willingness to give up all your bad habits, are you willing to sweat? Are you willing to get your self dirty, are you willing to put your body to the test? Are you ready for your journey? If not then get your self ready. Step up to the plate and be prepared to be tested. Because there are people like me that will test you to the max.

Because I know that you don't know shit. Because I know that I didn't know. I also know that I have been tested and have been sent through the fire. I can also tell if you have so your self. A gun hand recognizes another gun hand.

I also know that there are sharks in the waters. And have had to swim with them a few times. I have been bitten lots of times. But then yet haven't we all. This is getting funny isn't it.

To be the master you have to accept all these concepts and more and accept change. So far in your life the way you have done things is going to have to change. Your thinking and old thought patterns have to change. The world is rapidly changing. Prepare your self for this. Your thought process that got you were your at won't get you where you want to go. You cannot get to where you want to go without radical change.

You cannot get to where you want unless you have an obsession. Obsession: preoccupy intensely or abnormally. If you want things to be different in your life then you have to change things in your life. You can't do the same things in life and expect better results. If you are unwilling to do all that is necessary then you will be considered a loser. And remain a loser.

If your not growing then your stagnate. You cannot stay in one place for very long. Are you going forward or are you going backward. You can only start where you are at and that's alright. Starting out toward your goal is the first thing in front of you. You can't jump from 0 to 10 automatically. You have to begin exactly where you are at.

You move and grow on a systematic basis. Success is not a theory. Success is over coming every obstacle that you encounter. Success is attained through stages and levels. This means a whole lot of hard work. But the hard work should become a labor of love. Which means it's not really work.

As an artist I have made hundreds of pieces and each one was a labor of love. Sometimes a piece may take me a week to create, but it was not an unhappy experience. I have spent lots of labor on my property doing hard physical labor. Never once was it burdensome. I go to my job just to rest. But my job is what is stressful.

If you are not teachable then you cannot get to a higher level of knowledge. Only you can choose how far you are willing to go. How far your willing to push your self. But when you start the path and you get a little taste of the fruits of your labor you will feel the excitement. This is natures clue your on the right path. Then your belief will go up. Once your belief goes up and you plateau for assimilation then you are ready to move up a little higher with renewed confidence. When your willingness to learn goes up then your willingness to change will go up as well.

One way to get and keep your desire is for you to find some one to be around that wants what you want. When you get what you want, your willingness to learn goes up. Buy your self some information that you can listen to over and over again. You have to read and listen to something more than once to get it into your head. You have to change your pre programmed mind. You have to get the useless weeds out of your mind and give it something else to grasp. Bad information produces bad fruit. Good information produces good fruit. When you read something a third or forth, or a fifth time you always get new information out of it. By doing this you are reprogramming your brain. The old programming is designed to fail.

So, by you having a high willingness to learn and a high willingness to change, and being teachable, and having a pulsating desire (vibrating), you elevate your self one stage at a time. You will recognize each level. You will feel where you are at. This is an on going process. The reason that you reread and listen over and over is because your mind will play nasty tricks on you. You will turn right around and forget what you heard immediately. You can look your self in the mirror and say to your self some thing, then turn around and forget it. So you must make it a habit to reread. Frequency is key here. Fear will creep in. Jesus said something similar. He said when sowing good seed the evil one comes in and steels it away immediately.

Fear worry and doubt are enemies of progress. You must combat them instantly. You have the power to out witting Mother Nature.

When you are born into this material plain, you were given a body and a mind. You are neither your body nor your mind.

Your body and your mind are yours. You are the watcher. You are the decision maker. You are the director. Your body is the hard where. Your mind is the software. Your software is faulty. It is lost, and separated. It will lie to you constantly. It will believe in things mystical. It will produce bad results. This is why your circumstances will buffet you. Reality always wins. You are the manager. You are the regulator. You are the governor of your being. Your mind is the command center. As human creatures we are lost because of our sinful nature. You cannot help it, it just is.

It is through your command center that decisions are made. But your god power is there. He is hidden from you in plain sight. Your pre-program mind is designed to keep hidden from you your true potential. Humans have a special destiny. Our whole society is structured to keep hidden this knowledge from you. Not even your boss wants you to get smart. He too is afraid for his own job. Our whole system is designed to burden. The more of a burden mind you have the more you have on your mind. The more you have on your mind the more burdened you are. The more burdened you are the more you are not aware or your true potential.

When God created man He brought the angels together to pay homage. Not all the angels agreed to this. The angel of truth did not agree and was cast down. Lucifer did not agree and was cast down. In fact one third of the angelic host did not agree with the creations of humans. Two hundred million are awaiting in the abyss for their time to come out and play. Revelation declares their arrival. They will be let loose and their mission will be to torture the ones who have the mark of the beast.

True power is only obtained through knowledge. Your brain is naturally not in the alpha state. To learn, your brain has to be in the alpha state. In the alpha state your brain is synchronized. This state combines both the hemispheres of the brain. This can only be achieved through a comfortable atmosphere.

Today's work environment is purposefully designed to be hostile. This fills our lives with negative feelings, negative images. It takes advantage of our negative programming and perverts it to its own benefit. These negative experiences produce ambiguous views. Opposing views as you will. This sends your vibrations into over time. Your energy level becomes hostile.

I became unfocused, confused, highly irritated, always pissed off. This is the natures signal that my energy was in reverse. I was stagnate. I came to a place where I had to shift my priorities. I had to make some new decisions. This means my beliefs had to change. But I procrastinated for a while. This decision did cost me my job. I see now that there were signals that I did not pay attention to here. My god man was talking to me and I was hearing but I did nothing. So it cost me anyway. My mind virus got in the way. My mind virus said that I need my job and I cannot let it go right now. So I hung in there and ended up losing it anyway.

So this is the reason that if you feel bad then it's time to move on. If you hate where you are at then where your at hates you. Quit listening to those who are constantly bringing you down. By disowning them is not a right or wrong issue. It is an energy issue. It's bad energy being passed around. Where is your energy going? Is it going to the fixing of others? Is it going to the fixing of your too many issues? I'll tell you where its going. It's going in too many directions. This is the problem with most people. This is why everybody is stressing. There is to much unfocused energy going around every where. I see it all the time.

Most people carry this frown around with them like its part of their attire. Most people walk around and I swear they act like they have shit in their pants. They don't leave home without it. Lets name this thing PMS of the mind. People are stagnating. People are sick. Your sick. Your momma and dad are sick. Your family is sick. The signs are clear as a bell.

Once you start feeling bad and even terrible it is because you are not moving forward, you are standing still or moving backwards. If you are not growing then you are dying. When your magic is in motion you will know it. There is forward magic then there is backward magic. The blessings and the curse. You will experience the energy around you moving. It is a stir in the air. It is not always a good feeling. Something is coming about. Something is about to happen. You will know what is about to happen by what you are feeling. Things will appear in your experience.

When you are smiling you will notice opportunity that you didn't see before. This is what the ruling class do not want you to know. They don't want you to see opportunity. The opportunity that is self evident is made harder to attain through rules and regulations. This is purposefully put into place to keep your mind occupied and weighed down with unnecessary bunk.

In addition to, that is the laws and by laws, Threats of force if you get out of line, along with fees and fines and even jail. It's all pitiful. The ruling class fears that if you ever found out about your true power then they will lose their hold over you. They will lose their power to control you. You will become a threat to them. This is a control mechanism.

Once you cross this line you will be marked for extermination. But your stupidity is already being used against you and you are being taken advantage of. So what is there to loose?

Success favors the bold. There is another concept called the training balance scale. Your training, your balance, and on what scale. You can only eat your meal one bite at a time. You have to learn the basics before you go any further. On one side of the training scale is the thing that deals with the thoughts, like dreams, desires, goals and objectives.

How you think.

Then there is energy, vibration, frequency, and intention. This also deals with thoughts. This also deals with how you feel.

Your emotions are the other side deals with action, physical movements. What you do, Techniques and strategies, action steps, plans activities. These are the physical actions that you do.

So you have the thinking, feeling, and action steps. The thought is the why; the action is the how. There should be a balance between these two. One is almost useless without the other.

The idea is to transform from the incorporeal to the corporeal. There are ideas whose time is come then there is ideas that is better left unseen.

So, you should always be working on your goals, dreams, and wants. Your thoughts, attitude, and your motivation, and you should be working on the how, skills, techniques, and the methods. Learn exactly how to execute your actions. You should learn equal amounts of both.

We live in a split society. One is the rich that lives off of your labor. The other is parasitical. The lower is the slaves that make everybody rich. The parasitical class wants you to believe you have opportunity. There are hardly any opportunities. They make it hard. Their goal is to keep you a slave. This rich class is the one that burdens you with taxes, laws, fines, and even jail. Anything and all things to keep you struggling. They have made things impossible. The myth is to allow you to believe your free. But in reality you're a slave.

This is what is said being a slave to the grind. Ninety seven percent of the worlds population are in the slave class. You are no better off than picking cotton. Ninety nine percent of the population die without ever having their dreams come to reality. This is very sad. Also ninety nine percent of success is credited to the thought process.

Thinking and the thoughts are ultimately more important then the how. It is said when your attitudes right the facts don't count. Because what you think are facts are not really facts. They are just peoples opinion.

The how is not as important as the thought process. You must discern fact from opinion. Work on the thought process. Do not worry about the how. Worry about that later. Most people fail because they worry about the how.

There is four basic steps your mind goes through while your learning. The first is "unconscious incompetence". This is when you don't know that you don't know. Second is called "conscious incompetence". This is when you know that you don't know. Third is called "conscious competence". This is when you know that you know. Forth is called "unconscious competence". This is when you know and it happens automatically. This is called auto pilot. You need to understand the four steps and how they work.

What your looking for is the auto pilot stage to where things happen automatically. This is the stage where you don't have to think about it. This is the stage where magic happens. Things come into your experience easily. To arrive at the point of unconscious competence is by doing it over and over again at the conscious competence level. By then it's completely internalized.

This creates neuro-pathways in the brain. When you have the opportunity to observe others you can also come to unconscious competence. Being around others like a mentor you see first hand how things are done. This is monkey see monkey do. Success does breed success. Success does rub off. There is such a thing as unconscious competence and doing it the wrong way. Most people don't have a mentor and therefore must improvise.

To be the best you must learn from the best. People fail because they have wrong information, or have a low teachable index. Sometimes they have the right knowledge just an unwillingness to accept change. Such people continue to keep doing the same things over and over again and refuse to change their pattern.

Those patterns are neuro-pathways in the brain. Neuro-pathways can be likened to a grove in a record. This is why they keep doing it the same way all the time. You have to be willing to get out of this grove. Unforeseen circumstances will sometimes force you out involuntarily. New neuro-pathways create new What ever you want to be, do, or have patterns.

Another reason people fail is because they waste mind energy on how am I going to do this. They spend too much time on the technique or the skill. Too many excuses like I don't know how to do this or that. I don't have the skill. I don't know how I'm going to get the money. If you're going to become great at something your going to have to give it lots of attention to be good at it. You can only build up as your foundation is deep.

You have to have a fertile environment for this kind of information to grasp, grow, and develop. Your soil must be prepared. It must be fertile. Without it nothing will grow.

What ever it is you desire what ever it is you want, you have to call it forward. But you must prepare your self first. Once you do you can give the command and your god man abilities will manifest it in your experience. It is said that your wish is your command. What ever it is you have to call it forward. What ever it is you desire you can give the command and manifest it in your experience. Whatever it is that you want to see in front of you, your god power will be your help mate. What ever you want to be, do, or have is to give the command. Align your self up with your desires and then give the command. Your imagination will bring it to you.

It is a well known fact that women are more in tune with their feelings. They are more intuitive creatures. They know how to use this power more than men. They are all the time putting their desires out there. Are they not? Sure they are and largely getting their desires fulfilled because of it. They are using the magic of their genie. Because of their gift of nature they are more in tune to this frequency that men.

That's why it is said that behind every successful man is a woman. Women have a gift to accomplish things with amazing speed.

To know and not do is to not know. Who are you modeling your self after? Think about this for a minute. Who is your mentor? Who are you following? If you are like me then the answer is nobody. This pays off in the worst possible way. Who is it that you want to be? You cannot continue to go it alone and get what you want in this life. You have to involve other people. Your creator works through other people. He uses the frequency of other people to communicate to you. Consider your self a life time student. Even when you become a master you are still a student. So be a student or apprentice all your life. Surround your self with real people and real successful situations. Get away from fictional.

Books are magical. Books are powerful. Read books of real people. If they are deceased, so what, you can still associate with them. Books allow our imagination, our brains to be utilized. Through books our brains create sights, sounds that create new neuro-pathways. The power with books is known by the ruling class. You should read books with emphasis on the four basics.

Which is:
1. Who can you listen to?
2. Teach ability index.
3. The training balance scale.
4. Master the basics. If you want to be a master you must master the basics. Mastering the basics is focusing on the fundamentals. There are a lot of fundamentals. The false belief is that there is all these concepts to know but that isn't true. This is another secret the ruling class do not want you to know. The true key to success is to master the basics.

Take one thing that you love then learn all you can about it and in short time you will have knowledge that no one has. There is no right or wrong about any of it, because in the end the only thing that matters is your own happiness and success.

How do you use the law of attraction? The law of attraction works whether you know it or not. Your brain transmits frequency twenty four hours a day any way and the law of attraction is always in motion. You cannot turn it off, So whether you know about the law of attraction of not doesn't matter. It is there and working already. You might as well come to the knowledge of it and put it to use with deliberate creation.

There is creation then there is creation in reverse.

Creation is bringing forth your desires. Creation in reverse is you take your creations creative ability and destroy people things. When you stop and see it right in front of you only then will you see it. This is why The scriptures say "stop and know that I am God."

The law of attraction has been working for you and against you depending. Only you know where. If things are going your way then it is working in your favor. If not then it isn't. Then again things may be developing.

Every thing in this universe vibrates. All things vibrate at different frequencies. To get what you desire you must tune into the frequency of the thing. Once your tune into the frequency you are able to not only see it in it's entirety. But you gain control of it. You cannot gain control of something you cannot see. So awareness is key here.

You as a human have the ability to choose into any frequency you wish. You also have the ability to focus with power and intensity for long duration any frequency of like kind. It is here at this point the magic starts to happen. The more you can focus on any one thing the more you see into this thing. The more you see into this one thing the more you see it deeply. There fore you begin to see all that it is. This means its weakness and strengths. The more clearly you are able to see it the more you can deliberately control. There fore deliberately create.

This means you can have, be, or do anything you desire. When you magnetize your self to the thing the thing magnetizes it self to you. The more you focus on this thing, the more this thing appears whether it's bad or good. The more you focus the more you see the more you see the more of it appears. The more of it appears the more you become aware of its existence in all its energy form. When you are able to see it in all its energy form then you are seeing as a creator. Now you have the power to deliberately create.

Now you have the ability to call forward and by the law of attraction it will come in its own time. This is the secret the ruling class does not want you to know about. When you have come to unconscious competence things will happen with record speed. You will be able to dial into the frequency you want until it activates. This is the very reason they say you need to keep your friends close and your enemy's closer. It is an energy thing.

You must become a student or an apprentice till the day you die. You have to have a willingness to learn. You have to be teachable. You have to always have a willingness to learn from somebody. Read a book over and over again. Each day you're a different person. You are not the same person as yesterday. So by re reading the same material you will get new information. So read books constantly. You also learn by doing. Learn then apply.

You actually learn more by doing than reading. For instance, you love food. You know what you like to eat. But when you get your self in the kitchen and cook your own food then you will really learn about food. One day cooking your own food you will learn far more about food than just by reading about it. Same principle applies to every thing else. By doing things this way your attention to detail will help you.

You are preparing the way for manifestation of your desire. There is real desires then there is the desire of the ego.

Your desire gets put on hold and you end up getting something else, something less desirable. Probably something you deserve. The reason is simple your ego is not the real you. It is the false you. So if you desire something from the false you then what you really want will be altered to compliment the false you. Your ego is the self elevated view of your self. It is also your false front.

To bring your true desires to manifestation you have to be your true self. You will get what you project. To get back from the false you, you must descend from your lofty stance.

In other words humble yourself. This requires self honesty. A more accurate analysis of your situation is this is the point you have to stop lying to your self. Stop making excuses for your screw ups and take responsibility. No matter what your creative power will work for you. But the quality of your life is in accordance with your quality of thoughts. The universe's job is to always respond to your command and that's exactly what is happening in your life. Good and evil is the play ground in this existence. So it is justly ordered that honesty to what is be paid attention to.

The rewards and the penalties are there and are self evident for those who understand what is going on. So if you are not getting what you truly want you only have to look to your own thinking to find the answer. This is a sticky point for most people. Their mind virus gets in the way. This is where they lie to them selves. And believe false tenants. So what you want must truly come from the heart backed by strong reason.

Earths vibrations are very slow so a buffer of time is always required. Your angels is so ordered by its creator to obey the laws of attraction and all of the other laws of the universe. It is the same laws the gods are ordered to obey.

When you set your sights on something it is said you must work for it, sleep for it, pray for it, eat for it, study for it, look for it continually till it comes to pass. What this is saying is that when you align yourself with its frequency then your god man can bring it to you. But you are required to do your part. If things look impossible then just remember that all things are possible. It's just figuring how to get the job done.

Your god man operates in the eternal realm. He represents you in eternity. His mission is to assist you in your life. But the door that is there between the two worlds is open. This door is in the form of energy. Your energy is directly linked to it. This is the reason why when you ask it is already given. This is also why when you pray it is heard and whatever you pray is answered. The problem is if you deserve the thing or not.

So your every desire is waiting for you in vibrational escrow. Your job is to get it out of escrow. So the door is always open. Your wants are always there. So it just stands to reason that what you want is only hidden temporarily. This is because it's in escrow waiting. So a deeper truth is that it really is not very far from you. In fact it is just barely out of sight.

In light of this fact all things that you want and the way to get them is right in front of you. You just have to wake up to this fact and realize that you are the problem. Your stupidity is your problem. You will truly parish because of your lack of understanding.

There is your egos' wants then there is your true self's wants. Your deepest desires are written in you heart. This means they are deep with in you.

Life is like a game. It's all serious but do not take nothing personal. It is said we gravitate towards the things that we secretly harbor in our hearts. So place your self there always. You were meant to live in this special place. Eternal love is the only thing that's real all else is illusion. So it is this place that you feel love. Where there is love there is good vibrations. So when you have dreams and wants keep them to your self and cherish them. Cherish your ideals. Don't let anybody steal them away. If this happens then you will have to live someone else's dreams. This is suicide. If you cherish your ideals then you are less susceptible to losing them. Always operate in secret and tell only when you feel good about it.

If it is like a magnet pulling you then gravitate to it. This is you moving and shifting. This is the universal language. All things are in motion. You can make your thoughts and dreams your own or others will make you a slave. They will use you to make their desires come to pass.

People are experts of heaping upon you guilt, fear, humiliation, causing you to feel rage, and anger. They have a screwed knack of killing your dreams. Once you are off of your true path then the frustration of life kicks in. You feel it. This is your clue to get back on track.

Unbelief is the worst enemy of human kind. It limits severely. The greater truth is that you are limitless. The spirit of unbelief comes in many forms. It always comes in the form of well wishing. To counter balance unbelief is done with hard work, and determination. Unbelief is a blockage. It is a stop sign. It comes in the form of excuses. There is a whole array of stop signs. There is a world of excuses that comes your way.

You have to just say no to them. This becomes the battle ground. The battle ground of the mind. These negative vibrations are all designed to keep you and your god man out of the lime light. It is designed to keep you from your creative ability. It is there to keep you in your lower place so that you don't rise to the knowledge of who you really are and the capabilities that you truly have.

MAN-CREATOR

There are walls made of word bricks and they are strategically placed between you and your desire. The ruling class know this. The societies know this as well. What do you think they are keeping secret?

So we come back to who are you going to listen to? Those voices that are your excuses are not the real you. The ones that vibrates deeper within your being that make you feel good are the real you.

Are you teachable? What kind of training are you going to put your self through? There is a saying when the student is ready the teacher will appear. What this means is that only when you become teachable will you be ready to learn. Always have a high willingness to learn and change.

Understand the four stages of learning. The fourth stage is unconscious competence.

All around you is a psychological battle going on. All hell is alive in your mind and available to you and to everyone else. I heard it said that even love is war. Every kind of crap is available and in abundant supply. It is there purposefully put in place either by the gods, the system, or the punishment of the creator. So there is a multi dimensional cause.

We have become creatures of habit, we must become creatures of change. We are creatures of the clock. We have got to stop looking at the clock. The clock is an illusional device anyway. Start looking at the great clock of time. We are creatures of ego. We have to learn to put our ego aside.

We are creatures of excessive pride. We must put our pride away that is destructive away. The pride that divides. We are creatures that pollute. We pollute our bodies. Our minds and our environment. We pollute each other purposefully with all vile thinking. We have to start cleaning things up. It is not the majority that won't. It is the minority that won't. They are the ones that are destroying all the earth. In the end they will be brought to their knees.

We are creatures that love the lie more than the truth. This is why you are feeling destroyed. The curse of the earth must pass through the humans to the material plain. We must choose honesty. I didn't say truth. I said honesty. Being honest to what already is. The things that are present and self evident. This burns out religion and leaves open the energy channels to you and your creator. We are creatures that want all things that are no good for us. We must learn to be satisfied with what we have. We are creatures that hate what is good and love what is bad. This is a perversion of nature.

Because of this you reserve special judgment. The creator of your god man will not be mocked. We are creatures that destroy nature. We have to stop this. But in reality this is not possible. We have gone down to the point of no return already. But from here forward just take care of your own ass. We are creatures that love our manufactured pills. We need to find alternatives to these toxic substances. We are creatures that fight and kill each other for no apparent reason. We need to stop this madness. Woe to the generation that calls good bad and calls bad good. We are creatures of resistance. We must stop resistance. Stop going up stream. Nothing you want is up stream.

We are creatures that practice the wrong way over and over again. This is why many people are losers. Practice doesn't always make perfect. Perfect practice makes perfect. You have to practice the right way. By practicing the right way you make the right groves in the record; the record of your mind. This means your ways of doing things.

Some of us are creatures that think that we know it all. But the truth is that we don't know shit. We can't see what is off the radar screen. We know in part and can only see in part. Think wide scope. Be of the mind set that this universe is full of possibilities. . Unforeseen happenings are always on the horizon. Think about this for a minute. Un-foreseen happenings? Have they found you yet? Why yes they have. How about those negative unforeseen happenings. How do you think they found you. They found you because you were not paying attention that's how. So how to avoid is the question.

Ninety nine percent of things not seen is off the radar screen. My point being is this, you have to watch your ass in everything you do. You can't just go blab your mouth about shit you don't understand. What you sow, you will reap. If you're not growing and learning then you're going backward. Water doesn't have to sit long before it becomes stagnate. Stagnate water is rotting water.

You become what ever you think about most of the time; or you become what you think about most of the time. What ever the mind can conceive, and brings itself to believe it can achieve.

This is because you as a human being are a mini creator. This also holds true because you as a created being in the god class are limitless in your abilities. This is possible do to your god power.

You have been designed to create. Look around your world and what do you see. There are all sorts of things made with the hands of man. Man and their machines.

We as humans have shaped this world to where it is today. Anything and everything is possible. Is there something you don't see in your experience. If not, then it's up to you to create it. Only you can see this special thing in your mind. This is unique. The universe gave that to you. But also on the other end of the scales is this. Someone else is thinking about the same thing somewhere. It is the one that takes this idea and cherishes it. It is the one who makes this idea their own. The thoughts that you think are not your own. They came from some where else. You just picked them up on your radar screen.

All things are energy. This energy field is every where. You are energy. The thoughts you think and speak float around into the ether and get picked up by others. Your words and the feelings you express activates this energy field. Everything is affected by your very presence alone. If you continue to think the same thoughts you always have then you will continue to get the same results. You will continue to get what you have always got. The same shit different day. The brain is both a receiver and a transmitter of vibrational frequency. Your words and feelings activate earth's energy field.

Your destiny is determined by your words and deeds. This is why what you do here on earth follows you into eternity. This same energy field is a model after the one in eternity.

Every cell in the body emits a different frequency.

Everything on earth emits a different frequency. Everything on planet earth is made up of energy. You as a mini creator is made up of the same energy. What you think and feel affects all things in your environment. Why do you think music is good for your plants. Because it makes them feel better. Frequency is called a vibration. It is quantifiable and measurable. Your DNA at the lowest level emits a unique frequency. Every atom emits a frequency. Frequency passes through all known matter. Capture this energy capture the matter. This means to capture the energy surrounding your desire, and you will capture the desire. Your frequency pierces the ether and zeros in on the frequency of the matter thereby capturing the matter. This is called mind over matter. Your frequency cuts right through matter even though they are walls of stone, brick, or steel. It passes right through it. It is such an incredible thing that today's scientist cannot explain this.

These frequencies are smaller than atoms, smaller than electrons. It's smaller than the smallest known particle on earth.

So when you emit frequency they are picked up by other human's brains. They also pass through the ether and affect other physical matter. So the moment you think of something your thoughts go into the universe and float around into the ether only to go around and be picked up by somebody somewhere. Your personal frequency has the unique ability to by pass space and time. It does not necessarily go in a straight line. It goes anywhere and everywhere at the same time. Your brain is the most powerful transmitter and receiver on the planet, and it's the fastest known.

The law of attraction says that what ever frequency you emit that exact same frequency is attracted to you. There is a magnetic attraction. There is a magnetic pull. This is what the ruling class don't want you to know. They purposefully send out screwed up vibrations to send you in the wrong direction. This is why some say the system is fixed. There is also a scriptural bases for this.

What you sow is what you reap. What you put out you get back. Some call it karma. Some call it your karmic dues. So your real magic happens through your own brain, the magical command center. Think of it this way. Imagine inside your brain as a sparkler. The genie him self is the magical universe. Your angel is both male and female. Your energy is the sparkles, Is it sparkling black or is it colorful?

There is a law of gravity. This law is definitely not one to defy. But there is another one called the law of lift. This is the law that aids birds, definitely senior to the law of gravity. But the law of attraction is senior to both of these laws. It will defy any physical law. This is why it looks like magic or luck. The reason why we don't hear about the brain emitting energy is because the ruling class simply doesn't want you to know about it. Think about it. If you wanted to keep someone a slave would you want to empower them? Of course not. So you having your own magical creating ability is the worlds biggest secret. Now if this secret got out then it wouldn't be a secret anymore.

The controllers of monopolies are the ruling class. They are nick named the manipulators. The manipulators have kept this secret with in their own elite class for thousands of years. This is their biggest secret. This is what is being kept secret through the secret societies. They have done a fabulous job at it I must say. The world has been enslaved. They are rich and ruling and we are slaves, miserable and poor. The manipulators are the magic controllers of necessities. This includes the divine right to rule. This includes you are suppose to be their slave. This explains why we all feel like we are a slave to the grind, because we are. These manipulators are rulers of countries, rulers of people. All the royal families of the world, the elite world class. The controllers of monopolies which is the ruling class of necessities. Which include but not limited to oil and food. If earth was a star ship we should be set for a course for maximum destruction. This is earth's final destiny. They also believe they are genetically superior. They also believe they are smarter thinking and are genetically programmed to rule over the vast majority of the earths population. The genetics they are referring to is vibrational. The DNA of the ruling class remain with the ruling class. This is why they inter marry. They want To keep their blood as pure as possible. That way their frequency remains in the family.

The DNA, I refer to here is called the blue bloods. The blue blood comes not from human origin. It is reptilian. Origin.

The reason why the royal families and aristocratic families have been referred as blue bloods is because of the increase of copper in their blood. The copper based blood turns blue green when oxidizing. This is not human origin blood. It goes way back to the nefilim. The nefilim are the fallen angels that bred with humans. They planted their DNA with human daughters. "They took the daughters of men as wives and befouled the earth with their deeds. And in all times of their age were lawless and promiscuous. Giants were born and marvelous big men and great enmity. And there fore God punished them with great judgment. They are now located in the fifth heaven where they await judgment. There are called the Grigori. Their appearance is human and their size greater than that of great giants and their faces are now withered, and the silence on their mouths perpetual, their faces withered and melancholy. They are bound in the fifth heaven, sometimes with one great voice breaking out with song. As one voice their praises go up to the Lord of light pitifully and affectingly." Affectingly: arousing pity and sorrow. This is the destiny of those that disobeyed the lord of light. Their DNA now rules the earth through the ruling class. The ruling class has the same judgment awaiting them as well. But for now the blue bloods vibrate at a higher frequency than the lower class. There fore throughout history the ruling class has made sure the lower class vibrates at a much lower frequency.

That way we are kept as slaves. This is the very reason why we have drugs. Drugs are the number one toxic substance that keeps you at your lower frequency. We are a pill popping society. We have all the drugs we can stand. Drugs keep your frequency very, very low. They put you in the class of stupid, dumb, and unfeeling. They are the number one cause of your lack of self awareness. Simply put, they keep you from your god power. Now who do you suppose is the supplier of pills?

Big brother pharmaceutical. Who also is the biggest supplier of street drugs? Big brother that's who. Except they have to keep that a secret. They play both sides of the war on drugs. That way they totally control every thing.

By you being drugged up makes you more docile. You are never having a want to achieve anything great in your life. It also stops you from rising up and becoming a challenge to them. There fore the rulers remain the rulers. The slaves remain the slaves. Perfect, every body in their place.

So through history, what the ruling class have desperately kept secret is the fact that your brain is a transmitter and receiver of vibration and energy. Through this knowledge comes the understanding of you and your god man. This is the biggest secret in secret societies. As simple as it sounds it's true. They desperately don't want you to know about this that's why it must be kept a secret. If you knew about who you are and your superior ability then you could activate your very own magic.

Now think about this for a second. Imagine a world where every one knew about their own superior abilities. This would not be the same planet today that's a fact. Since they have had this knowledge for ages, they have had time to structure our world to the point where they have done every thing humanly possible to cut you off from you magical god.

All damage has already been done. They have had their day on earth. Their time is up. It is the dawn of a new beginning. There is a change in the wind. The time of the end is at hand and the promise of the bright eternal future is active in the heavens. The Heavens and all that is therein are a million times larger than this earthly experience. Eternity has things under control.

Here on earth things need to be played out to the end. The ruling class is to remain the ruling class while you and I remain their slaves. You must not always remain in your lower state.

You are considered a poor pitiful human. Not only just pitiful, but worthless. Their reptilian blood allows these rulers to be heartless, and cold, uncaring and unfeeling. They are also the ones destroying the earth. Their judgment awaits them up the north side of the third heaven. "It is a terrible place. It has all manner of tortures: cruel darkness and un-illumined gloom. There is no light there, but murky fire constantly flaming up. It has a fiery river and every where is fire. Everywhere frost and ice, thirst and shivering. The bonds are very cruel and the angels are fearful and merciless, bearing angry weapons and merciless torture. This place is for those who dishonor God and practice sin against nature. Which is enchantments and devilish witch craft. It is for those who boast of their wicked deeds. Those who steal, lie, and slander. The envy, the rancor, fornication, and murder. Those accursed ones who steal men's souls, who take away goods from the poor, and make them selves rich, injuring them for their own good. It is for those who corrupt children through sodomy, who perform magic. For those who, are able to satisfy the needy, made the hungering die. For those who could cloth but stripped the naked; and those who knew not their creator, and bowed down to soulless gods. Who are deceived by vain gods. For all these is prepared this place for eternal inheritance.

Does this sound pretty inviting. I should say not. Their time on earth is just for a little while longer. Your brain is like a radio transmitter of frequency vibration, or energy which are all interchangeable.

Every thing on earth is made of atoms. Atoms used to be the smallest particle on earth. But later they found out that the electron was even smaller. An atom consist of an electron circulating around a nucleus called a protonelectron. Which is smaller than an atom. The thing that holds the electron around the nucleus is a thing called energy, vibration, or frequency. So, the electron is made up of vibration. The electron is full of holes. It is not solid. It is vibration. This is a proven scientific fact. Your cell phone is a frequency. The cell phone frequency passes through known matter. It is energy, it is vibration.

This means that this frequency permeates all space. This signal is not in a straight line. It is gasses that permeate the whole ether with a vibration. This signal virtually permeates every space. It's like this gas and fills up every space. It goes and passes through trees, buildings, walls, elevators, brick and steel. It's every where. This is called quantum physics. We can't see it but it's there. Every thing on this planet is made up of these same atoms and electrons, which is made up of nothing but energy, frequency, or vibration.

There fore everything on the planet is the same. It is only the combinations of atoms that's different. So the number of frequency combinations is virtually endless. It's infinite. So, every thing you see, taste, touch, smell and feel is a combination of different frequencies. Every thing you see is nothing but energy. Every thing is vibrating. Your brain is a transmitter and receiver of frequency.

You have the power to create any frequency you want with your brain and transmit it. You can either put out a low frequency or virtually blast it out with huge amounts of power. Since your brain is a transmitter, you have a volume control. Your brain transmits frequencies similar to a satellite frequency, a cell tower, or a radio tower. The only difference being your brain is much more powerful. Any frequency that you transmit is picked up by other brains and affects physical matter. Not maybe but does.

There is massive scientific proof that what the brain transmits affects all physical matter. We have the ability to transmit any frequency we want with little or high intensity.

This is the reason the rich is the rich. They understand this perfectly. They desperately don't want you to know this. So they have kept it secret for thousands of years. Generous of them isn't it.

The ruling class kept this secret to them selves only.

Another secret is the law of attraction which is senior to all other laws. It supersedes all other laws. It has the most power of all laws. The law of attraction says that vibrations that are the same attract.

Homeopathic remedies' is based on this theory. Their theory is like cures like. This is like the law of attraction. Like attracts like, it neutralizes and cures it. The rich under stand this and are the major users of homeopathic remedies. This is called energy healing.

The law of attraction says that like will attract like or that which is similar. So vibrations that are similar attract. This is where the magnetic pull comes into play. When you transmit a frequency this is your command. When you want something turn to the frequency and give the command and it will come.

You will become what you think about most of the time. You get what you think about most of the time. How do you use the law of attraction. The law of attraction works whether you know it of not. Your brain transmits frequencies 24 hours a day. It receives frequencies whether you are consciously aware of if or not. Everything on earth vibrates whether you know about it or not. So whether or not you know about the law of attraction it is there and working any way. The fact is the law of attraction is working in the life of every one 24 hours a day seven day a week. It is right in front of you. All you have to do is take notice of it.

Once you tune in to it and see it you will instantly know how it works. You will understand how you have gotten the things you have in your life. It's just co creating from there. You can also see where you have failed and, What you have to improve upon. The more you tune into the frequency of the law of attraction. The easier things become. This law has been there all along working on your behalf all your life. It doesn't matter whether or not you agree with this or not it is a biological fact. It happens.

But those who have figured it out are doing great. If you purposefully do it successfully then you will do fantastic. Everything is energy that vibrates at it's own frequency.

Humans have the unique ability to tune into any frequency. Humans also have the ability to determine the power and intensity and the duration of that frequency being broadcast. So by putting out a frequency with power and intensity, for long durations, a matching frequency will come to us. It will be like a magnet as fast as you can imagine.

When you have come to unconscious competence it will happen faster and faster. You will be able to dial into the frequency until it activates. Once you hit the frequency it comes rushing towards you. What you want wants you. All you have to do is activate it. It will come rushing towards you with magnetic pull. This is the secret of attracting your true love.

You can attract things, people, places. You can also attract bliss, happiness, success and, friends. You can have, be, or do any thing you desire. Any thing the mind can conceive and come to believe you can achieve. This is the way you can have any thing you can dream of anything you desire. If you believe you can get it you can have it. If you dial into the frequency and send out thoughts with power and intensity and believe you can have it then by the law of attraction your magic will bring it to you. It has to it is a law. Your genie has to obey the law of attraction.

The law of attraction is senior to all other laws. It is how everything works. You can't deny it and. you can't explain it away. It is scientifically proven. The most famous people in the world use this technique.

The ruling class know this to well and that's why they send frequencies to the slave level of intimidation, fear, along with fines and fees to and threats of force to punish in any way possible. It is put there purposefully to send a frequency of frustration, discontentment, and anger. There is a whole host of other feelings that is there as well. It is designed purposefully to mislead and divert your attention from your true self. It is not a right and wrong issue, it's an energy issue. The ruling class has structured this system to keep your nose to the grind stone, quite literally. They need to keep 95 percent of the population slaves. To fill positions of corporate need.

I heard it said this is the United States of Corporation. Better yet The Jewnited States. Nothing against Jews here. So define your dream with specificity. What this means is you must clarify, define, or know what it is that you really want. Doubt kills it. Doubt delays it.

Praying is vibrating. Praying is calling from you. Prayer is like the telephone line. You putting your order in.

Life is like a restaurant, you have to order what you want. Success is said to come to one thing and that is to define your dream. In other words you have to order it from the menu of life. Determine and define exactly what you want. Get a burning desire, which is a pulsating desire which is a strong emotion. Pulsating: Expand and retract rhythmically.

I have to say there is not much reading material that I have found that covers this principle. It is out there though. This was never mentioned in school. I wonder why.

Your number one goal and should always be is to feel good right now. Each and every moment of your life is to feel good and feel better. Don't wait for tomorrow. Don't say I will when this or that happens. Bring your self in the moment, and stop putting off. Do it now. Make your self feel outrageously good. Being happy, being content, being secure, being grateful, feeling blessed, feeling bliss and joy.

They all describe different emotions but they are all good emotions. When you put your self in this state you are in your natural state. You are in the state that you were designed to be in. It is out of this state that you are square with the universe. While your in this state you are more able to see things more for what they really are. You are better able to determine real from fiction. See reality with greater clarity, and not for what your preprogrammed mind thinks it's supposed to be.

Feel good and look good. Once you decide what it is you want, make it a single, solitary chief aim. You start moving in its direction. Ask your self what are you craving. Full fill your craving. The major indicator that you're on track is that you get what your craving for, the healthy kind that is. Break your day down moment by moment; hour by hour if needed to feel good now, and then to feel better.

When you define your dream, you can either be specific or general, of not define anything, this all depends how you feel. But just concentrate on better feeling thoughts as this is the process. You might be a bum wanting to be a CEO. Well you are going to have to go through a lot of changes to become a CEO.

So it's taking mini steps toward your goal. So every decision you make you have to feel good about it.

You can't get what you want in this life feeling angry. Anger repels. Most people Know how to lose friends and make enemies naturally. But the more specific you are the better you can define it the better you are. To be able to see it clearly becomes a prerequisite. If you can see it clearly, If you can feel it clearly, If you believe it is within your ability to get it which means you must me lined up with it. Then you are in the perfect position for it to be attracted to you. The powers that be are put in place by the laws of attraction. You must pass through a vicissitude of changes.

This is why you must have a high willingness to learn and to change. Because your going to have to start shifting your energies constantly. As your shifting you are moving towards your desires. So everything around you is to be used. You use your house, your car, your loved ones. When I say used I don't mean abused. I am referring to allowing all things to remain in tack.

To be used means to use all things as a tool. The word conjure comes to mind here. If thoughts are things then to create out of the mind the thing hoped for is kind of like conjuring. But to entreat is the clean definition. You must create magnetic pull by any means necessary. Put all options on the table. Leave nothing unturned. Don't limit your self not one little ounce. Remember, love is war.

Your thoughts send out particles into the universe known as frequencies that are picked up by all things. All things I said. This explains why when you walk into a room other people get a feel for what you are about. They get strong feelings about your presence. Those who get good feelings about you will be drawn to you first.

So to develop magnet pull is through personality only. So your personality is where you should put your focus. This means thinking the right thoughts, feeling the right feelings and also having accomplishment under your belt. This creates presence, also known as success. This is why you build on your strengths. But to strengthen your weakness gives you wider latitude. That's why great trials are healthy. To think about something great you want and you know its not going to be easy. Then for it to come to pass you are going to have to think about it all the time.

Remember this earth is dense. So you have to give it all your thoughts all the time. You will see all the obstacles that are in your way. Start to remove these obstacles one by one. This takes time and patience, continual focus and determination.

Now your god man sees you doing this and you are working together. What you want wants you but not right yet as you are, it is repelled from you. Your job is to remove the repellant. Your stink as you will.

I know a lovely little butterfly that I can see her in public She is my dream girl. I can smell her. I can taste her, I can see us together every where. When I'm alone I talk to her. But in reality I never see her. Truth is she has a repellant around her. She has an unwillingness about her. She is not open to anything. But also a greater truth is that I must have one too.

So there is work to be done. And along with that time is to be used. Allow the stars to line up. In time all good things come to pass. When my desire goes from I want to I want because, then I will have a greater purpose. I will have further defined, there by drawing just a little bit. Then What I want comes from a deeper inner level. It is from this place that events and circumstances are created.

Your outer circumstances are first created in the mind through thought. It is from this deeper level that you conjure your abilities to move mountains. Jesus said if you have just the faith as a mustard seed you can move mountains. Now, a mustard seed is pretty small.

The law of attraction has to work. So, guess who brought you all the things you currently have. That's right your god power did. It is your relationship with Him. It is the two of you working together. Through the law of attraction your god man will start shifting things around for you in the incorporeal realm and time your desire to meet up with you at some point and time.

When you ask for something there are complications that do arise. There are variables that have to take place. There fore your angel cannot get it to you right away. When you ask for some thing your angel goes to work on it. While your angel works on it you have to work your end as well. You have to move toward it. You have to magnetize your self to your desire. You have to keep looking at it. You have to keep reminding yourself of it by continuing to want it because. You really don't know how your angel will bring it to you or when. Just know it will happen. You know it will come because you feel it.

Your radar screen can only see a little bit at a time. So most of the time the things you want are off of your radar screen. So the trick is to call them into your radar screen.

99% of the things you can't see are off the radar screen. It doesn't mean it isn't there. It just means that you can't see it.

So, you first start out by wondering and thinking. Most people look at their radar screen and don't see it and become frustrated. Well what you want is not on your radar screen. This is the big reason people fail. They put all their hope on what they see. This is where you turn to your angel and ask him. Your angel sees everything not on your radar screen. The vast majority of every thing is happening off the radar screen.

You can't see it. You can't even imagine it. You first start by calling if forth. Then wait for it. There are millions of variables, lots of twist and turns. Different road ways and highways before it comes into your experience.

But how far away is it? Only you can tell. You know by how you feel. Does it feel close or does it feel far away? When will it come in? If you believe it will then start looking for it.

The universe will start the process of bringing it to you. Things will start to shift. You will start to experience people, and circumstances and events that will come into your life and out of these events you will see new direction. Every thing will point you in the right direction. You will know how to get there by how you feel.

Each situation you find your self in, ask yourself, is this where I want to be? Your answer is self evident; if this place isn't then move out of this place onward. If you remain in your place that causes unbelief then what you desire cannot come to you. What you want wants you. But it cannot come to you until you put out expectation for it. Because opportunity does come knocking sometimes. When it does will you be ready. You will not be ready without your expectation. So, deep down do you really believe you deserve what you want? The level of expectation will depend on your answer.

This means what is your value. How high of a value do you place on your self. If you have a high value on your self then your belief goes up. But believing in something and not believing you can get it sends out counter vibrations that cancel each other out. If you have a low value on your self then your unbelief goes up. So, what you have now is intention and counter intention being broadcast simultaneously that cancel each other out.

On an energy level you have a want that is like a magnet. Then at the same time an unbelief which is like a repellant. This is a major reason people fail. So you start in the place you know you can believe in. Your feelings are your guide, your gauge. Your feelings are your telescope. Feelings tell you if your lined up with it. Your feelings will tell you if it is in your sweet spot.

When you define what you want it has to be some thing you can believe in. Believe in something you know you can easily get. Start out on things that you feel good about. Then move toward them. The sweet spot is defined as the goal, the desire. The want that you feel good about makes you smile, get your juices going. The sweet spot is something that you really, really want. It produces high, high excitement. When you think about it, it lights your fire and at the same time you absolutely believe you can get it. The sweet spot has to include both.

Success builds confidence. So, in the beginning you have to get some success. The sweet spot has to be a goal you can get. It gets you all fired up and gets your juices flowing and makes you feel good just thinking about it. So, which one of your dreams do you have a burning desire for and a high level of belief? There is what is called a success cycle, and a motivation cycle. When you do some thing for the first time and you see it work, your belief goes up.

Even the scriptures state. Ask and it is given. Knock and the door will be open. You have not because you ask not. Ask and believe and you shall have what so ever you ask.

Continually pray and make you supplications known. So, what is your belief level? If it is low then don't think about it. You will only get frustrated. Set it aside for now and focus your attention of what you can get. Picture your self in it.

Imagine yourself already having it. Feel the emotions of how good you will feel having it. If you feel annoyed, or irritated, that means it is not in your sweet spot. It means your level of belief is low. Put it aside for now, it will come later. How do you get your level of belief up? Remove all doubt.

The rules of attainment are simple. If you want money, then you first must desire money. If you want love then you must desire love. If you want a great job then you must desire a great job. Your want is your wish. For your wish to be your command then you have to understand desire. Desire is the chariot you ride on to your goal. It is the emotional energy to carry you to your goal. Your angel sees you putting all this energy behind your goal with desire. He will start his process and work just as hard as you. Together you two can bring in to pass with record speed.

The universe is alive. You are alive. Your wish is just that, a wish. Want is stronger. Want leads to desire. All three must be lined up. What you want is alive. The more you think about it the more you activate it. The more you activate it the stronger it gets. The stronger it gets the more you feel it. The more you feel it the more real it becomes. The more real it becomes the chances of it coming in happens much faster.

Desire activates the energy of it. You as the creator call it out. You then line your energy up to the energy of your want then the magic happens. So when you vibrate at a high rate at a high level of intention with long duration; your angel sees you, he hears you, and he feels you. So make your self available. Your maker did not leave you stranded.

How you feel is an indication of where you are at. If you place a command about something and don't feel good about it then guess what, it won't come to pass. If you want some one to fall in love with you and they just won't have it then guess what.

Things aren't lined up. You and their vibrations are not lined up.

Your feelings are a gauge of your thinking. Thinking activates feelings. Belief determines what thoughts. Feelings determine actions which mean outcome. Out come is manifestation of thought. When things are lined up then at the right place at the right time the universe will deliver something. It may not be what you totally wanted but it is a step in the right direction. It all has to happen naturally. So, naturally you must be lined up. If you want something desperately and believe you won't get it the chances are you won't get it. This is because your feelings are disallowing it. It is called intention, counter intention.

Listen to your gut feeling. Your gut has cells in them that communicate with the cells in your brain. They are in constant communication. This is where you get intuition, which leads to decisions. You can choose to ignore it or pay attention to it.

Out of this choice you will activate a result. Be it good or bad, want or un-want. You angel are always there waiting, and watching. They always have eyes on you whether you are aware of it or not. His job is to bring to you that which you command. If you don't know what it is you want he will do his best to accommodate you. He brings you both good and bad. But he is always bringing you what you commanded. So we can say more accurately that your command was your wish. There is a saying be careful what you wish for you just might it.

Did you ever get a feeling what you wish for didn't just feel right? All out ward factors pointed south, but something about going south just didn't feel right. So, you went south anyway. By going south you did not get the desired results intended. But if you would have listened to your gut feeling then the results would have been a better outcome. This theory runs contrary to feel the fear and do it any way.

If you come into a situation where your desire is in front of you and your afraid, guess what, you need to feel the fear and get it any way. You still need to listen to your gut feelings. They are always right. Just the out come is not always desirable.

Personally my decision in tough situations is the most restrictive one.

Your emotions are your guiding system. They are your indicator, and your regulator. They are your red light, yellow light, and green light. Your emotions will tell you what to do. Your emotions will tell you when you all lined up. So the getting of the thing in your life should never be about right or wrong. Right and wrong is vertical thinking. We are thinking wide scope. It is horizontal. Your decisions should be more about is it what I want or don't want. So, the more specific you are the better. In the end result it is not about having the thing. It is ultimately about the feeling of having it.

So, from beginning to the end it is about your feeling good. This is why you drive the car you drive. This is also why you wear the clothes that you wear. This is why you have the mate that you have. It is about the feelings that they bring to the table. These people and things bring certain good feelings into your life that you like. It is what you are attracted to. So you allow them to stay.

So, whatever you have good feelings for has good feelings for you. What ever you have bad feelings for has bad feelings for you. Now, your angels know this, your angel stays out of your feelings. He just responds or reacts to what your actions are.

His job is to give you what you deserve, whether it is good or bad. How you feel is your responsibility and yours alone. He has orders to stay out of this area. He operates in the incorporeal realm. Your angel works for you or against you.

You are truly the decider. You decide by your actions led by your thinking, feelings and your belief system. Your belief system should be likened to your immune system. Your immune system is your internal medicine cabinet. Your mind is the internal command center. Your belief system leads you to your earthly destiny, and ultimately your eternal destiny.

GOD-CREATOR

In short your angels obey the eternal rule book. He has the rule book to go by. So as soon as you know the rules the better. He has at his command the rules of heaven the rules of earth and the rules of hell. His job is simple though when it comes to you. He gives you what you rightfully deserve. He delivers to you what you got coming. This is his job. He has to make sure you reap what you have sowed.

It you lived a stupid life this is not his fault. This is yours alone. If your always feeling bad this is not his fault it is yours alone. If you are not getting the things in life that you want this is not his fault. You got what you asked for.

Since you are the creator of your experience, then your attention should always be deliberate. Your being less than you can be by being a victim is laying down. How about the reverse theory? The phrase your feelings get in the way. Well if your feelings are getting in the way. It is detrimental to you. Then it's time to let it go.

So, being specific is good but being general is also good. Which ever feels better at the time.

Success in life is no more than a decision away. Failure in life is no more than a delusion away. Delusions always look sweet and right. But the end is bitter. Are you eating of the fruit of knowledge of the wrong tree? Whatever tree you eat from you will become just like it. Each tree has its own vibrations.

Bad things happen because we are in tune with the wrong vibrations. Both are decisions only you can make and make them we do.

Let's say we had success for a while then it turned into failure. We did not listen to our feelings strong enough. Believing you are doing the right thing is one thing. Following your feelings is another. They both have different roads. I believed to stay in my job was bitter. My belief was noble but unfruitful. When you make a decision and it makes you feel good then it is in the sweet spot. Once it is in the sweet spot it is in the realm of possibilities. Chances are greater that it will happen.

The law of attraction works forward and backward.

Either way you are the director. So, if you reverse your focus to the negative then you go backwards. It is at this point you will feel it. It doesn't feel good. This is your nature saying you are not being what you are supposed to be. You are being less than what you are created to be. If you focus on the negative you will get it. So, if you are in the negative then get creative.

Let go and let God. Un attach your self to the thing.

Over this course of your life you have developed this big ball of energy. What does this big ball of energy consist of depends largely on what you have fed it.

I heard a story one time about a native American. He had a dream one night. He told his grand son he had a dream about two wolves that were fighting. One was good and one was bad. His grand son asked him which one won. He responded by saying the one he had fed the most.

This big ball of energy that is yours is continually fighting. The one you feed the most will win. Your beliefs are the feeding ground. Your thinking is the food. The wolves feed on what you provide them. Your thinking makes it so. You have been thinking your whole life a certain way and it has brought you to where your at today. You have to take total responsibility.

You have developed neuro pathways. This is your grove of thinking. Set patterns. These patterns need to change. It is your set patterns that is causing your misery. Your pattern's of thinking is in accordance with your mind disease. When you understand this then and only then will you stop being a victim.

We tend to blame other people, and circumstances. This is your disease. Truth is we allowed other people into our lives and allowed the circumstances to come forward by doing nothing when the circumstances was forming. All you had to do was step into the mess. We created our own circumstances. We also create our own luck. We make our own bed and we lie our selves in it.

But you say I didn't see that coming. This is because you were not looking and being watchful. But by experiencing the contrast you will get a better perception on things. This is the very reason why failure is the road to success. This is how I have arrived.

This reality that we call earth is very dense. The quick creative power is not evident. This reality is considered an illusion.

WE are missing our heavenly abilities. This is why we all lie. The power of lies is self evident. They work. We lie because we don't know how to tell the truth on a deeper level. But we will pay for it along the way.

Our heavenly bodies have been stripped from us but only for a little while longer. We live in darkness and don't know it. The veil is across our eyes. This reality is full of contrast.

Earth is our psychological hell. The physical reality is hells realm. All manner of war fare has been unleashed on humans. It has always been, but it will not be forever.

But things will get worse before they will get better.

Earth's realm is just a tiny piece of eternity. History shows and records show that gods roamed the earth long ago. They have their place in legend. But the god's are no longer here. Some of those demons are still here. There place is below, to inner earth. They are subject to man. They are awaiting their judgment Along with man. We are not allowed to see them. But they are there. They are not allowed to dwell with man. But it looks to me that man is here on earth subject to the gods of the underground. Man's association with these creatures is the cause of the whole earth's demise.

"After the creation of things God did not give them bodies. He has decreed this from the beginning". All the sons of disobedience are in different locations. But all are awaiting judgment. There are those who are in the abyss. There are those who are in inner earth. This may be the same place, who knows. Then there are those gods that walked the earth who are in the north side of the fifth heaven. They all await judgment.

But their influence can be felt through out the earth. The whole earth lies in the power of the wicked ones. As a human we have a perception that we are insignificant, that we are worthless, and that we have no value. But nothing can be further from the truth. If fact it is to the contrary. We as humans have a special eternal destiny. Problem is we just don't know what it is yet.

We as a creator class of beings have been put to the test. Not all the heavenly host will pay homage to man kind. This is the reason for their rebellion. Humans are special but we sure don't always feel that way. We have been programmed to lose because the gods have designed it that way because they hate you.

You feel worthless because they look at you as worthless. You feel unwanted because they don't want you around. You feel used because they are using you. You are sick because they are making you sick.

So what does this have to do with your creative ability?

Glad you asked. Your creator did not leave you with out a way out. Your magical abilities are there. They have just been manipulated away from you. They have been hidden from your sight. This magic you desperately need. But there has been an assault on your humanness to keep you from knowing it. All manner if psychological hell has been unleashed on you mind, knowing this key here. What stops you from knowing is your lack of gratitude. Your inability to see beauty is a direct result of your mind disease. There is a barrier between you and your sanity. Between you and your eternal abilities to see who you really are. These barriers must be removed. This again is where Jesus Christ comes into play. He has removed these barriers. It is through Him only.

This is what He came to accomplish. This is what he was trying to tell every one. "For give them for they know not what the do." This is what He was saying.

Your over all state of mind is on the opposite end of the spectrum from where it should be. A better analogy is that you have inner desires that come from your center. Then there is the accomplishment of those desires. But in between you and your desires and there fulfillment is your mind virus. Your mind disease stands in the way.

First order of every day should be to stop the madness in your own mind. This means you have to go on a path to enlightenment. The reality of this is that this way of thinking is actually a way of life. This is your life's journey. So determine from this day forward to get the disease out of your mind and then out of your body. Then along the way get it out of your life. Once you do this then you are now ready to get on with co creating. Get your self out of your box. Raise your self above it all. Step out of it all. But you must want it to make it happen. "Your will" will be tested. So you must have iron resolve.

Give your attention to other things than what makes you angry. As humans we do not have magical in of our selves, but we have magic power access. We do not have the power of the gods but have god power access. You are a god man-woman. We are designed to create magic together, with each other, Side by side in a spirit of cooperation. But we are heading in the wrong direction. Our mind virus heads you south. You true nature is north.

Two brains together generate the power of three. Jesus said, "where two of you are gathered in his name there he is also". This is what he meant. He is the third mind. Jesus is the third eye. Let me remind you that you have a third eye. Develop your third eye. This is your Jesus eye, seeing things as He sees them. You develop this third eye by first understanding the eternal deities that are incorporeal. I believe it is seeing with your spirit. It is the combination of all your experiences that you develop your third eye.

This is the place of knowing. The third mind and the third eye is the key to success. The reason being is because you as you are, are born to lose. When you combine the third mind, the third eye, and your magical god man together you get an unbeatable combination. The third mind is the mind of the universe. It is an awareness of all things. I heard a story about gods that came from the Draco star system.

They were said to have superior intelligence because they were both sexed. What I'm saying here is simple, female intelligence in more intuitive than male. So align your self with female.

In this dense reality, you need intuition. You have to see things for what they can be. Quit looking at what things are. This takes faith. Start looking at things for what they can become. This is faith in action. Things take time to materialize from the incorporeal to the corporeal. The knowledge of this art has been stripped away from the education system. This is also knowledge that you cannot find in book stores. This knowledge is considered to potent.

Your god man and your angel work as a team. You do your part and he does his part. Your domain is the corporeal. His domain is the incorporeal. You are team mates. You give the command of the desires that you want with power and intensity. He will hear you immediately. You are granted it right away. But getting it to you is the problem. Man does not get what he prays for but he gets what he justly earns. So it is a matter of earning it.

He will start a dialog with you. In fact he has one with you already. When you have a conversation going on in your head, who do you think your talking to? You are talking to your angel. He makes recommendations to you all the time. But do you do them? Probably not.

This is why you are where you are at. Sometimes we default. So you are without excuse. This is an indication you are in your pre programmed failure mode. You don't do what he asks you to do. You decide to ignore all signals he brings to your attention. You end up doing it your stupid way with your stupid pre programmed self. Then bam! Failure, There is reality then there is delusional reality. It is here you must know the difference. Delusional reality always brings disappointment. They both run parallel with each other.

There are things to accomplish for this worlds betterment with no eternal rewards. Then there are things that are to be accomplished for this world's betterment with eternal rewards.

If you are experiencing failure, then you just have your self to blame like all the rest of us. Imagine a world where every one takes responsibility. You alone are responsible for all the things that happen to you and for you. Blaming some one else is weak and sick. Blaming any thing is weak and insane. But we all do it. I do it all the time. But it is still weak and insane. Blaming is weakness leaving the body.

You may not understand what I am saying. But I challenge you to lock your self in a tiny cell with you and yourself for one month. When your month is over your view of things will dramatically change. This means that when you were free you were under the delusion of life. When you were locked up you had to face the ugly truth as to why you were there. Then you realized that you were lying o your self your whole life.

Blaming your self is judging your self. I heard it said long ago that if you judge your self here on earth then there is no judgment day for you because you have already done so.

Scriptures bear witness with this principle.

You have walked among men on earth openly and in front of the gods. They have witnessed you rightly judging your own life with discernment and wisdom. This life is cruel why should the after life be any different. I also heard it said that what you do here on this earth echo's through out eternity. This too is a scripturally based truth. "Your deeds follow you into eternity."

What this says to me is watch your step. Even a Satanist thinks twice before putting a curse on any one because they know it boomerangs. They know it better than anyone.

Chances are your knowledge of eternity and all those who inhabit them is limited. You and I do not really know who we really are. Our god like powers lay hidden, quite and mostly unused. But they are there never the less. This very fact is hidden from most of earth's population. It is purposely done so. The reason is to keep you stupid. Ask your self do you feel stupid. I do all the time. Fact is I am. I do not know what I do not know. The true knowledge of who you are is the knowledge of the hidden societies. This is what they don't want you to know.

Your earth domain is yours. You get to see only .01 percent on your radar screen. Your angel's domain is the invisible realm. He has 100 percent on his radar screen. This is the reason why you don't know what you don't know. Your angel truly is your best friend. The fantastic way he does things is legendary. Put him to the test today. He has access to the throne. He has the power of vastness. The secret powers of heaven and earth and those living under the earth know of their powers. In fact that is why they are where they are today.

Now let me remind you this angel that I speak of is know the universal energy field that is called vibration. The whole universe including the earth is built on. Your angel has the same power the gods rely on. This is how they create. How do you think they do it?

The hole of mankind is fascinated with magical powers. It is inherent in the physic of humans to have magical powers. Some thing in us all feels something missing. This is very reason for our frustration. We know we should be able to have what we want but we just don't know how to get it. In the beginning man was created with two faces. He also possessed a heavenly body. He was as large as the distance between earth and heaven. Then he was put asleep and woman was formed from him.

It is at this point that things went bad. The reason things went bad is because delusional reality was introduced. They ate of the fruit and became paranoid. They became ashamed of them selves. This sounds like to me they did a drug. Hey! Maybe the fruit was not really a fruit. Maybe the fruit was a drug introduced to them. Now we know that where there are drugs there is all matters of sin. Is there a connection? You tell me.

Adam and Eve became small. When you do drugs you become small. You become beside your self. Drugs separate you from your self and it puts you in a delusional reality. This is the universe of delusional reality; a reality without God. Is it real? Absolutely! But you are there without God and without His permission! God does not want you there. Why does god not want you there? I believe that drugs are a gate way into dimensions not meant for man. Will you go to hell? No! But it further separates you from Him.

What this is saying to me is that it takes more than two people to figure things out. One mind only puts out so much power. But two minds are more powerful. Today's problems are so complex that most of the time we don't know how things will work out.

Providence is your leverage. This is your way out. This only happens when you make up your mind. Once you make up your mind providence kicks in. This an energy transaction. This is where your paradigm shifts. This is where you discover your destiny. When you feel that energy run up from the base of your spine this is the real thing. This is a life force. This energy will run from then base of your spine to the top of your head. It is called the serpent of life.

Worry is said to be negative goal setting. Don't sweat the small stuff. Your energy should be focused on dialing into the frequency of what you want with power and intensity. Live life with high expectation and then you will begin to see things associated with those desires. Every thing is inter connected. Your angel will immediately activate when providence kicks in. After all this is his purpose.

This universe is governed by this supreme law of attraction. It defies all other laws. All the gods know this power and use it. Call it the power of the gods. The power behind the gods. The power behind creation. Or better yet, your personal god power.

We as humans are in the god class of creatures. But here on this earth the energy is very dense. Things have slowed down to what seems a crawl. Time moves by too slow. Every thing takes forever. But the world does turn. The sun comes up in the sky every day and it does go down every day. One day you're a child the next day you sitting in the retirement chair.

In the mean time we have no clue of who we are.

All we know is that we have done this thing called life. The best kept secret in the world is the fact that we all have the power of creation. After all you created your mess didn't you? Lots of people create them selves a real stink hole. A real genuine shit hole. Nice. They create for them selves a stressful environment. The true nature of humans has been kept under ground.

The under ground gods rule over mans mind through the system. The gods want to use your talent for their purposes. Your true nature has been kept from you so that the gods through the elite class will rule over the earth's masses. The masses are all slaves to serve their system. Their system is in place to control them. The rich serve them and then we in turn serve the rich. Jesus says that he came so that we are not to be slaves anymore.

After all the gods need dumb down working slaves. Control of the system is covert. It has been covert since the foundation of this country.

The elite class devote them selves to the gods. The gods in return make them kings and queens. Bring them riches beyond measure. So you know there has to be sacrifices. Perhaps this is where all the missing children have gone. This is a down side to their ways.

The gods are awaiting for judgment day. Those who are in league with them are in the same judgment. The time when man fell from grace. "The moon did not obey." Therefore the moon was punished. It lost most of its brightness. The earth will under go its own judgment next because of the activities on it.

Your Angel is subject to the laws of eternity. We are in the same class as mini creatures. Humans are tiny gods. So we are tiny gods living in earth's dense reality, being mini creators.

Your angel is not a god. He has the power of the gods. He is not the laws of the universe he is the enforcer of the laws of the universe. He is not a deity in any way or form. But he has the power to creation. The word commands and he goes forth. The angel has only one owner and that is his creator. He does neither good or bad but grants you either. His job is to not judge but simply stand by as you judge and are judged. This is the nature of your angel.

This dense reality of our existence will cease in a very short time. Humans should, in the meantime start to wake up to the new reality of their true selves.

When the earth's population starts to realize their true nature then things will change for the worse. The powers that be and their manipulators will become very distressed. There by distressing the earth. Chaos will be the ruin of all things.

You have to under stand you have been lied to all your life about how things really are. You have a veil over your eyes and cannot see the other reality that God has for you. You have scales over your eyes. Removing them takes time. You have a life time of perception to change. Your trials bear witness to this.

The system that you serve and pay taxes to looks upon you as a low chaste slave, nothing more. You are expendable. You are a number. You are to be used, nothing more. The under ground gods view of humans are of slaves to serve them You are to be mislead, lied to, slaughtered, sickened, poisoned, fed food not meant for consumption. You are to be bombed, and terrorized killed, and murdered, misled, taxed, fined, and controlled. We have been treated like cattle. We have been penned in fed pro feed, then slaughtered. Our bodies today are chemically altered, our minds as well. The under ground gods govern the masses thanks to the elite class.

So, it is mans alignment with these reptilians that is causing man and the earth to come under sever judgment. The earth is already showing signs of the coming distress. Mans destruction of him self is Gods judgment upon man.

This is the agenda of the underground gods. Their aim is to destroy all that God has made. They use man and they try to get man to destroy. Replace all that is natural with artificial or synthetic. This way the under ground gods control all the earth through artificial means. Look around you my smart little friends and what do you see. The goal is to have complete control over your mind, body and soul.

This way your spirit is so laden and heavy it cannot lift from this atmosphere. The idea behind all this is to keep your soul trapped in this dense reality. In other words the devil wants your soul. There is nothing your angel can do about it. The reason is simple. Your angel is not your master. He is the power aligned with the deities.

So follow your feelings. If you followed your belief system versus your feelings you would not be in the same place today. You belief system is what is screwing you up. You have this belief you must do the right thing. Well you doing the right thing has got you where you are at today. Tell me how do you like it.

Your God feels what you feel. He feels your energy. He understands what it is you want. But he cannot bring you your hearts desire until you obey the rules of attraction. Your job is to feel the feelings. Have the belief system. Line your self up. Get rid of all doubt. Stop worry. Have patience. Express your desire and keep the faith. Stay on the watch. Look for signs. Carry on a dialog. Be willing to listen to him. Recognize his voice.

His voice always leads you to what is better for you. Stop being dogmatic. He always has your best interest in mind. Your universe is bringing you what it brings you. Be happy with what you have today. Obey the rules of eternity and live long and prosper.

Praying is communicating. Pray with out ceasing until you have what you are asking. Is this not the command? Pray and let your request be made known to God. Ceaselessly pray. This is vibrating. This is an energy issue. The scripture is telling you and I this secret, That the universe will respond to your frequency. The more you pray. The more you are vibrating. The more you are vibrating the more you will tune into the frequency of your prayer. Then the more you will be able to see how to bring it to pass. The ability to bring it to pass has always been there but you have not been able to see it. That is until you prayed about it. Then your eyes began to see. So what happened here? How about your third mind and third eye was opened?

No church has ever told me this information. Once you understand this information, the easier it is to under stand all things. All entities, all humans, all animals, all systems and all earthly conditions. All things.

To create means to bring into being. There is a law called the law of conversion. Conversion simply means to change. The taking of raw materials and change them into some thing else. Again nothing really new upon the earth, same materials different product.

Once you become consciously competent you will become consciously aware. Only then can you deliberately co create. Every thought that you have is converted to energy. This is why you are vibrating a frequency. Your thoughts are creating energy. So the more intensity you put into your thoughts the more power it generates. When you have emotions attached to that thought whatever that emotion; this is the power behind that thought. This is the power of co-creating. The longer you think that thought this is duration.

Every time you think of a thought, your brain is putting out a frequency. The first thing it will do is attract other like minded thoughts. This is generating. Generating leads to conversion. Because the more you generate the more you will realize. The more you realize the more you are going to change. You will want to change because you will not be satisfied with where you are at. This means your growing. So by putting out the right thoughts you get the right response. Once you get the right response your belief will get stronger. So, you under go a conversion. One of unbelief to one of belief.

But just starting out you have a ball of energy. It is filled with massive unbelief. Your thoughts create your feelings. So how do you know your thinking the right thoughts? Look to how you feel once you think them. If you are feeling doubt, worry, or fear, then you are on the wrong line of thinking.

To make things stupidly simple, monitor your thoughts all the time. By doing so you will be more in tune with how you feel. Monitor your thoughts and there impact on your emotions. This is your area of focus. Your god man will take it from there. Worry is caused by looking at the impossibility of things. Stress is caused by looking at the impossibility of how things will get better. Separate your self emotionally right here. This is your God's job. Let him worry about these things. This frees up your energy field to focus on more productive things. If you feel good your objective is to feel better.

You cannot see events off your radar screen. If you can't see what you want, then you can feel what you want. It is from this place you start. Stay its frequency. Match the vibration, then the magnet kicks in. now what you want wants you. It wants you because it is designed to feel good and be healthy.

But as you were it will not want you. You have to make it attracted to you. I heard it said attraction isn't a choice. This must be because you have the power to command. You command attraction. Like is attracted to like. So the first thing you must feel after a decision is to feel good about it. By feeling good about it things begin to shift in your favor. In other words you can say anything you like as long as you smile about it. Get to the feeling of complete expectation. You may have to go through a process of complete change, or a conversion as you will. Just so the thing that you want wants you. Your job is to be willing to take action steps to make it so. As you go about the process things will seeming change. Different things will come into your experience. This is the process. The name of this process is called life.

There will be experiences that will materialize out of no where. But if you keep steady at the wheel of thought, then in due time you will have what you asked for. You cannot put a time limit on things. You are on the great clock of eternity. Once you put a time limit on it this produces the ability to increase doubt. This is self sabotage.

Your body is an important element here. If your body feels bad then you will feel bad. So it's important to make your body feel food. You must eat good food. So eat food as close to nature as intended. Most foods today have been genetically modified to keep you from realizing your full potential. They are full of body altering, emotion altering chemicals. They are loaded with hormones, antibiotics, and all sorts of other chemicals. These substances keep your vibration low.

Drugs are the biggest factor in keeping you vibration low. Artificial sweeteners block the ability to send out vibrations. Another thing that will block your abilities is toxins in the body. Toxins in the food you have been eating all you life. Toxins in the water you drink and shower in. Also toxins you pick up in your work environment. Toxins you breath from the city air. The number one toxin is drugs.

All drugs. We have more legal drugs than illegal. If it's green, it's good. If it's an herb it's better. Taking drugs even just an aspirin will weaken your ability to focus and transmit vibration. So the more drugs the doctors can get you to take, the more powerless you become. It reduces your power to create. Drugs are specifically designed to get you to be less powerful. Your body is loaded with toxins. That's why you can't ever feel good. They are also the reason your angry and pissed off all the time.

So, clean your body out. Do some cleanses. Your body is your engine. Your oil is your blood. Your window is your eyes. Positive input is your fuel. Your vibration is your life force. Your mission is your road map. Your value is you worth. Your brain is considered your command center. Your thoughts send out vibrations that literally affect all physical matter around you. Your four walls are affected by your thoughts. They also affect others that are near you. They will either react or respond to it.

One important way to feel better is to exercise. The number one cure for depression is going out for a brisk walk and looking at things far into the distance.

Also read every day. This helps you to focus. Find a mentor and listen to them. They will help you go in the right direction. There should be no better mentor than your parents. This is not always the case.

Hugs are a good way to feel better. Most people today don't get enough contact with other human beings. Laughing is the biggest factor in feeling good. When your feeling good your vibrations are good. Out of this you will attract things and people that are good. The more you laugh, the better you feel. Laughter creates an alkaline state in the body. This counter acts your acidic state. There fore helps to restore balance. The act of smiling changes your vibrations. Most people go around with a scowl on their face.

Dancing is another way to feel better. Go stand in the sunshine. Do something with your hands. When you are feeling bad, you are thinking what you don't want. Everything you want is in your own DNA. So, you are automatically vibrating what you want. But if you are vibrating an opposing vibration, they won't mix. This blocks energy in the body and you feel horrible.

This is the mechanics of how it works. This is why it's important to think about things you know you can get. That you'll believe you can get. Scripture gives us a hint here when it states that hope deferred makes the heart sick. It's bad for your bones. The negative is very powerful. It also has attractive pull. If your ball of energy is attracted to the negative then you will experience negative results. This is the cause of depression. So if your depressed then you should consider dream building. Dream building is looking at things that you could potentially want. This means expanding your mind to possibilities. Look at things that are opulent, clothes, exotic places, houses, and cars. Pay attention to the things that you want or places to visit.

Get out of your head and into your body. It's you being in your head that's the problem. When your experience becomes real your belief level goes up, and the anticipation level increases. Then imagine how you will feel having those things.

This is something you should be doing constantly. Work on building up your dreams. One thing you can do all day every day is appreciation. Start looking around and appreciate what you have, where you are at. Feel appreciation for the people in your life. Forgive them for they don't know they are stupid. Feel a deep pity for their dumb ass. If you can't then it's time to start the process.

It is said that familiarity breeds contempt. What this means is the loved ones in our lives we hate them. This in turn brings negative vibrations. This is bad for the dwelling place.

Ask your self instead, what are you thankful for? If you are not thankful for them perhaps you should do without them for a while until you do feel good about them.

Try living without hot water in a cold environment. You will learn to appreciate hot water when you live in an icy environment. If you can't find something any reason to appreciate then you should look harder at things.

Remember, nothing is what it seems. Abuse it and lose it. There is a whole universe of things to feel thankful for. Once you experience this emotion the universe will move mountains on your behalf. This universe was not created to be conquered. It was created to surrender to. So it is through surrender that you find happiness.

All things are frequency, vibration, and held together by energy. It is the emotion of your energy that causes things in your life to move, shift, and change. All things are in motion. You are in motion. Everything is alive.

GOD

Walk into a room full of people and observe who is affected by your appearance. This universe is justly ordered. All things are justly affected. Every thing is happy when there is harmony, love and appreciation, All things are happy when they are healthy and there is no stress.

Your water is happy when you're happy. Water forms crystals when it's happy. This explains why plants grow taller when you play music and sing to them.

Scripture gives us another hint here when it says if man doesn't give him praise then the rocks and the trees cry out to him, Also, when Cain slew Able the grave screamed injustice. All things flourish under the right conditions. Justice is the order of the universe. When an evil ruler parish who will miss him. But the righteous rejoice when justice rules. The universe, which include all things respond to your emotional energy.

Look no further than you pet. I'm pretty certain your pet does not understand one word you say. But they do respond to your energy. This is the secret behind the horse, and dog whisperer. Your words to them are filled with vibrations. I play around with this concept on my cat. I tell my cay when he meows I say cat you are a flea bitten scrounge, You came into this house just for me to kick you didn't you. That's why you are meowing. But I say it with love. He just purrs and responds to my vibrations. He doesn't care about my words. But he knows what makes him feel good.

So, your goal is to feel good now. I also have lived with a heard of horses for the last fifteen years. This concept also extends to them. A horse will feel your intensity or passiveness. They will know exactly how you feel the moment you step into the eye view. They know exactly what you are feeling. Wild animals are the same. I have stumbled across deer and not even seen them. Until I suddenly look at them then they seem frightened. This same thing happened with a cougar one time. I did not see him watching me. But once I turned my attention to him he vanished.

Veterinarians say pets are an extension of their master. The master is sickly so goes the pet. Healthy is the master so goes the pet. If you are fat then so does the pet. If you are stupid then so is your pet. If you are stupid they are stupid. If you smarten up so do they. You are the master not the beast. If you are sickly they become sickly. If you are in good health they tend to be in good health.

So, the better you feel about all things the better. Feeling good allows you to in crease desire. When you write things down with pen and paper it is much healthier than typing. When you write it your feeling the thought, Not so with typing. Writing activates ten thousand neuro-pathways in the brain. So write every thing down. Write your dreams and goals down.

Control your thoughts. What an impossible thought. But if you can do it then you control your tongue. If you are able to bridle the tongue then you are able to harness your power. Therefore steer your life in all the right directions. Your natural way of thinking keeps you from knowing about your god man. By controlling your thoughts you will be able to harness the power of creation. Harness the power of the creative process.

You will have to get into your mind and clean things up first. Some times you have to tear things down before rebuilding. Once in a while you have to totally destroy and build a new structure.

No one knows the grand scheme of things. No one has any idea the intricacies that must take place to get what you want. This is why you must have a high willingness to change and learn. As long as you are teachable you don't need to worry about the variables. This is the angel's job.

Worry is negative goal setting. When you think about something long enough and it happens it's no surprise. One thing is for sure, if you don't believe you cannot have something then you will never have it. That's a fact. To believe is a positive equation. To not believe is self destructive. It is you denying yourself. Unbelief is the poison that kills.

Unbelief kills just as surely as the bullet but not as fast. Man can walk on water? When Peter saw Jesus approaching them when they were on that boat, during stormy seas Peter was so elated that he totally forgot he was in a boat on the sea. He stepped out thinking he was on dry land. He jumped right out of the boat and started walking towards Jesus. He had not even realized what he had just done. When he did realize what he had just done he then caught him self. When he caught him self he doubted. At this point he started to sink. Jesus said why did you doubt Peter?

The potential for great things is there right in front of us. We are just too blinded to see it. To fear and doubt seems the natural thing to do. But it never works. We must be re-programmed to have no fear and doubt. So the ball of fear energy, doubt energy is stronger the belief energy. We must under go a conversion. We naturally have it back wards. So we go unnatural. Therefore we must have faith at this point. Walking by faith is not natural and cannot be understood by the natural mind. What this is saying we must let it go and let God.

What you really, really, really want you'll get. Like wise, what you really, really, really don't want, you'll get as well. This is the rule. It's the thinking that makes it so. So what ever you are thinking about you'll get.

So, to get what you want, you must first define what it is that you want. Anticipate its arrival with emotion as if it's already there. Repeat this often every day for at least five minutes . Simply believe you can get it. This will make you feel better. If your feeling as if you've achieved it then that's the ultimate. If you think about it and start feeling doubt, then this is your clue your not in alignment with it. This is your nature telling you are not looking out for your own best interest. Then this problem is in your court. You now have the ball. This is God's signal you must do something different.

Doubt, worry, and fear are illusions. They are not real. Oh they are very real alright! They are real delusions. In other words they don't work. What is real is what works. I heard it said that ninety nine percent of fear is said to be non reality.

Your DNA is your hard ware. Your brain is your soft ware. You are vibrating all the things you want. Your programming is flawed. It's getting in the way. This is the one and only belief system. Your belief system is not the same as your feelings. Our belief system thinks its way through life. Our feelings system feels it's way through life. I heard it said lots of times to follow your feelings. I have rarely followed my feelings, but when I did awesome things happened. Beliefs and feelings inter mix. You must come to where you consciously know the difference. This is an art. Both have a say in your life. But it is you that chooses.

So choose that which is good for your organism. It is you who chooses who and what to listen to. God chooses who is put into your life you choose to let them remain.

Everything you want is vibrating within you already. It is you who must choose who to listen to it or not. Your belief system does not always include your best interest, unless your feelings are involved.

Your mind program is faulted to failing. This is why we are always making decisions that we regret later. It comes easier to fail than to succeed. That is because we are naturally failures. We are a fallen mini god-like creature. But a god-like creature never the less. If the actions that you take daily are not a joy and a pleasure then you should not be doing them. If you don't agree with this statement, then that means you have a long ways to go until you do accept it as fact. I have lived my whole life living and doing things I absolutely hate. So I know what I'm talking about. If things are a burden then you need to start the process of stopping them. This is bad for your organism.

When you love what you are doing things come into your experience a lot easier. This is because there is less resistance. When you are doing things you love the energy around you is without resistance. Resistance is the opposite of surrender. It is only through surrender to reality that is that you find peace.

Your bad feelings are you fighting the universe. The universe is fighting you back. In other words you will always lose. So in the mean time you are losing. Get it.

But there is a buffer of time from the point of resistance to death. You may resist unto death, that's alright with me. But the universe is kind to you and does not kill you right away. In the end though, it is you who destroy your self. And in between you're a miserable, lousy, sick , angry, unhappy human. I live very close to a few of them. But when bad things seemingly occur this is not necessarily a bad thing. Just because it seems bad does not mean that things will not work out. It just means that the universe has something else in mind for you than the path you were on. Your path is altered. Don't resist it. Go with the flow. Out of this seemingly bad thing comes new ideas, and a new way of looking at things and a brand new direction. It also means the end of the way it was. But the reason why it happened has some thing to do with what your vibrating. You somehow unknowingly created it. So, be careful what your asking for you just might get it, or get something else.

This is an instance where you did not know what you were doing. This is why Jesus prayed to the Father and said "forgive them Lord for they do not know what they are doing." Out of one eye you see the physical world for what it is.

Then with your imagination you can envision what it can become. The third mind is your makers mind together with yours co-creating together. This is your new awareness. The third eye is your ability to look into both incorporeal and corporeal simultaneously. This third eye is your creating ability using the universe as a backdrop. This third mind is your mini god like creating powers connected to the gods.

It is under standing these simple but powerful concepts which gives you the ability to command your god power. It is the entrance way to deliberate co creating. Once you understand this you will start to become the master of your environment, and stop being the slave.

You will start becoming a winner instead of a loser. You will start to move with purpose. Your days of sitting around whining will be over.

This entrance way is also achieved through the feelings of tired of being sick and tired. This is the signal from your nature that all that your doing is not bringing you good tidings. To me this is an indication It is a time to die to that which is. Then simultaneously be reborn. In other words doors are being closed. If so, then look for windows, preferably windows of opportunity.

All humans are not lost to this ability. The ones that are, they do well. Your god like ability, and god like thinking are in your DNA. They just need awakening.

I access mine through the strong feelings of screw this bull shit. It is in this state of mind that I discover new abilities that help me over come. When I get angry at something that is not going my way I find the energy through anger. This is why this emotion pops up. I use it to plow through my problem. Through this state of mind I have discovered I can achieve greater heights. I have over come insurmountable odds with my attitude. But then again I'm a man. They used to call this grit. But today this meaning is lost. It is frowned upon. This leads me to where I am today. It is not I who is lost. It is those around me that just don't have any grit themselves. I am a man that knows long days of heavy labor. When it came to hard labor I did not shrink.

The reason that your desires are in your DNA is because at mans creation it was deliberately put there. But through the ages this ability has been shelved as mankind descended into slavery. Humans are all born into slavery. But soon and very soon we will all be reunited with our heavenly bodies.

When Enoch ascended into heaven God told the escorting angel to clothe Enoch with his heavenly body. After all, humans are all fascinated with the world of magic. This is the realm of all possibilities. The third eye and mind directly connects you with the realm of all possibilities. It connects you to the magical way this universe works. In a sense it is the gateway to the universe. Once you open the gateway, your god man will be more seen.

Jesus is the Word made flesh. So, start by using your words wisely. Your words are very powerful. Your words backed with powerful emotion creative the right vibrations. Start by using your words to command the storms of the soul, and say peace be still. Start to use your words and say to your personal world all things will get better. Use your words to create your relationships the way you desire. Words are very important because they help focus your thoughts. They do two things.

They help create things and they help you focus your thoughts. So your words are used as leverage in your life. So by saying words in a certain way it will help you focus.

All things in the universe used to be something else. All products that are made start out to be raw materials. This is the same thing with creating your dreams. You take the raw materials which is who and what your presently are and wrought them into the image you have in your mind. If you don't like who you are then start the process of conversion. Try it you might like it. I did. I have recreated my self over many times. It is always an exciting process. New things, new thoughts, and new places. Hey! This is earth. We were born to live on this earth.

All things are the result of a mathematical equation. It's called conversion. This is what money is all about. You labor or produce for money. To convert means to change. Exchange is the giving or taking of one thing in return for another. Does compromise come to mind. This means to settle differences by mutual concessions.

This means you have to start developing some new speech patterns. When you start saying the right things you will create new neuro-pathways in the brain. Develop some new dominate thought patterns. This will create new vibrations that transmit out of your brain, which will in turn cause different things and events to occur in your life.

This is being a conscious creator. The conscious creator looks at what is and sees it without resistance. The negative that is there is not to be ignored but instead used to your benefit. The negative will always be there. You cannot escape it. So experience the negative vibrations. But be consciously aware of it.

See the solution from within the problem. Always know deeply that every thing will work out fine. You don't know how or why but you just know that it does. Expect miracles and get miracles. Your goal is to have a life of more pleasure and less conflict. The third eye and mind is the eye and the mind of the universe. It is watching you. It sees and hears everything you do whether in public or private. Whatever you have coming to you, then it will deliver. But then again, what you have coming to you can be delayed, be it either good or bad. Again all depends on what its will is.

Your negative energy is destroying everything around you. It causes all division and destruction. It causes all soul destruction. It is the cause of all tears. But negative is not all bad. Negative is a force to be used. Jesus did all the time. There are fruits that are acidic but alkalize the body. There is negative that seems lowly but turns out to be very wise. Know the difference.

This world is backwards and upside down. So right your self up. What you sow is what you reap. The best time to create things in your life is when things are not going well. This allows focus through discontent. Through your discontent your shift occurs because your feeling unhappy and you want to feel better. Your desires are strongest. Your focus is sharpest. Pain sharpens the senses. So your unfortunate circumstances forces you to focus on what you want.

The scriptures also declare that we should feel blessed when unfortunate circumstances visit us. You have been found worthy to endure it. I have even heard it said it's time to pop the champagne. So the universe has things in store for you beyond your understanding. Some times all you can really do is acknowledge it for what it is and move on. When things happen to you, you should say I don't know how things are going to turn out but they will turn out to my benefit. Then start to turn it around. Then start to focus on what you want to happen. This really allows you to clarify your thinking. So, clarify what you want.

Look at life like a buffet. There are things you like to eat then there are things you don't like to eat. By eating some things you don't like you then know what it is you don't like.

Life is the same way. Life is always throwing things at you that you don't like. Trials are events that teach us what we don't want. Then and only then can we be clear about what we do want. This is why when something bad happens in your life you should pop the champagne. Because when something bad happens the bigger it is, the worst it appears, it allows you to sharply focus with a massive beam and massive power and massive intensity of what you do want.

This trial now becomes an advantage. It is only through your trial that you have the ability to generate massive power. True change only occurs when you are sick and tired of where you are at and with what you have. What you are feeling and what you are experiencing. This is when your shift occurs.

Because you are sick and tired of being sick and tired. This is when you stop looking at these bad circumstances in your life. When this happens this is the moment to stop looking at it, turn your back on it, and say I'm sick of this. Then realize what you really want. This is when massive desire is born within you.

Massive clarity is born. Out of this is your self being reborn. Shake off the old and put on the new. This will cause you to become obsessed. You will find your self thinking about it all the time. And you become what you think about most of the time. Because what you are vibrating most of the time is what's being attracted to your life. People have a bad habit of putting a negative spin on everything which causes them to focus on what it is that they don't want.

Worry is negative goal setting. So to get from where you are at to where you want is a seemingly impossible jump. What you are feeling is where your sending your self. Your goal is to always move up the emotional scale. So, you start where you are at. Your goal is to always feel better. Catch your thoughts along the way. Your thoughts and feelings are an indicator of what will be attracted to you; which in turn what will happen out of it. So we must always look to the possibilities of all things. So instead of telling the story of what is, you begin to tell it like you want it. This is deliberate creation. Hey! Wait a minute here I am sounding like Esther Hicks here. I think this is where I got this.

Look at only the possibilities that c an come out of your situation that will benefit. Discard all the rest. Your words are very important. But what's more important is the vibration attached to your words. So always use your words as leverage to lift.

Your words have the power to sink or lift you. The law of lift is superior to the law of gravity. So pay attention to them. If you get a sinking feeling then you are sinking. If you get a lifting feeling then you are lifting. Words are used to create or change. Always look for thoughts that bring good feeling. Choose your words wisely.

Stop lying to your self, and stop lying to others. Start being honest with your self about everything. Say things that accurately describe how you feel. Stop putting a negative spin on everything. If you truly feel horrible then say it. But don't say things that you don't really believe. Other people change or influence your vibration. All in the end it's not about achieving anyhow. It's always about the feeling. It's about how you will feel getting it. It's about how you will feel having it. It is about how you will feel experiencing the rewards of it. So be honest about the reason why you want it.

Another thing, what you think is the best method is probably not the best method. But if you let the universe bring it to you then you will feel so much better about it. I have heard it said time and again to write things down. There is magical things that happen when you write things on paper. Through this method you predict the future by creating the future. So, predict the future by mini creating the future. This is key because it goes right along with being a god like creature.

You are a fallen god like creature, but a god class creature nevertheless. Your not allowed to rule the world. You are allowed to rule your sphere. Create your right now. Let tomorrow come and then do it again. Build your eternity one day at a time. Do what you want for eternity. If you can figure this one out you've got it made.

Every one is responsible for themselves because they created their situation. Bring your self to the point where the anticipation goes up and up. When your there then it's getting closer. When your feeling bad about something, then it's an indication it's getting father away. Your feelings are your tracking system. Your feelings are your guiding system. Your feelings are your predictor. Your feelings are your thermometer. Your feelings are your guider counter. So, go through life feeling your way thru. If you are feeling fine then things will be fine.

When it appears to be the worst, know it's the best. Because it means something big is taking shape, and it's right around the corner. It means that it will have more magnetic pull than ever before. How fast things will occur is irrelevant. It doesn't matter when it occurs. When the time is right it will happen. When the student is ready the teacher will appear.

You cannot get caught up in the timing. It comes when it comes. You care but not that much. This applies to money as well. You must keep your options open in case the universe presents other offers to you. But remember, what you want wants you, but probably not as you presently are. Not believing you can have something stops the process of it coming into your life.

So, doubting, unbelief, worry, and fear are truly the destroyers of progress. Because the god like creature that you are knows that you can have be or do anything is truly true. It is the ultimate truth. This is so because of the law of lift backed by the law of attraction. But your pre programmed ego stops you dead cold.

Eternal love is the only thing that's real all else is illusion. So, all things are available to you. All things are in front of you. What you have to work on is your self worth. Your self worth is tied to quality. Quality of self equals quality of things. But your big ball of negative energy stops you from having it. Your negative neuro path ways stops you because they are not working to your advantage. They are not creating your life the way you want it any way. They are creating for you what you don't want.

Everything in your own life you brought it to pass, that's the fact. So, it just stands to reason that you can re create something else, something better, Something more pleasing using your thoughts. Every thing is energy, vibration. Capture the energy capture the matter. Life is like a roller coaster, you go down then you go up. It's all one big thrill.

Your number one objective is to feel good right now ands if you can feel even better. The better you feel the better your thoughts. That means the vibrations going out are on the things you want. Laugh and sing all day long.

Ninety nine percent of creating anything is your thoughts. It's using your brain to put out a vibration. So, by the law of attraction, the universe will put you in situations, bring to you people and offer events that will help you create that which you want. The law of attraction will bring into your life that which you are vibrating. It will give you situations, people and events that will give you matching feelings. What ever your emotion your vibrating the universe will respond to that vibration.

When it comes to money, the first thing is to want money. This is the first thing, you must want it. Specifically money and at what level you choose. Determine how much you want. What ever the amount it must make you feel good. If it makes you feel good then it's in your sweet spot. If it makes you feel bad then it's not in your sweet spot. If it feels bad then you will be drawn to the lack of it. So, how you feel about it determines the magnetic pull. The magnetic pull is what draws you to It, or it to you. So, how you feel about it determines the magnetic pull. Everybody's amount is different. Initially you need to come up with a dollar amount that you feel good about. If you can't do that then be general.

Look for the thought that makes you feel good. The good feelings and the bad feelings all have magnetic pull. Your thoughts determine feelings. Feelings determine direction. Direction determines outcome. Outcome is all stemmed from thought. You cannot put a time limit on things either. Always think on what you want and, not on what you don't want.

Through experiencing what you don't want, you can become clearer on what it is you do want. If you are looking at what you don't want then this is what you will get.

Always put wants, dreams, goals, and desires in the affirmative. That way you are focusing on what you want. Always fine tune your dreams and what you want. Don't become dogmatic about anything. Stay open minded. Always be ever more specific on desire. Because the more specific on desire the more power and intensity and you get a higher level of belief, which means it comes into your existence faster.

So this means that you must have a chief aim. A chief aim means to have a primary focus goal when it comes to money. When you vibrate anything with power and intensity you must draw energy from other mental areas. Which means you must give up other thoughts going to other subjects. This is considered off balance. So to get what you want you can't be balanced.

You can't live a balanced life. You can't juggle one hundred subjects and focus on a chief aim too. You have to make sacrifices. You must be focusing on a chief aim most of the time. If it's your job, it's your job. If it's your health, then it's your health. You become what you think about most of the time. So, stop and take a long hard look at where you are spending all your energies.

You must be obsessed with what you want. Obsessed is defined as: Preoccupy intensely or abnormally. Because that's the only way you can focus. By being obsessed your broadcasting with intensity what you want. That's the only way you can continually clarify it. That's by broadcasting the vibration with power and intensity and have the duration long enough to create it in your life. You can only do this by being obsessed.

You get what you think about most of the time. What this is saying is that you are putting out thoughts on fifty different things. These things will come into your life in varying degrees sooner or later. But if you want some thing to come into your life with record speed, then you must be obsessed. Which means you must be broadcasting it all the time. You must develop a burning desire. Desire is defined as: Feel desire for. Request, Strong conscious impulse to have, be or do something.

So determine what your chief aim will be, then have a pulsating desire for it. Believe you can accomplish it. Set your sights on it. Feel good doing it. Forget or forsake all things in the way. Have eyes only for it. Virtually keep at it till it comes to pass. Burning desire is massive obsession. This means you must live for it, eat for it, breath for it pray for it think for it, Sleep for it. Believe all the while it's yours. This translates to having no doubt. You make it your own. You take it shape it, mold it like clay and form it. Bend it to your will with your will. You will the thing.

All things will eventually bend to your will. But this takes an iron will. This is how you bring some thing to pass with record speed. Having a balanced life is very good do not get me wrong.

Scripture gives us a clue here. The apostle Paul writes that we must run the race with endurance versus enduring the race we run. The first one means with power and focus. The second means to just barely get by.

When you have massive obsession you will love and enjoy what you are doing. There fore there is no burden. If you are not enjoying the activity then that means your not feeling good. That means that you are thinking about the lack of it. This is "doubting" that you'll get it, and therefore you won't get it. So, you must be obsessed.

Explore how you will feel about having money. Lots of money, and all the things it can do for you. If you say I want, I want. Add to this and say I want because. Then say I want because I need too . Then add to this and say I want to because I need to do this for a greater purpose that only you can determine. Here is where you vision comes in. This is fine tuning.

This means you have specific reasons. Don't you know that knowing is just not going to jump out of the sky and fall into your lap out of nowhere. Although it has been know to happen. More than likely they have to be manipulated into existence. Manipulated is defined as: 1. Treat or operate manually, or mechanically. 2. Influenced by cunning. Cunning in defined as; Crafty, clever, appealing skill, or craftiness. When you were created you were created to have all the things you want. You were designed to have it all. And have it anytime you want. This is still in your hard ware. You are living and pulsating your desires right this very minute. So, again what you desire is in you DNA.

But this earth's density has come to what appears to an absolute halt. But this is only an illusion. This universe is alive. It is all energy. You were specifically designed to live in this earth. You were not designed to life in heaven. Every thing seems to be in slow motion. But in motion never the less. I heard it said that the wheels of justice turns slowly but they do turn.

So start by looking at your eternal value. You are worthy of all things. Nothing is too good for you. Nothing good will be with held for all those who love and appreciate this good earth.

Today's society is structured to turn you in the opposite direction. It is designed to keep you not only from knowing this information, but keep you penned in like cattle in all manner of the word.

Think of your life like a car. When you are driving in a rain storm at night. You have to have an intense focus. You bother less with your rear view. You must keep your attention straight ahead. Your past is your rear view is nothing. Where you have been is less important than where you are going. The most important thing is that you get there safely. So, stop looking in the rear view. People get stuck looking in the rear view. This is what bickering is all about. This is what gossip is all about. This is what arguing is all about. Your stuck looking in the rear view. This is wasted energy massively. This is why you are crashing.

I heard it said more than once that arguing with a woman is the same amount of stress as defusing a bomb. I believe this is true. People's lives are a wreck. People any more are a nervous wreck. That's because they are always crashing. They have wreck less relationships. They have wreck less jobs. They have wreck less home environments. They are emotional wrecks. This is because they are always crashing. Day in and day out all day long.

Wreck is defined as: 1.Broken remains after heavy damage. 2. Some thing disabled or in a state of ruin. 3. An individual who has become weak or infirm. 4. Action of breaking up or destroying something. This suggests that you must be always in a state of repair before you can rebuild. You rebuild by dream building. From daydream to dream build. Go out and look at things is good. Touching them and feeling them is better. Start building new neuro-pathways.

The secret to riches is all in the mind. The ruling class want to keep you from it. So they helped design your wrecked life. Our society is specifically designed to wreck your life so that you are always crashing. Because the more your energy is sucked up here the less likely you will figure things out. Your mind is always preoccupied. Your life is in a constant state of destruction. This system is also specifically designed with road blocks, stops, dead ends, hindrances, to abolish, kill, suck away your time or wreck and destroy. These are all energy stagnation. Purposely put in place to keep you from knowing your true nature.

Going one step further, this stops you from knowing about your god man and its power. We are experiencing a real live psychological hell here on earth. Truly all hell has been unleashed on mankind.

To have money you must get obsessed about it and think about it and feel good about it all the time. This is 99% of it. Your life is already structured to consume all your energy. The things you do daily sucks the life right out you. These things make you focus on stuff that don't really matter. Chances are your giving your attention to crap. Your wrecked life, your broken self. To things that bring no return or satisfaction.

So, work you slaves, and put out massive energy for crap and get peanuts in return. The work place is a trap. It is killing you. Ninety nine percent of success is created in the mind. If you believe you must slave 24 hours a day seven days a week then guess what, this is true. It is the thinking that makes it so. This is the secret. Here are some views from the rich and famous:

1. Persistence beats education. You don't have to be smart to be rich.
2. Make your own luck. Create your own luck.
3. Gamble but wisely. The rich and famous follow their feelings. They make decisions based on feelings, gut intuition. They do things based on how they feel. If their feeling great about it, it always works out. That's because they are predicting the future. They are creating the future.
4. They know their market intimately. Associate with people and situations that is involved around their particular market is so they know their market intimately. Intimately means they have a feeling or sense about the market. So when they think about their business, they are following their feelings, which is how it works. You get out of the thinking stage and into the feeling stage. Think with your head and feel with your heart. When it comes to your self use your head. When it comes to others use your heart. Because when your attitudes right the facts don't count.
5. Focus obsessively, and work, work, work. This means having a chief aim. Put the blinders on and think about what you want to happen all the time. Timing is everything. Depth of vision. You have to see the future. You have to know exactly what you want. You have to see the potential of things. This means you

must go beyond what you see and discover what it could become.
6. Quit looking at how things are and start looking at how they could become. You must develop the inner ability to see things further down the road. You have to place your self at the right place at the right time. Luck has a lot to do with things. But then again you can create your own luck. So, when you focus on something obsessively, the universe will give you circumstances, situation, and events that match your vibration. In other words the universe will put you in the right place at the right time.
There are always other people who have the same ideas as you. But you must take action. It is always up to you to go with your feeling and do something. Take action when it is presented. Right at the most opportune moment. Look to your intuition.
Circumstances and situations often present itself always in the form of ideas. But will you answer to the call is the question.
I heard it said long ago prepare your self for what your about to receive. If you do not prepare your self then the desired thing will come into your life and catch you unprepared. So you must take action steps to prepare. Prepare your soil.
7. It is not just about the money. It's about the feeling that having the money will bring. So you are truly working on the feeling. So, first define how you want to feel. Better yet, what you want to feel. Like security, maybe a sense of accomplishment. Safety, prestige, love and respect. The money is secondary. The vibration is what makes the money.
8. It's not the skill you have, it's the smarts you have. It's not the technique that matters. it's the vibration that matters. When you are thinking about what you want and you are putting it out into the universe on a high

intensity frequency. This brings you what you want. It's the thought process that matters. Whether you are doing it unconsciously or automatically, this is how it's done.

This is the technique everybody is using. So, the key is you must be thinking about the money and the feeling of having it all the time. But the most important thing is the feeling of having money. The feeling of being happy, blissful and fulfilled. It doesn't matter if you are totally in debt. Doesn't make any difference if you are poor, or live in a camp ground in a tent. When the rich vacation, they spend big money to live like a bum and love it. When they do it it's worth every penny.

They usually have the time of their life. What life is really all about is feeling good. Feeling blessed. Feeling blissful.

MAN

Blissful is defined as: Compete happiness.

The greatest happiness that you can get is by adding value to society, and to help other people. This is what being human is all about. Money is only one part. Every body has different amounts they would like to generate. From a little to a lot. So, choose how much you need to generate. What ever the amount you must feel good about. You can have any amount you desire. There are opportunities all around you. But want do you have energy for. If you work for someone else you are pretty much limited on the amount you can make.

When circumstances present itself you will not be able to see them, much less act on them. If you are wasting your time with bad energy then chances you will miss opportunity when it comes because you are preoccupied. If your boat came in today to rescue you, would you recognize it?

If you want to make serious money then chances are your job is not the place to be. But real money is going to come from a business of your own. A business of your own allows you to make more money than your job. Generating money and building wealth is almost the same.

There are two ways to make money:
1. You earn money. Which means you go out and make money.

   Your efforts make you money. Nothing wrong with this as long as it's pleasurable. However, there is a limit on the amount of time you have and do everyday. So, when you earn money based on your own efforts, your money is limited. Then there is duplicating your own efforts. This means you have others helping you make money. Meaning you hire others.
2. The second way to make money is when money is working for you. Instead of you working for money, money is working for you. This is basic investing. This means you have money to put into a business and with your efforts your money begins to grow. So, you must find an investment vehicle. This is where your money is making you more money. This is where your money, math, and magic knowledge come into play.

This is how super wealth is created. This is where you want to place your self. Once you are at a place where your money is generating more wealth. Then and only then can you be free of debt. You are never free as long as your in debt. Being financially free is truly what freedom is all about. Debt is bondage. So start transmitting the new thought process. Maybe for you this will become a reality. There is still a few basic concepts required.
1. Getting out of debt.
2. Establish credit. You must become aware of how the free flow of energy works. Debt is negative. Debt is bad. Debt makes you feel bad. Your thought process will come easier when you have reduced your debt, or you are on your way out of debt, and your only using credit. All the thoughts flow easier. So, reduce or get out of debt now. Say to your self I want to be debt free. I want to have no bills.

Saving up money frees up energy. Reduce the taxes you pay. Reduce your insurance premiums. Use corporations to gain access to lines of credit. there is one major character trait that you must develop to become successful :

1. Develop a pleasing personality. When you develop a pleasing personality you attract better people into your life. The higher the quality the better. What ever personality you have, you will attract like minded people. Attract is defined as: Draw to one self. Have emotional or aesthetic appeal for. Aesthetic is defined as: relating to beauty. If you have a pleasing personality, things will become easier. You will go farther, and get more accomplished.
2. Work on improving your communication skills, your persuasive skills, your sales skills, and your negotiation skills. You will need and use these skills in all your business negotiations and transactions. These skills are on the right side of the training balance scale. This means you must learn how to ask questions and listen. You have two ears and one mouth. Use them proportionately.

So, when you are meeting people listen more and talk less. Nothing will work until your thinking is right. If you don't have the law of attraction working on your side things will not work out.

Then you must manage your priorities. Some refer to this as time management. Some call it really priority management. It really is called energy management. This means getting more done in less time. You get more done when you are not all stressed out. If your thinking is right you will not be feeling any stress at all. So, you do need to prioritize. The number one thing you should do daily is

1. Read books all the time. Leaders are readers.
2. Listen to cd's everyday. The more you listen the more you get new information. Listen to your cd's over and over again.

3. Associate with people that have what you want. Associate with like minded people. Listen to people that have what you want. Listen to them and observe them. Then duplicate. Copy cat. Five years from now your income will average to those five best friends that you have. Besides when you have others that are like minded, master minds are created.

Thoughts create vibration. Vibration brings in the money. So, in essence thoughts create the income. So, be careful what vibration you put out into the universe. You may not like the results.

If you get a feeling that you need to get new friends, then guess what, your right. Associate with people that have income levels that you want, the higher the income the better. Observe them, watch them, mimic them, model your self after them. Listen to them and learn from them. Soon after you will start developing neuro-pathways like them and achieve like them. It's your thinking that does make it so.

Your bliss is your direction. Once you give up the game is over. Your chain of desire/ un-desire is totally in your mind. You are imprisoned by your mind, or you are set free by your mind. Your mind has to be rearranged.

You hesitate because of inner resistance. We all have self imposed limitations placed on our selves. The chain links are your self imposed limitations, woven together by the ego. Your ego is the other self that is your invisible enemy/friend. The only way out is to follow your bliss.

You have created every thing in you life. You have the ability inside you to re create a whole new life. But you must die to ego. Preferably at the same time. Out with the old and in with the new. There is nothing that can't be different. In fact, the only thing in life that's a dead guarantee is that of change. Change is just a decision away.

Once you decide to get rid of your bad situation watch and you how much better you feel. You will see magic happen. This is the power of your nature. She was just waiting on you to make the decision.

Focus on what you want and look to it with anticipation. As if you've already received it. Anticipation is defined as: be prepared for. Look forward to. It should make you jump up and down with happiness. You will be then broadcasting a frequency with power and intensity. If you will broadcast that frequency consistently things will start to change real fast. You will attract like minded thoughts around you that want to associate with it. This in turn will attract into your life exactly what your transmitting.

But also be aware other crabs will pull you back down into the crab pot. Listen not to them. Leave them behind. You are forging ahead. But do so quietly. Your new life will begin. You will start to attract into your life circumstances, events and situations, experiences and people that match that vibrational frequency.

This translates you will have in your life the emotions, or feelings that you are broadcasting. This is because that thing is a vibrational frequency, that thought of a thing you attach an emotion to brings into your life circumstances, people and events that give you the same emotion that you were broadcasting.

It is exciting to know that what ever happens in your life there is no such as something bad. What ever came from you came from an emotion which was a thought first. This blossomed into act. Now, you have circumstance. So there is space between thought and circumstance. Your circumstance unfolds exactly like you designed it. Better yet you got what you got. It came out the way it came out, If you like it that's fine. If you don't then change the way you do it next time. Adapt and survive.

If you stare at what you don't want for awhile then this will help clarify what it is that you do want. This is something that is in your court. Your angel will take it from there. The energy between you and your angel is an ongoing affair. It never stops.

Don't keep wasting energy on things you don't want. Look at it only long enough to clarity.

You feel bad for two reasons only. One is that you are looking at what you don't want, of two you are looking at what you want but don't believe you can have it. Either way you feel bad. This seems to be the energy field around most people. So, your attitude is wrong or your unbelief is higher than belief. Either way your thinking is wrong. What ever your belief is your body will still respond to it.

Good thoughts produce good fruits. Bad thoughts produce bad fruit. Good and healthy thoughts build up. Bad thoughts and vibrations bring down and destroy. Your environment as well as your body will respond or react.

Either way you are the god man like creature shaping your environment. If you have a strong body, your thoughts have made it so. If you have a sickly body, your thoughts have made it so. So, stand tall, head up. Throw your shoulders back and have a spring in your step. Your body will move with power and confidence when you are feeling good. When you are feeling bad your body responds. Your shoulders begin to slouch. You begin to hunch over. You walk a little slower. You frown, Your voice gets lower. You become tired, depressed, and annoyed all the time. You are o my o my fearful.

The most permanent way to feel better is to change your physiology. Like put a smile on your face. You will instantly feel better. Once you feel better this means your internal focus has changed. Now you are vibrating good thoughts and feelings. Now you are ready to attract more good thoughts and feelings. This builds your positive ball of energy. Now your negative ball of energy goes down. But when you go around with a frown you are building you negative ball of energy, and your positive ball goes down. You will know which way things are going by how you feel.

The key element here is to feel good all the time. Because you get what you think about most of the time. If you think about what you want and then to think about not having it cancels each other out. When you feel anticipation of having it that's when things are flowing into you. This is broadcasting it with full power and with full intensity.

You have no resistance on the line. This is the law of attraction working and the universe is bringing it into your life. Ninety nine of all variables that help bring it to pass is off your radar screen. You can't see them, you can't even imagine them. You can't even dream of what they can be. But there are millions of bits of information and data and particles that are being flowed and moved and adjusted and it's all being done to work and bring it into your life.

So, once you ask it is given. Your angel has his work cut out for him. This is your god man at work. As you put the law of attraction to work for you your angel takes it from there. But your dialog with him does not end there. If fact it's only beginning. Your angel works behind the scenes. He applies the magic. Your job is to keep the vibration going. Stay tuned to your frequency. This means that more thoughts come to you and they get better and better.

The physical manifestation will soon appear. But there is always a buffer of time. You will always be faced with disappointments. How do you handle them? You will always have experiences that you want to go one way but don't, and you get a feeling of disappointment. You try something and fail then you feel bad. The reason you feel bad is based on your habits. What you think is disappointments are nothing more than your thoughts are on the lack of it, or the not having it.

Your thoughts are on the fact that you are not going to get what you want. The fact that you don't have what you want, you feel bad. This happens because it's a habit. This is nature's clue that you are on the wrong neuro-pathways. This occurs as a result of your pre programmed mind, which is to ingeniously fail.

People at higher levels know this stuff. This is why they are where they are at. They don't get emotional about what appears to be failure. Failure is only a misstep only, nothing more. It is the emotion of disappointment that brings to mind failure. Nobody succeeds at everything. Every body has miscues, and missteps. So, say to your self, wow, I had a misstep, I must be getting closer. This should become your next habit.

The people at the highest levels knows this secret. A disappointment is only something that didn't turn out the way you planned. There are only two reasons why it did not work.
1. It is something that you caused. The vibration that your putting out.
2. Some thing incredible that you cannot imagine is about to happen. So, the thing that you want to happen is not happening it means that something bigger and better is happening. This is another clue from nature. It is her way of saying she heard your request and sent your circumstances as proof. But this circumstance is only temporary. Remember the prophet Daniel. He prayed for something to happen and did not get an answer. The answer came at a later time. The messenger angel said God heard your prayer Daniel and he sent me right away to answer, but the angels of darkness stopped me along the way. They held me up. But I told them the Lord rebuke you.

So what you are wanting and praying for is only held up on technicality. So this is scriptural proof that what you are praying for and not getting does not mean it's failure. There is hindrance in your angel's world. So, your logical step is to check your vibration to see just what you have been broadcasting.

Look no further than your feelings. Your communication with your angel is through thoughts, coupled with emotion. If you are broad casting the right feelings then the no your receiving is not really a no. It just means that it hasn't been released to you yet. Remember, you can't see what is not off your radar screen. So, your feeling disappointment is a bad habit.

Your point of attraction is that it's not happening. If you feel bad then let it go. Draw in and let go is the definition of pulsate.

This is what desire is. This means to draw back and refocus. If you pull back and refocus and still you feel bad. This means that you are far removed from the frequency. This is your nature's clue you that need to work on your self. This means you have to change your beliefs. Your dialog with your feelings is moment by moment. There are always open channels. Your maker has made this so. He communicates with you through intellect and emotion and circumstances. As well as through all the things created.

Everything you want is there you and I just can't see them. So we have to adjust our selves to where we can see it. The biggest problem is your mind disease. It is constantly in the way. Once you kick your die-ease to the curb you will find your true self, because that's all that's left.

Always be willing to change and adopt new strategies. Always adopt new strategies that feel good. When you can't see any thing good on your radar screen then it's time to use your belief system. Just have faith as they say. Faith is defined as: Confidence. From incorporeal to corporeal.

Your belief system I likened to your immune system Your immune system is your bodies medicine cabinet. Your belief system is the command center. You as a god man like creature have the ability to call out things as though they were even though there not. This is called faith. When you practice faith you are exercising your god man power.

Your thoughts affect your immune system. Likewise your thoughts affect the universe. In reality, you and your nature are one. This is the simplest form of it, although the reasons are very complex.

Your belief system is the light unto to your lamp. Your words are the telephone line. Your emotions are the electrical current that transmits feeling through the line. Your whole being is an extension of the whole universe. Better yet the universe is an extension of you. You and the universe are one.

This explains why prayer activates all things. This is why when you ask it is already given, because all things in this universe are yours anyway. All material objects are all of the same basic material as you. We are not separate from anything. This is the illusion. But the deeper truth is that all things are the same.

There is just a wall of resistance between you and your desire. There is a veil that blinds you from knowing this fact. Then to top it off there is your destructive other self, your ego. The only way that I know of that will bring you out from behind the veil is to move your emotions up to a higher plain or place.

Excitement and a complete abandonment of all rational caused Peter to walk on water just for a moment. Until rational caught up with him, interesting isn't it. So to discover exhilaration is essential for deeper discovery to higher consciousness. This can only happen if you look up. Your person goes where your eyes go. When you are driving into a curve, you are supposed to look into the curve. Because where your eyes go your car goes. This is the thinking behind it. So where ever the eyes of your mind go so shall your body.

You are the controller. The controller, the watcher and the observer. The deeper truth that is hidden behind the veil is that you and the universe are one. The problem lies in the fact that this knowledge has been purposefully hidden from you and I. Our society is structured around the illusion of things.

Like the illusion of the time clock. Under standing this truth puts you in direct contact with the power of your god man. Things are not what they seem in this illusion we call reality. But this reality that we have come to know is so deeply ingrained we cannot believe any thing else. So the deeper truth is that we have it backwards. Now answer this, don't you ever get this feeling that things just are not right? Look around you and tell me things are not upside down, or backwards. Everything is backwards and upside down.

The answer to our problems are right in front of us, we just can't see them because we have the wrong coordinates. When you have the right coordinates you will be able to move up on the emotional scale easier.

So this all goes back to your created being, your ability to know who you are you are lost to. This is why the whole world is lost. The lost are enslaved to the wicked one. The problems and the answers exist at the same time.

So, when there is a problem there is an immediate answer. If this is true then why are there so many problems? The reason is simple. The answers are hidden outside the veil. They are hidden only because you are hidden. But deep inside you know the answers. But the outside forces suppresses you from applying them. This is the psychology of our structured system. That's why what you think is the right thing is not the right thing. It is actually backwards.

This is the reason for our anxiety when dealing with the system. If you feel bad after being criticized then your not feeling secure about your self. Being criticized should be a non issue. This is a clue you have the wrong perception of things. What we as humans need to work on is our awareness of who we really are. Enter heightened awareness and you will discover you are the director, and the actor.

Your god man is the producer of things. Your angel is there only to work for you. So, become the star. Direct your own reality show. Everybody has their own truth which could be anything.

If You become offended by what people say it is because you are separate from your true self and there is an understanding gap. This means there is a vibration gap. The only way out of this swamp of garbage is the attitude of Damn this shit to hell. To hell with this shit attitude is the way out of your preprogrammed self. That attitude of I am not putting up with this shit anymore. I am tired of this bull shit. I am getting the hell away from this crap. This is the right coordinates. This is what it takes to punch right through your stink hole. That is the spirit as they say. There is a reason you are feeling these emotions. This is your true god man commanding and waking you. He finally got through to you.

This is a break through. You are finally getting something. Go with it. Lose your self to find yourself. Let go and let God. Screw it. Fuck it. Get lost.

This is a vulgar and extreme form of energy. But you are starting to shift from one place to another. There has been and will be a greater hell unleashed on earth. It's all on its way. Just read the signs. Get your self in order and prepare your self for the coming storm. This is your prep-time.

We are pre programmed to be sensitive to the negative things other people say. But again we have the wrong coordinates. We should not have to worry about the negative things people say because everybody is in the wrong vibration already. So what they say don't mean shit. Think of it this way every body is swimming up stream. Everybody is fighting the current. Have you found the end of your rainbow yet? Do you know anybody who has? I rest my case.

This is because we all have the wrong compass. Our compass does not point north. Our compass is pointing south. Going south is a metaphor I use that means that all of the world is going to hell. Set your compass heading the opposite direction which is true north. Look to the north star. This is where it is believed that heaven lies. Behind the vast dark space behind the north star.

The only way to break free of your resistance is this attitude of yours. It is through your bad attitude do you have the energy, the boldness, along with the will to break through the wall. It is called the wall of resistance. It is an energy thing. You already have deep groves in your record. And you instinctively know what is real and what not is real. You see and feel all the wrongs things around you and feel helpless.

Don't worry about saving the world. You were not meant to do this. You were born into this world to find what it is that you want and move toward it. That's it period. So, stop your resistance and turn and go with the flow. Stop your kicking and screaming because all you are doing is bringing every body down. Quit looking down. Quit looking south. Get out of your head, or get into your head and straighten it out. Get out of your head and into your body. Lose your ego to find yourself.

If it is not good for your organism then it is not good for you. Are you playing your record in tune with the universe. The universe is the ultimate record. Chances are your record groves are in tune with all points south. Where do you think this phrase comes from? Think about it. We are all headed south because we are manipulated to go there. Now ask your self what is south and who is the commander of south. It is the grave that's who. Who do you think rules the grave? Death that's who. Who is the chief of death, the underground manipulators, that's who. Who are the manipulators, the fallen ones that's who. The ones who are underground awaiting the final judgment that the ruling class is connected through their blood line. They are the ones responsible for pointing our compass south. This is the reason why the world is lost, because we are in the power of the wicked one. The fallen ones hate human beings. They hate all that God has made. They want nothing more than to destroy you and I. They live out of sight and are held in their place because of it.

So, now this goes back to who can you really listen to. Are you teachable. Are you willing to change. Do you have a high willingness to learn. Learning who you really are is pointing your compass true north. The dialog you are having in your mind right now is a dialog with the universe. Is it fruitful or not fruitful. If it is not then your heading in the wrong direction. If it is leading you into chaos then again it's heading south. All points south are illusion.

If I say your energy and the universe's energy are two separate entities. This would make some sense. But if I say you and your universe is of the same energy essence, this would make more perfect sense. Because the latter is truest.

The same energy matter that made this world and all that is in it. Nature to is energy matter. The very same as a matter of fact. You are a product of the universe. The creator used the magic of the creation to make you. God is a pure power source. He is the machine that gets the job done. Both you and Him are interchangeable. The god man lives inside of you. The problem is your awareness. The god power is a part of us all.

This is why you compass is purposely pointed in the wrong direction. You have been programmed to believe that you are separate and left all alone. But this is the illusion. But you and god man are one. You and him are inter changeable. Your God is the power behind your creation. You and him have already created your world and everything you possess. He has been with you the whole time.

But you cannot see him because of your preprogrammed dark hole. God man has been darkened out. This dark energy has stopped you from seeing and knowing him. This dark energy has stopped you from seeing, knowing, communicating, and understanding all things as they were created to be. The purpose of the under ground manipulators is to replace all that is natural and replace it with all things artificial. When this happens complete control of the human race is possible.

To make things worse for us is that daily we have circumstances that activate out dark energy to meet the worlds end. The only way to dis-empower it is to see it for what it is. It is the elephant in the room. Pointing out the elephant in the room is in essence taking away its power. But you must want it. If you are a person that doesn't want to do what it takes to make your mind a better place to dwell then we have nothing further to talk about. But me I have put my self on a quest to make my body and mind without pain and sorrow. To rid my life all that has and is causing me grief and sorrow. My life has been filled up with sorrow and grief and now pain. My lively hood has been one fire storm after another. Sparks always breathing down my neck.

As a human we live on the earths plain but we come from the eternal. Our angel is still in eternity. We have connection with him through intelligence. He is still with us. The relationship is custom fit. We create from the incorporeal to the corporeal. Our angels does the very opposite. From incorporeal to the corporeal. Both are interchangeable. The direction of our angel is true north.

If you are feeling anger, depression, worry, doubt, or fear. Then your compass is pointed south. Learn to use these emotions to the glory of God.

If you think this is nonsense then look at your body language. If you lie to your self, your body will tell on you. All negative emotion is illusion. Eternal love is the only thing that's real, all else is illusion. All negative emotion heads to all points south unless it is discipline.

We are not totally lost and with out power. Our creator has allowed us to become confused. When you are feeling these emotions you are, in other words, not your original self. You are the other self that's beside your self. There are two entities here The false you and the real you. This other negative self lives in your body and occupies space in your mind. The results of its presence is destructive. This other self's job is to tear down and destroy. To separate and accuse. This other self creates personality disorders. Because the personality is disorderly. This causes your true self to sit on the sidelines and watch.

But even through this your god man is still there working with you giving you exactly what you have coming to you. He is bringing to you both all the good and the bad. When you ask it is given should become when you ask something is given. So when you ask watch for changes. Things may not go like you like them. But remember you asked for it. Maybe you might get the complete opposite. You have not because you ask not. You were designed to ask and to receive. Here on earth the eternal is hidden from view, out of sight out of mind. But that doesn't mean it is non existent.

The eternal is far bigger and vast than little old earth. There are as many angels In heaven as there is people on earth. This is the reason why everybody has their own guardian angel.

We as humans are sent to earth to experience the contrast and to make choices. Here on this earth we must learn things the hard way. To get what you want you have to be your true self.

There are things for both selves. Both selves may live this life together. But your true self is the better one. Your ideals are your children. They want to be born. You have to plant the seeds. Water them and take care of them. Cultivate them. They want to live. Your ideals need you and you need them. Your angel is there to help. After all, your creator did not leave you helpless.

It's all about growth. You have to want to grow. You need to grow. Grow up or grow cranky.

Back to focusing on a chief aim. When you find a chief aim and get tired of it, then it's time to put it down for the time being. When something starts to feel burdensome then take a break. Go back to it when you feel better.

All art is inspired. All creation is inspired. All things created are inspired. If there is no inspiration then there is no forward momentum. The artist needs inspiration. Most people don't understand this very important concept. Inspiration is positive forward focused energy. It brings to the artist wide scope and depth simultaneously. This allows the artist to float to a higher frequency. Then bring it to us who are on a lower frequency and do it in color. If you love what you're doing then you will love doing it. If there is no burden then there is no wear and tear on your person. If it is not burdensome, then time will fly. You will feel great doing it. You will have the time of your life. Art allows you to escape from your past, gives you intense pleasure in the present tense. Art brings you into the here and now. So does reading a good book. So does cooking. When anything becomes drudgery this is your nature's clue to stop it. This is your clue to stop and reevaluate, refocus, rethink, and re approach. Either way you go back at it your desire will give you the feelings for it. You will feel it in your bones.

The game of life should be about pleasure. It's about discovering, uncovering to find more pleasure. When your experiencing pleasure only then can you realize how pleasurable life can be. We were not sent here to just sweat and toil. We were sent here to experience the buffet called life. Choose what we want and then move toward it. We secretly move toward what we desire or love. If you sit in one spot to long your bottom will hurt. This is a signal that you must shift your body, same thing in life. If we stay too long in one place we become stagnate. This is the reason for vacations.

Motivation is like the dance. Dancing with an ideal is like seeing it fresh every time you look at it. The universe is always in flux. This means you are never at the same place. The truth is you are not because every day you wake up your not the same person you was the day before.

When you are stagnate you will feel bad. Being stagnate does not feel good. Your river of life should stay in constant motion. In fact the faster it moves the more clear the water because it is always washing out the lower funk. So, by having a chief aim you become motivated. Your chief aim is your purpose.

Your purpose is the anchor that will help you through hard times. Purpose generates burning desire. Burning desire is pulsating desire. You always know you are in the right place at the right time when you are feeling happy. Your happiest when you are in the process of bringing about your desire. This is your nature's clue that you are in the right place at the right time. True happiness is the progressive realization of a worth while dream. It's the process. By being in this special place you by pass the preprogrammed failure mode. This is out witting mother nature.

To dream build helps you to desire. It fuels desire. So, fuel the fire of desire. It's so very important to follow your desires. If you don't then you will be doing something else for somebody else. Follow that which gives you the greatest sense of bliss. If you follow your bliss continually you will live an extraordinary life, one that's truly worth living. You will live on this earth in all its glory. There is no right or wrong about it. It is cut and dry. If it is good for your organism then it's good for you. You and your god man working together feels right.

After all he is your life long side kick. Your goal is to know what you want, align your self with it, then move toward it. The only thing holding you back is your huge ball of black energy. It's how you are choosing to look at your self. It's you being untrue to your self. It's you putting limitations on your self. Making magical moments makes life magical. Magical moments magical life. So now you have your own god man. So, now you have your own magical lamp which is your own mind. Your wish is at your own command. Your angel can and will grant you any wish you want. You have the power to call forth. You have the belief, you have the knowledge, and you have the energy. You have the time. You have all the essential ingredients. There is so much more available to you than you can ever imagine. You can go any where, any time, and do anything.

You can achieve anything you want. You can have, be, or do anything you desire. You have the power to manifest. To conjure: To bring to pass all your dreams and desires. There are ways to make all the money you want. You can have great relationships. You can have the job of your dreams. You can have the car you have always wanted. You can wake up each day feeling exhilarated. You can have vibrant health. You can come up with ideas and inventions. You can learn new skills. You can travel all over the world, and eat at the finest restaurants. You can live a more secure more fulfilled life. You can experience any and every emotion you want. Adventure, excitement, and enthusiasm. You can feel passion, power. And achievement. You can add value to society, to others, and your community. You can change your world. Right now your at unconscious incompetence. You have to physically apply it. You have old patterns. You have old negative thought patterns and energies that are activated. They are constantly making you feel bad. But now you know that you have the power to change. As you start the process of change your negative energy will diminish. Its magnetic pull will get weaker and weaker.

The neuro-pathways that you have established will get less used and will get weaker and weaker. Newer neuro-pathways will be established in the brain. Then they will get stronger and stronger. Then the next thing you know the big ball of positive energy will get bigger than the negative ball of energy. Once this happens it's all down hill from there. When this happens the momentum is on your side. All of a sudden things will go your way.

At this stage your in unconscious competence. This is the stage that things happen automatically. Instead of jumping into negative habits and patterns. You will jump into positive habits and patterns. When things occur in your life that you don't want, you will smile and say I don't know how this is going to turn out but I believe it will be to my benefit. Compared to the old way which is o my God this is bad. This positive change will eventually occur. It will not happen over night. For you to magnetically attract what it is that you want it has to occur. When it does life will get easier, more fulfilling and more exciting. You will feel more secure, more content. You will fall in love with your positive emotions and with their intensity more than ever before. You have what you need. You already possess all you need. You have what you need in the palm of your hand. It's up to you to use it. This is your power. It's simple. This is what everybody is using. It's backed by universal law. Whether you consciously apply it or not it will happen everyday anyhow.

Every time you think a thought you are broadcasting a vibration, and attracting a like vibration into your life. Every time you are feeling a feeling You are calling forth more circumstances, situations, and events, and people into your life that give you similar feelings.

You have been a ship without a rudder, no engine and have been tossed about by the waves, wind and have been a victim. Now you can be a ship that's a nuclear powered vessel with unlimited power for the rest of your life. You can steer your own ship by your own will by your own choice, and by your own decision power you can point it in any direction and go anywhere anytime any place you choose. Now that you have your god man, you can add value to your own life and become someone people want to emulate. Someone people admire.

You'll find out at some point it's not what you have that counts. It's not about the things you've accumulated that matters. It's who you've become that truly matters in the end.

For many people they will never figure this out. In the end after you have attained all you want in life you will find that honesty, integrity, character, love, and forgiveness, giving, gratefulness, will become your crowning glory. This is what it's really about. Life is truly about feeling good right now.

Every step of every moment, regardless of what you're looking at, regardless of your situation. You can live life feeling really, really good. Your life should become the most blissful, exciting experience you can make it. It will be and can be for everyone. There are two kinds of people in the world. Those who add value to society and those who live off of those who add value to society. The latter are parasites The greatest experience is being a value creator.

YOUR BABY

Thought imagined is seed. Your initial thought is only a seed. These seeds are a gift of the universe to us all. In the beginning was the word. The word was made flesh. Thoughts become words and words become things. So this is somewhat saying that thoughts are things. Thought from imagination is seeds. Christ is the seed giver.

To call forth thoughts is through commands. Commands spring forth from desire. Desire is the emotional fuel that drives the word. The word spoken backed by the emotion activates the field of intelligence. The field of intelligence which hears you responds and records all things. This creates your aurora. Your aurora is what people feel emanating from you when they come in contact with you.

Once a single idea is accepted as worthy of time and energy. It will begin to take root. If you cherish your ideals then this thing imagined will not only germinate but will take root. So the question remains how good is your soil? For any good idea to come to fruition there has to be good soil.

Every seed produces after its own kind. Good thoughts produce good fruit. Bad thoughts produce bad fruit. If the soil is toxic then nothing good can grow in toxic soil except maybe weeds.

If you cherish your ideals then this brings value and validation to it. Once it passes this initial stage then it is a matter of how to bring it to pass. Naturally we will immediately see all the ways we cannot bring it to pass. Then with applied determination we will begin to see how we can bring it to pass. Determination implies resolute will. A resolute will is an iron will. An iron will produces in us an indomitable spirit. This is below surface thinking. This is deep inner feeling and thinking. It must be a deep inner command from the center.

So to have an iron will means this baby your trying to bring forth must come from the deepest place within your self.

Thoughts imagined are but seeds of desire that need to be born. But they cannot enter our plain until the creator brings them forth. You are the creature. They are seeds from eternity that want to be part of our earth. But they cannot come here until you bring them forth. You are the god like creator that has babies that need to be born. They are your babies. They need you and you need them. This is why it is said that you must cherish your ideals and cherish your dreams. You must open the doorway (Star gate).

Your babies are asking you permission to be born. You will never be really happy until you give birth to your desires. So ponder upon your ideals. It takes physical action to convert these ideals into this earthly plain. So the more you think upon them the more you are able to see them.

The thoughts are only the beginning. The more you give them your attention the more of this thing you are able to see. The idea is to bring them into sharp focus. Put them under a microscope. Call them forth out of eternity into reality.

This is saying to me that essentially your imagination is your reality. You have the ability to take from imagination and make it reality. Question is do you have the iron will to bring it to pass? For most people the answer is a resoundingly no! It is too hard. It takes to much energy. Well then! Push baby push!

It is said what is it that you have energy for? Thoughts create energy. The more the thinking on the desire the more energy is generated. Now we are talking. Kind of like a generator. Generator and vibration is essentially the same thing. Praying is generating power. Power generation is praying.

The Bible says to pray without ceasing. This is God's way of saying you have to generate energy to bring forth this desire.

God made man in his image. This means His created ability image. Humans are god like creators. So become god man and god woman like in all your ways. Jesus used strong emotion in his life.

Jesus was a God-man. He was the ultimate God-man. He is our example. When Jesus raised Lazarus from the dead, the

Bible says He cried with a loud voice, "Lazarus Come forth". Jesus used strong emotions with authority. Christ let loose the ultimate command. This tells me that He did not ask for anything but that He commanded and the grave obeyed. In other words the grave is alive and he commanded and it heard and obeyed. So be not timid.

So if you cherish your ideals then you can have intimate contact with your baby in the imaginative realm. The more you give it your love and attention the more of its potential you are able to see. Remember the thought is only a seed and it must go through a process before it becomes real.

Some thoughts incubate for a life time and yet nothing comes from it. This is because you are not doing anything about it. Tell me, how do you feel about the ones you have? I rest my case.

What thoughts are you entertaining? Are you entertaining thoughts from others or are they your own? For me there is only one way to tell. That is to be alone for a time and the ones that bring me excitement must be from me.

All growth is a time oriented journey. The human race has a nine month span from conception to birth. In between is growth and preparation.

FAITH:

What is faith? Faith is dropping off reason at the cliff and stepping into the beyond. Our natural minds cannot understand faith. It can only be achieved by eradicating reason. Reasoning is a mind activity. Faith is beyond mind. The Bible says faith is the thing hoped for yet not seen. This suggests to me we are to believe in the impossible. This indicates an iron will. How else can the impossible come to pass. Faith therefore is the attainment of the impossible. Attain the knowledge of the unknowable. This puts our life force into the throne room of the Most High. Faith is a letting go of reason and trusting. Faith moves things in the spirit. Faith is the eyes of the spirit looking into eternity, using the power of eternity to make things shift in your behalf. Faith is the scepter of the god-man.

TIMING:

Everything in its own time. Time does not mean the clock time. There is an eternal clock of time. This is the only one that matters. Success starts with using time wisely. Your seed that becomes your baby brought forth grows with time. The market place will determine if it is the right product or not at this time. Your time is always in the now. We are wasters of our time. All time is valuable. Time is the most important commodity we have. We hoard time. We waste time. We spend time. We do time. The right answer is that we should be investing in time. This to me means to bring forth a baby then nurture it to bring forth fruit. No matter what time will pass anyhow. So find something to grow with you.

I looked upon a pregnant woman the other day who was holding her stomach. She had a far away look in her eyes. I pondered on her far away look and realized that she is seeing into the future her and her new baby. The men in women's lives come and go. But far into the future is her and her child together. She is seeing these things fully and prophetically. You and your baby must have destiny together like the mother and her baby. Her baby is worth every minute of her time and energy. Time matters not. It's the moment.

Prayer is energy generation. Prayer is vibration. You are an instrument. You are a tone. Your life is one song after another. Your deeds spring from words. What song are you singing with your life?

So pierce the ether with sharp crisp commands. Speak it with the voice of authority. Have eyes into eternity. Know the will of the gods. Think, speak, and command and have no doubt and you shall have.

IMAGINATION:

What ever it is that you want you first imagine it. To pull it out of imagination is calling it forth. Time and effort is the magic formula. Your time is the most important commodity we possess, your time along with effort.

The thing imagined must be blown up 1000%. The more time spent the more clarity it gives in return. Your time into it allows you to see it with more clarity.

Imagination is far away vision. Zoom it in for greater view. This means exploration. See it in pictures. The more time and attention the bigger it becomes.

The creating of the thing is the applied magic. It all takes magic you know. This is how from out of the mind ideas into the material plain how things come to pass. It's kind of like a baby wanting to be born.

It is essential to subject your mind to thought discipline. This is called focus. This is because your mind is a frequency transmitter. Tune into the station of the thing imagined. You have control through the power of your will.

Now you see your baby in eternity. Do you want your baby? Your baby wants you. Your baby wants to be born. But can you do it? Resolute will! Lock your ways into the frequency. Zoom into this thing. Blow it up 1000%. Get a good picture of it. Imagine all its beauty and purpose. Cherish it, Love it, want it.

What will this baby do for you in this world? Will it bring you happiness power, money or influence? Perhaps all three. Whatever it is it is good for you. This to me is opening the door. Let's make this more cosmic here. I shall call it opening the Star gate. Ask your self, "What is it I must do using time as an ally?" You must cosmically embrace this baby. When you apply magic you are breathing life into it, giving it breath. Making it come alive, giving it soul.

All this time this has to be brought to the light to be examined. This cannot be born in darkness. What can you see in the dark? Nothing that's what. Bring it into the light to be examined.

EMOTIONS:

Whatever your emotions are they have to make you feel good. They have to hit you in the sweet spot. This is all good on one end of the emotions spectrum. On the other end now that you have it in your sweet spot it is locked into memory. You must immediately dismiss your emotions and now dig deep to no emotions. Your emotions are now to be used in bringing it to pass. You will pass through a vicissitude of changes. Your emotional scale will go off the chart off of both ends. This is what I will call birth pains. My mental state is this: Nothing personal just business.

The reason is simple. You are now thinking for two. You see things on your radar screen. You also do not see the things off your radar screen that are vital. The thing desired is a life force. It is a living organism. So are you.

EMOTIONAL ATTATCHMENTS:

So you have to call them forth as well. This is forward momentum or falling forward. It takes intense focus. Most of the time my emotions are not good ones. During baby creation I am intensely focused. I am experiencing all range of emotions. Others are not aware of what is going on inside all they see is the intensity. No worry, just tell them you are having a baby.

If you have problems in life, then so what, they will become small. You will plough right though them with intensity. Because you are having a baby. And your baby is calling you. So get to it! Nothing is more important than giving birth to your baby.

Any attachments that are a hindrance to bringing your baby to pass must be done away with, unless of course you have energy for all things. The more you give up the more free energy you have for you and your baby. During the time of creation, cling to nothing and give up all the things that are stopping you, because they are robbing you of your baby. You are a creator. You must understand this deeply. To get is simple. Giving up is a prerequisite. I'm sure you have heard it said you must give up something to get something. Get it? I shall call this the maneuvering dance. You are maneuvering you self to a right place and dancing with this eternal baby. It's kind of like catching a fly ball.

You have the eyes of your spirit into the spiritual realm and you have two eyes for this material plain only. Use them together.

DANCING WITH IMAGINATION:

You are a mini-creator. The Bible states faith. Faith to me means using your spiritual eyes to see what things can be or the way they are suppose to be. Keep praying, keep imagining, Keep looking and keep pursuing the thing that is worthy of your precious time.

Nothing is more worthy of my time than creating my baby! Want your baby, Create you baby, Breath life into your baby. Your baby is out there in eternity waiting for you to call it forth. It wants to be here. You and your baby are one. Your babies are calling you to be born. But it is all a process.

To do all the things necessary is the dance. Your dancing with time, energy and circumstance. Your time, your energy and your circumstances. Ok! So you must learn to do the tango.

Another reason it is a dance is this, all things are in flux. All things are in motion already. Nothing stays the same. All things change from one day to the next. You change daily so does everything else. We just don't see it. This is what I will call a hidden reality. It is right in front of us all. All you have to do is stop and look at it. This is the very reason faith in the unattainable does in fact work. So, what are you calling your baby?

First rule is to expel all negative influence. Fear worry and doubt are destroyers of dreams. Unbelief always brings with it undesired results.

NEGATIVE ENERGY:

Jealousy is a mild form of insanity. Jealousy is suffering. People hinder, doubt, stop, question and influence all things south. It is madness. Negative energy is vibrations in disease mode. Negative vibrations are a result of negative thinking. If you encounter these forces then it is time that you depart company. Negative belief is the belief of I can't. I won't. It cannot be done. They also come in the form of well-wishing. This unbelief, this fear is unfounded. If you encounter this just remember this unbelief is just that, unbelief. This does not mean that you cannot accomplish your self. Unbelief is sickness in action. Jesus always made mention the unbelief of those around Him.

If I say you can become anything you desire. This is the ultimate truth. But if I say you are here to discover who you truly are and this is what you must become because you cannot become anything you want. This is also a viable truth. So become what you are supposed to become and then become some one greater. This is a blend of them both. Either way negative influence will stop you from entering either. Fear and unbelief are belief factors that are infantile. They are designed to control. These are not real to your organism. They bring stagnation and death. Look to your own organism for verification of this truth. Listening to these voices will only bring undesired outcomes. Your job is to therefore punch right through them. Pierce their unbelief with sharp criticism. Slap them across the face with belief verbology.

You are a god-man and a god-woman. You are a mini creator. This is what you are by design. You are the one that is in charge of your destiny. You are the star of the show in your life. You are more adept to imagination than reality. So shape your reality through the use of your imagination. It can be as you think it can. You can only go as far as your beliefs take you. Your beliefs are the super highway. Do you dare believe in your self? Why not? Let it all hang out baby! Leave it all on the field of play. The earth is the play ground.

Let's get a little perverse here. I used to consider my self a man after God's own heart. While this is still true in a greater sense. How about we turn it upside down for experimental purposes. How about we say I am a god after man's own heart. Is this perverse? Probably so. But we are in a perverse generation. This is using insanity to your benefit. But it's smart. This is cunning and crafty. Everybody does it that is in business they just don't come out and say it. This is why businesses are entities. These entities are after man's own wallet via business.

If the world is in motion then the world is one big living organism. Then it just stands to reason that everything is alive and ever changing. Every thing is in motion. The sphere of imagination is also in flux and all things are moving. We are living in a power evolving universe. You are included in this power evolving universe. You have power yourself. I want you to know this.

All things created are first in the imagination. So from this day forward you are to think like a god-man, god-woman mini-creator. Think like a mini-god after the earths own riches. We are in abundance on earth. We have riches beyond measure. There are billions of dollars floating around out there. Jump in and claim your share through your value creation. Your value creation is your baby.

Thoughts are things are creator thinking. All things were thoughts before they became things.

Imaginative thoughts equals imaginative life. Live life with wonder and awe. Our humdrum lives have us living life in stagnation. Death is at our door. We have to beat off unbelief, stupidity, negative influence with a bat everyday, enough already. I can tell you stories about people's unbelief. I can assure you that the old adage is true that you cannot change the stripes of somebody else. Call out your own destiny. Do your own will. That is what you're here on this earth to do nothing else. If you think that you must do the will of God is your reason for being. You are on the wrong path. This is a Christian illusion. Let me offer you this question. Does He say what you should be doing exactly? The answer is a resoundingly no! He stays out of your will. God will not tell you what you should do. But He does state that He is the giver of the seed. The rest is up to you and I. Imagination is the seed.

Jesus also made mention having the river of life flowing through you. Is your current job offering you a river of life? The answer again is a resounding No!. The river of life He is referring to is the abundance of excitement that you feel when you have a baby, when you give birth to one of your children, when you see your baby online pulling in massive orders and filling you bank account with rivers of cash and the numbers rising like the tide. Is this a perverse thought? To me it is not. It is my reward for all of my hard work. It's all how you choose to look at it my friend.

YOUR THOUGHTS:

Your thoughts are not the real you. Your thoughts are the energy for this world only. When you die so does your thoughts. Your thoughts are from the universe. That is where they come from. They are not your own they belong to the universe and they are borrowed. The real you is the mini-god. You are the watcher. In between thoughts is where you reside. All thoughts are from there source. They will return to its source when you exit your body. They go back to its owner. Its source is the power evolving universe.

But for most people their huge ball of energy is destructive instead of creative. This means they are using their power in a diseased way. This is why they have dis-ease. Dis-ease is dis-connect from its source and discontent is the feelings resulted. Out of our dis-connect we unknowingly create our undesired circumstances. What this says is we are sick. Our belief system causes our sickness. The dragon always intercepts our thoughts and then replaces it with his own. Therefore we conclude that things are impossible.

What you accept into your energy field is considered your boundary. You as the creator are responsible for what goes into and what comes out of your boundary. What you feed into or allow to enter is what will either give back to you or take away from you. This is seed after its own kind. So your responsibility is to let in only things that are good for your organism. These are the things that bring that river of life excitement to you. All else is illusion. So what you truly want is a river flow of life's energy flowing through you like gusts of wind. This energy brings with it miracles, healings, good tidings and ultimately the money. Massive money.

THOUGHT PLAYGROUND:

Since success is 99% thinking. I have learned to hone my skills in this arena for a life time. This has separated me from the general public at large. I have come to see that most people live in their own egg shell. They are not easily removed. I am exactly the same way. I am no different. The only difference is that I have made an attempt to straighten mine out. Our mind is in the eggshell. Your mind itself is the living egg. We are all cocooned in there own minds. The thought playground is where all the battles are fought. The ultimate destiny awaits your decision. It is a battle for your soul. Again I must reiterate that you are the god-creator. Create you destiny.

Mean while there is your dragon you must slay. The dragon my friend is the negative forces that keep you from reaching your full potential.

If this power expanding universe is the owner of your thoughts then you are inherently its child. The Father of this universe is Jehovah. He is the creator of Mother Nature. Out of Mother Nature we all came. Our mother is Mother Nature. (Universal energy.) We are tones, vibrations, instruments. We are human creators.

What will follow us into eternity is the things that we have done with our lives. What have we accomplished with this thing we call thought and energy? The mind is only a conduit to this energy source. What have we accomplished with this huge ball of generating electricity using the conduit we call mind thought.

Your mind is a conduit using thoughts generated from eternity.

We humans as well as all things come out of eternity to be present and accounted for here right now. Since our energy source is from the universe then it stands to reason that what we do here on earth will echo through into eternity. The Bible states this very thing. Our deeds follow us after death. So, my friend this says to me that you must watch your ass with observing ego. This means you are watching over your deeds.

FIELD OF INTELLIGENCE:

Your thoughts are the intelligence center. Your words and acts activate the field of intelligence. Your brain is the command post. It is where all thoughts accumulate and blend with belief system. When you move the field of intelligence moves in perfect rhythm with you. The field of intelligence is the universe of thought. To activate is to first generate. Generating brings with it energy that is converted to power. Power is the clarity it brings. Power and clarity along with your personal magic is the magic formula that brings your baby from out of eternity into this material realm. But remember you will have birth pains while giving birth. Don't get the baby blues.

ERNEST JOHNSON

About the Author

Dear Reader,

My name is Ernest Johnson. If this letter reaches your eyes and ears, then pay attention to the details. Our galaxy is fully occupied by the unseen gods. All of them are positioning themselves to bring about the Judgment of End Times. All heavenly forces and wicked forces have their agenda. They are all active. They all have hardened positions and winner takes all. Where we are at on the great apocalypse time clock is alarming to say the least. I speak to all conscious beings, both dead and alive, to support anyone, anywhere who can bring you deep knowledge that will enlighten our understanding on the unforeseen forces.

Deeply you know this subject I'm speaking of. You instinctively understand what is at stake. You know you heart beats to your dream. To be faceless is to be enlightened. Give up self to allow the energy of these forces to lead you to your destiny, whatever it is, for only you decide.

I have been from heaven to hell to bring to you the nasty facts of life. BS/No BS razor's edge, set on fire by the Holy Spirit. I can only be your friend by not becoming your friend. My material is not the light hearted. You may not be suited for my writings.

Duality is misleading if we judge from this place. Church is not what it seems. Hell is neither Christ or Satan! Truth is, your reality is only that, your own reality. I have brought to you Earth shattering, thunder thinking. You will learn by subjecting yourself to this new cutting edge, bone shattering thunder. Only then can you appreciate the spirit of man.

If you think this letter is either honest or deceptive, you are right either way. But do us both a favor, reread this letter. Act with love or hatred. Either one will work. Just educate yourself in any way you choose. But learn, you must do. We live in a world that doesn't understand deep inner things. But we all crave it. My material is my best that this hard-working man of iron can muster. Honesty and truth are not the same. The church is not what is seems. My material is designed to clear all the cobwebs, address the sin of man from a dual mind set, with quadruple points of view.

This is why nothing is as it seems. Learn why you're here. What your mission is. What your part is. Last but not least, where you'll end up.

This is how I present my audio. It's shut up, sit your ass down and listen to what the gods have to say to you. Period! But not all at once. Each subject is just that, one subject. But all combined, Yes! After continuing for a season you will understand this to be true!

Stand for something or fall for anything! The cosmic gates are about to swing wide. Support for this cause is paramount. Capture the energy, capture the matter. Live life on the run!

Whatever it is that you desire, first rule is to lock yourself into the energy of it. Look deeply into the subject and dive in. That's it. Secret revealed! All success is wrapped up in this key!
Ernest Johnson

www.ingramcontent.com/pod-product-compliance
Lightning Source LLC
Chambersburg PA
CBHW032039150426
43194CB00006B/338